Workshop on Data Science with Human-in-the-loop: Language Advances (DaSH 2022)

Abu Dhabi, United Arab Emirates
8 December 2022

ISBN: 978-1-7138-9107-9

Printed from e-media with permission by:

Curran Associates, Inc.
57 Morehouse Lane
Red Hook, NY 12571

Some format issues inherent in the e-media version may also appear in this print version.

Printed with permission by Curran Associates, Inc. (2024)

For permission requests, please contact the Association for Computational Linguistics at the address below.

Association for Computational Linguistics
209 N. Eighth Street
Stroudsburg, Pennsylvania 18360

Phone: 1-570-476-8006
Fax: 1-570-476-0860

acl@aclweb.org

Additional copies of this publication are available from:

Curran Associates, Inc.
57 Morehouse Lane
Red Hook, NY 12571 USA
Phone: 845-758-0400
Fax: 845-758-2633
Email: curran@proceedings.com
Web: www.proceedings.com

DaSH 2022

Data Science with Human-in-the-Loop (Language Advances)

Proceedings of the DaSH Workshop at EMNLP 2022

December 8, 2022

The DaSH organizers gratefully acknowledge the support from the following sponsors.

With support from

IBM Research

Introduction

We are delighted to welcome to you DaSH 2022, the Fourth Workshop on Data Science with Human-in-the-loop at EMNLP 2022!

The aim of this workshop is to stimulate research on the cooperation between humans and computers within the broad area of natural language processing, including but not limited to information extraction, information retrieval and text mining, machine translation, dialog systems, question answering, language generation, summarization, model interpretability, evaluation, fairness, and ethics. We invite researchers and practitioners interested in understanding how to optimize human-computer cooperation and how to minimize human effort along an NLP pipeline in a wide range of tasks and applications.

This year, the workshop program includes three keynote talks, two invited talks, fourteen accepted papers, and three 'Findings of EMNLP' papers. We received 22 submissions, each of which received at least two reviews from our distinguished program committee. The submissions and accepted papers show a strong mix of participation both from the academia and industry: 50% of the accepted papers have an academic provenance (the primary affiliation of the lead author is a university), while 50% originate in industry labs.

We hope to bring together interdisciplinary researchers from academia, research labs and practice to share, exchange, learn, and develop preliminary results, new concepts, ideas, principles, and methodologies on understanding and improving human-computer interaction in natural language processing. We expect the workshop to help develop and grow a strong community of researchers who are interested in this topic and to yield future collaborations and scientific exchanges across the relevant areas of computational linguistics, natural language processing, data mining, machine learning, data and knowledge management, human-machine interaction, and intelligent user interfaces. We are thankful to IBM research for sponsoring the workshop and best paper awards.

We hope you have a wonderful time at the workshop.

Cheers!

DaSH 2022 Organizers
Eduard Dragut, Temple University
Yunyao Li, Apple Inc.
Lucian Popa, IBM Research
Shashank Srivastava, UNC Chapel Hill
Slobodan Vucetic, Temple University

Organizing Committee

Organizers

Eduard Dragut, Temple University
Yunyao Li, Apple
Lucian Popa, IBM Research - Almaden
Shashank Srivastava, University of North Carolina at Chapel Hill
Slobodan Vucetic, Temple University

Program Committee

Chairs

Eduard Dragut, Temple University
Yunyao Li, Apple
Lucian Popa, IBM Research - Almaden
Shashank Srivastava, University of North Carolina at Chapel Hill
Slobodan Vucetic, Temple University

Program Committee

Maria Antoniak, Allen Institute for Artificial Intelligence
Jeffrey Bigham, Carnegie Mellon University/Apple
Su Lin Blodgett, Microsoft Research
Marina Danilevsky, IBM Research
Aritra Dasgupta, New Jersey Institute of Technology
Nemanja Djuric, Aurora Innovation
Anna Lisa Gentile, IBM Research - Almaden
Sayan Ghosh, University of North Carolina at Chapel Hill
Saptarshi Guha, Apple
Toby Jia-jun Li, University of Notre Dame
Katherine Luna, Apple
Shen Ma, Apple
Dominik Moritz, Carnegie Mellon University
Kun Qian, Apple
Rakesh R. Menon, University of North Carolina at Chapel Hill
Sajjadur Rahman, Megagon Labs
Huan Sun, Ohio State University
Mihai Surdeanu, University of Arizona
Kerem Zaman, University of North Carolina at Chapel Hill
Li Zhang, University of Pennsylvania

Steering Committee

AnHai Doan, University of Wisconsin, Madison
Marti Hearst, University of California, Berkeley
Sunita Sarawagi, Indian Institute of Technology Bombay
Daniel Weld, University of Washington
ChengXiang Zhai, University of Illinois, Urbana-Champaign

Keynote Talk: Decision-making in an uncertain world

Azza Abouzied
NYU Abu Dhabi

Abstract: Decision-makers in a broad range of domains, such as finance, and healthcare, need to derive optimal decisions given a set of constraints and objectives over uncertain data or models. Traditional solutions to such problems are typically complex, do not generalize, and do not scale to our modern-day massive data scales. The emerging research area of prescriptive analytics aims to provide declarative, and scalable approaches. In this talk, I discuss some strategies for addressing key challenges related to usability, scalability, data uncertainty, dynamic environments with changing data and models, and the need to support decision-making agents with emphasis on a real-life application of supporting policy-makers with epidemic intervention planning.

Bio: Azza Abouzied's research work focuses on designing intuitive data querying tools. Today's technologies are helping people collect and produce data at phenomenal rates. Despite the abundance of data, it remains largely inaccessible due to the skill required to explore, query and analyze it in a non-trivial fashion. While many users know exactly what they are looking for, they have trouble expressing sophisticated queries in interfaces that require knowledge of a programming language or a query language. Azza designs novel interfaces, such as example-driven query tools, that simplify data querying and analysis. Her research work combines techniques from various research fields such as UI-design, machine learning, and databases. Azza Abouzied received her doctoral degree from Yale in 2013. She spent a year as a visiting scholar at UC Berkeley. She is also one of the co-founders of Hadapt – a Big Data analytics platform.

Keynote Talk: Measuring what matters for human-AI teams

Saleema Amershi
Microsoft Research

Abstract: There is a significant discrepancy between the success metrics driving the AI industry and what people value in the real world. In the AI-assisted programming scenario, for example, a key value proposition is the potential for code generation models to dramatically improve developer productivity. Yet, offline metrics used to inform model development decisions and gate which models are deployed to people in the real world currently focus on generation correctness rather than correctness or effort with a developer-in-the-loop. Similarly, online metrics currently focused on acceptance rates overlook interaction costs to developers in prompting, reviewing, and editing generated code. In this talk, I will describe ongoing work from the HAX team at Microsoft Research to develop metrics and measurement tools that more faithfully reflect the needs and effectiveness of human-AI teams.

Bio: Saleema Amershi is a Senior Principal Research Manager at Microsoft Research where she leads the Human-AI eXperiences (HAX) team, building tools for creating responsible AI experiences. She also currently chairs Microsoft's Aether Working Group on Human-AI Interaction and Collaboration. Aether is Microsoft's advisory committee on responsible and ethical AI. Saleema holds a PhD in Computer Science & Engineering from the Paul G. Allen School of Computer Science and Engineering. Prior to UW, she completed a MSc in Computer Science and a BSc in Computer Science and Mathematics at the University of British Columbia.

Keynote Talk: Data Preparation with human in the loop - The Case for a commodity crowdsourcing system

Mourad Ouzzani
Qatar Computing Research Institute, Hamad Bin Khalifa University, Qatar

Abstract: Data science is becoming central to many industries as it helps extract insights from large amounts of data that in turn lead to critical actions in many applications. An important aspect of data science is data preparation that we broadly define to include data cleaning, extraction, matching, merging, labeling, and so on. It is often the case that these tasks are performed collaboratively by multiple users. Such collaborative work is often referred to as crowdsourcing. While much work has been published in this area, most focus on developing algorithmic solutions for point problems. There is very little work on how to build crowdsourcing systems that can be used widely. In this talk, I will describe our current efforts to build Cymphony, a commodity collaborative management system that effectively supports various collaborative data preparation tasks. We aim to build a platform that enables a uniform specification as well as efficient execution of data preparation tasks that require collaboration among a group of users. While existing systems may cover some aspects of data collaboration, they do not provide easy ways to express and execute the many collaboration scenarios that are often found in practice. In a nutshell, we define a simple workflow consisting of three basic operators, namely Assign, Annotate, and Aggregate. Multiple simple workflows along with basic data manipulation operations (e.g., SQL queries, sampling) can be composed to build more complex workflows. In addition to in-house users who can connect to Cymphony, we also provide integration with public crowdsourcing platforms such as Amazon Mechanical Turk. Early experiments show that Cymphony allows the easy specification and automatic execution of many practical workflows without having to write code to run them or manually connect parts of these workflows.

Bio: Mourad Ouzzani is a Research Director with the Qatar Computing Research Institute at Hamad Bin Khalifa University, Qatar Foundation. Before joining QCRI, he was a research associate professor at Purdue University. Mourad has played a key role in establishing the data analytics group within QCRI. He is now leading the Research Engineering Group whose mission is to productize QCRI's research. Mourad's research interests lie in the fields of data management and analytics with a focus on data integration, data cleaning, and collaborative data science. He was the project lead of Rayyan, the leading systematic reviews web and mobile app, which is now being used by more than 250k users worldwide. Rayyan has since graduated from QCRI to a start-up, Rayyan Systems Inc. His work has led to numerous publications in top tier venues including PVLDB, TKDE, SIGMOD, and ICDE. He holds a PhD from Virginia Tech, and a BSc and MSc from USTHB, Algiers, all in computer science.

Keynote Talk: Enabling domain experts to create their own NLP models: Notes from our journey

Yannis Katsis
IBM Research - Almaden

Abstract: Creating AI models for Natural Language Processing (NLP) tasks remains a daunting task for domain experts that have the need but lack the technical expertise and resources to create such models. To address this issue, at IBM Research we have been designing and developing human-in-the-loop systems that enable domain experts to interactively build their own NLP models. In this talk I will summarize our experience with building two such systems focusing on text classification and information extraction, respectively. After a brief description of the systems, I will focus on the lessons learned during this process and interesting research challenges that lie ahead in our journey to lowering the barrier of entry to NLP.

Bio: Yannis Katsis is a Senior Research Scientist at IBM Research - Almaden with expertise in the management, integration, and extraction of knowledge from structured, semi-structured, and unstructured data. In his recent work, Yannis focuses on lowering the barrier of entry to knowledge extraction by designing, analyzing, and building human-in-the-loop systems that enable domain experts to interactively generate knowledge extraction AI models that serve their needs. Yannis received his PhD in Computer Science from UC San Diego. His work has appeared in top conferences and journals in the areas of data management, natural language processing, and human-computer interaction, and has been leveraged for multiple IBM products.

Keynote Talk: Understanding and Addressing Uncertainty in Crowd Annotation on Subjective Tasks

Amy Zhang
University of Washington

Abstract: Uncertainty is an important factor that is crucial when it comes to understanding human judgments in subjective and nuanced domains. Whether it's annotators producing data used to train and evaluate machine learning systems for subjective tasks or online communities adjudicating moderation actions on nuanced content, many groups and individuals need to account for and address the uncertainty that comes along with conducting judgments. This issue is exacerbated as the application of computing technology expands to more areas that depend on social and cultural factors. I will present an overview of work consisting of a set of novel annotation tools and workflow designs that support capturing, distinguishing, and addressing uncertainty throughout each step involved in making group judgments. Specifically, I will talk about: (1) how we can use ranges to better capture and distinguish sources of uncertainty in scalar rating tasks; (2) how we can use precedents to interact with uncertainty in categorical decision tasks; (3) how we can address disagreements to reduce uncertainty through pairwise multi-turn deliberation; and (4) how we can dynamically select targeted interventions for reducing uncertainty.

Bio: Amy X. Zhang is an assistant professor at University of Washington's Allen School of Computer Science and Engineering. Previously, she was a 2019-20 postdoctoral researcher at Stanford University's Computer Science Department after completing her Ph.D. at MIT CSAIL in 2019, where she received the George Sprowls Best Ph.D. Thesis Award at MIT in computer science. During her Ph.D., she was an affiliate and 2018-19 Fellow at the Berkman Klein Center at Harvard University, a Google Ph.D. Fellow, and an NSF Graduate Research Fellow. Her work has received a best paper award at ACM CSCW, a best paper honorable mention award at ACM CHI, and has been profiled on BBC's Click television program, CBC radio, and featured in articles by ABC News, The Verge, New Scientist, and Poynter. She is a founding member of the Credibility Coalition, a group dedicated to research and standards for information credibility online. She has interned at Microsoft Research and Google Research. She received an M.Phil. in Computer Science at the University of Cambridge on a Gates Fellowship and a B.S. in Computer Science at Rutgers University, where she was captain of the Division I Women's tennis team.

Table of Contents

Program

Thursday, December 8, 2022

08:55 - 09:00	*Opening Remarks*
09:00 - 09:40	*Keynote Talk 1*
09:40 - 10:40	*Paper Session 1*
10:40 - 11:00	*Coffee Break*
11:00 - 11:40	*Keynote Talk 2*
11:40 - 12:30	*Paper Session 2*
12:30 - 14:00	*Lunch Break*
14:00 - 14:20	*Invited Talk 1*
14:20 - 14:40	*Invited Talk 2*
14:40 - 15:40	*Paper Session 3*
15:30 - 16:00	*Coffee Break*
16:00 - 16:40	*Keynote Talk 3 (Hybrid)*
16:40 - 17:30	*Panel Discussion*

MEGAnno: Exploratory Labeling for NLP in Computational Notebooks

Dan Zhang*, Hannah Kim*, Rafael Li Chen, Eser Kandogan, Estevam Hruschka
Megagon Labs
{dan_z,hannah,rafael,eser,estevam}@megagon.ai

Abstract

We present MEGAnno, a novel exploratory annotation framework designed for NLP researchers and practitioners. Unlike existing labeling tools that focus on data labeling only, our framework aims to support a broader, iterative ML workflow including data exploration and model development. With MEGAnno's API, users can programmatically explore the data through sophisticated search and automated suggestion functions and incrementally update labeling schema as their project evolve. Combined with our widget, the users can interactively sort, filter, and assign labels to multiple items simultaneously in the same notebook where the rest of the NLP project resides. We demonstrate MEGAnno's flexible, exploratory, efficient, and seamless labeling experience through a sentiment analysis use case.

1 Introduction

Data labeling is an important step in the machine learning life cycle since the quality and quantity of training data directly affect the model performance (Geiger et al., 2021). Unfortunately, existing annotation tools tend to consider the data labeling step in isolation from the broader ML life cycle, ignoring the iterative workflow of researchers and practitioners. However, activities such as data selection, exploratory data analysis, data labeling, model training, and evaluation do not happen sequentially (Rahman and Kandogan, 2022). Instead, continuous iterations are required to improve data, annotation, and models (Hohman et al., 2020).

To further investigate this gap, we examine the data annotation practices within the ML model development life cycle. Based on a formative study with six researchers from our organization, we characterize their annotation practices as a "dual-loop" model shown in Fig. 1. After data preprocessing (Fig. 1 ①), researchers define their annotation schema in terms of what labels to collect, how many data points are needed, and so on (Fig. 1 ②). As they explore and annotate the data (Fig. 1 ③), they often go back and refine the annotation schema due to their improved understanding of the data and updated mental models for the tasks (Fig. 1 ④). For example, in a document classification task, a user may start with loosely defined category labels and add more choices as she discovers relevant documents (Felix et al., 2018). Throughout this paper, we refer to this cycle as **data understanding/exploration loop**. Next, the labeled data is exported from the annotation tool and is used to train a model (Fig. 1 ⑤). However, in practice, ML model training is rarely completed in one pass and usually goes through many iterations of labeling, training, data, and model debugging (Pustejovsky and Stubbs, 2012). Fig. 1 ⑥ refers to the cases where researchers may need to collect more data (e.g., for the less represented classes due to a sub-optimal prediction performance of the downstream model) or further refine the schema. We call this cycle (i.e., model training, evaluating and debugging, collecting more data, and training again) **model evaluation loop**.

We find that the iterative dual-loop workflow

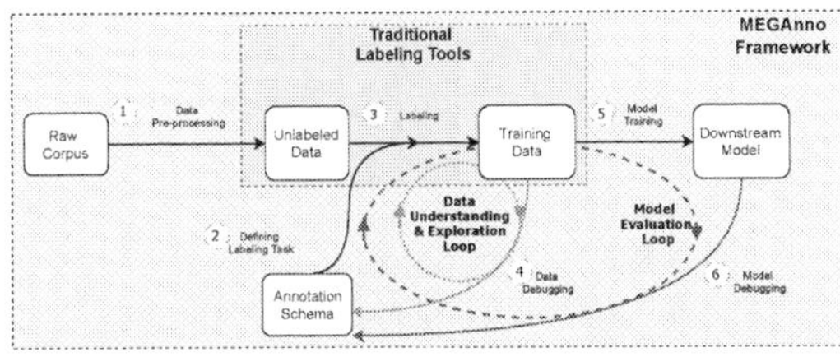

Figure 1: Dual-loop model for data annotation: (1) data understanding/exploration loop (yellow): iteratively update annotation schema while exploring and annotating data and (2) model evaluation loop (green): train and improve a downstream model over iterations by debugging data. Most tools are focused on the labeling step only (red box). MEGAnno aims to capture both loops seamlessly within the framework (green box).

* Equal contribution.

Proceedings of the Fourth Workshop on Data Science with Human-in-the-Loop (Language Advances), pages 1 - 7
December 8, 2022

of NLP researchers and practitioners is rarely supported in most existing tools. More specifically, we identified three main challenges towards supporting the full annotation life cycle:

- **Gaps between ML toolings.** Most of the existing tools are standalone and designed for a specific ML step, which results in frequent context switching and data migration overhead in the researchers' daily workflow.
- **Lack of customizable and granular control.** Not all data points are equally important. There are often cases where users might want to prioritize a particular batch (e.g., to achieve better class or domain coverage or focus on the data points that the downstream model cannot predict well). Although some recent active learning based tools (Montani and Honnibal, 2018; hua) can provide suggestions for the next batch, most tools do not offer customizable and fine-grained control with or with a downstream model (i.e., covering both loops).
- **Lack of support for project evolution.** Current annotation tools usually work with the assumption that the data collection task is well-defined and immutable and ignore that annotation projects can evolve as explorations happen and insights are gathered. Thus they lack the support to help users make evolution decisions, and their immutable nature makes it hard to apply these changes.

To address the challenges, we present MEGAnno, a flexible, exploratory, efficient, and seamless labeling framework for NLP researchers and practitioners. It provides a seamless experience where data pre-processing, annotation, analysis, model development and evaluation can happen in the same notebook, a popular daily working environment for data science practitioners. MEGAnno provides customizable interfaces to help users drive their project to the desired directions through rich heuristic-based search, automatic suggestion, and active learning based suggestions of the next data batch. With project evolution in mind, MEGAnno is designed to work with flexible task schema and provides a built-in analysis dashboard to aid decision-making. To our knowledge, MEGAnno is the first flexible, exploratory labeling framework that can support ML workflow seamlessly in computational notebooks (Fig. 1: green box).

2 MEGAnno

2.1 Framework Overview

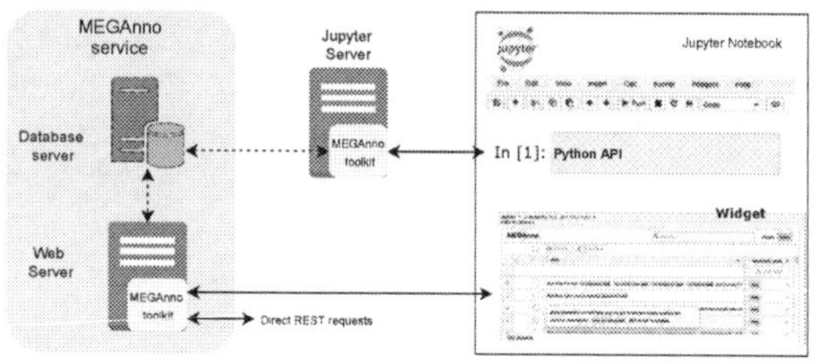

Figure 2: The MEGAnno framework provides exploratory annotation services through a toolkit (installable as Python libraries) providing programmatic interfaces, a web server providing language-agnostic REST APIs, and an internal database to store data, annotation, and related artifacts. Solid lines show programmatic interactions through Python APIs calls and REST calls delegated by our notebook widget or directly issued by authenticated applications. Dotted lines show internal interfaces where MEGAnno toolkit handles communication with the database and are hidden from the users.

MEGAnno provides service through 1) an internal database that stores the data, annotations, and various artifacts produced in the annotation process, 2) a MEGAnno toolkit that provides python API for programmatic and visual data exploration and labeling, and 3) a web server that provides language-agnostic REST APIs (Fig 2). After installing the toolkit on a Jupyter server, users will have access to our Python APIs and React-based widget to manage their project, explore and annotate their data from any connected notebook.

Data model A `Data record` refers to an item in the pre-processed data corpus for labeling. It can be a sentence, a paragraph, a document, or a flattened text from multiple texts such as a question-answer pair. A `Label` is the smallest unit of user labeling output. MEGAnno currently supports record-level (e.g., topics for document or sentence) and span-level (e.g., named entities) labels. An `Annotation` is a set of labels given to a data record by an annotator. `Metadata` refers to additional information related to the content of a data record (e.g., externally generated part-of-speech tags, embeddings) or of an annotation (e.g., time taken to label, disagreement among annotators). Such information can be helpful in various steps of the ML iterations. A `Subset` is a slice of the data records in the database. Subsets can be of random data records or can be generated through search queries that match certain characteristics.

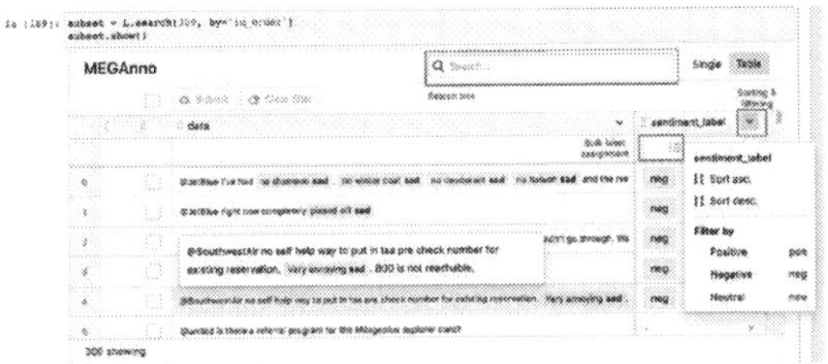

Figure 3: The table view to show multiple data records. Hovering over a data record shows its full text in a pop-up. This view allows exploration by searching, sorting, and filtering over labels and single/bulk annotation.

Task schema We support a wide variety of tasks through our customizable schema in JSON format. To collect a label, users need to specify the level (i.e., record or span) and provide a list of options to choose from. For a task, MEGAnno supports arbitrary numbers of both types of labels. We'll see concrete schema examples for a sentiment prediction and extraction task in Section 3. At any stage, users can always update the schema to reflect the evolution of the project. There are certain constraints to schema updates to keep the consistency of data. Adding new labels or new label options will always be allowed. Removal of labels and options will trigger a database query and MEGAnno will warn the user if there exist such labeled instances. [1]

2.2 MEGAnno Jupyter Notebook Widget

MEGAnno's interactive notebook widget features 1) our novel table view to facilitate exploratory and batch labeling and 2) the single view, which is similar to traditional labeling UIs.

Table view The table view (Fig. 3) shows data items in a `Subset` and their annotations if any. Each record-level label is shown as a column, and span-level labels are shown together with the highlighted textual span in the data column. Users can hover over an item to see full text in a pop-up. The search box supports three types of search (exact, fuzzy, and regex-based) to filter the data subset further. Users can sort and filter rows based on any record-level labels using the dropdown menu. To assign a record-level label, the users can click on the cell's arrow button and select from the dropdown options. Alternatively, the users can assign the same label to multiple records simultaneously by selecting those records and clicking the bulk label button.

Single view The table view is good for exploration, but the limited space makes span-level annotation cumbersome. So we also provide a single view where users can have a more zoomed-in experience. By clicking the "Single" button on the top-right corner or double-clicking on a data record, the widget switches to the single view (Fig. 4). In this view, users can assign record-level labels on the right side and span-level labels on the left side by selecting/dragging target spans and choosing the label from the options drop-down. Users can loop through the subset using the prev/next button based on the order specified in the table view. At any time, users can switch between the two views by clicking the top right buttons, and the widget preserves all uncommitted annotations during view changes.

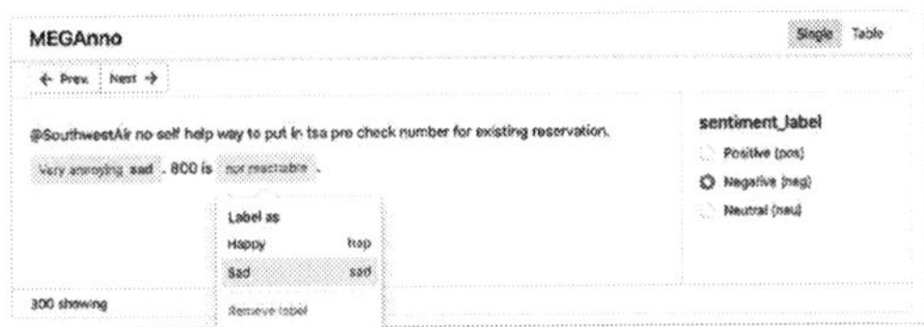

Figure 4: The single view to annotate data one by one. In this view, users can drag and label spans for extraction tasks.

Working with multiple annotators Annotation is rarely done by a single person. As an initial step towards collaborative annotation, MEGAnno provides virtually separated namespaces for each annotator. Users identify themselves by a unique authentication token while connecting to the service and only update their own labels through the widgets. MEGAnno provides a reconciliation view (Fig. 5) to look at labels from different individuals and resolve potential conflicts.

Figure 5: Reconcilation view showing the existing label distribution for data points.

Dashboard MEGAnno also provides a built-in visual monitoring dashboard (Fig. 6). As projects evolve, users would need to understand

[1] MEGAnno provides an option to clean up legacy labels and retry automatically.

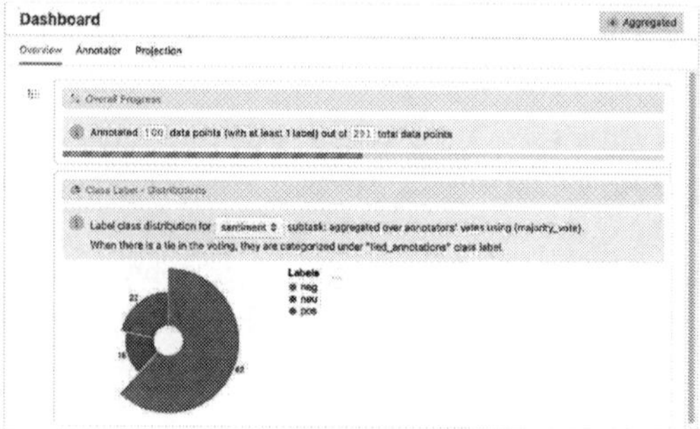

Figure 6: Dashboard widget to monitor the progress and statistics of the project and aid decision-making.

the project's status to make decisions about the next steps, like collecting more data points with certain characteristics or adding a new class to the task definition. To aid such analysis, the dashboard widget packs common statistics and analytical visualizations based on a survey of our pilot users. The "overview" panel shows statistics about overall progress and per-label class distribution. If multiple annotators are involved, the distribution reflects the majority vote over annotators [2]. The remaining "annotator" and "projection" panels are hidden due to space limitations. To help identify problematic annotators, the annotator pannel shows statistics like overall individual contribution and disagreement scores with others. The projection panel provides customizable visualization to project data points to a two-dimensional visual space. By default, we show the t-SNE (Van der Maaten and Hinton, 2008) projection of sentence bert (Reimers and Gurevych, 2019) embeddings.

2.3 MEGAnno APIs

Project management The management module provides various interfaces to configure and monitor the annotation project through the `Project` class. `import_data` loads the data records from CSV or JSON files into the database. `set_config` updates the project configuration as it evolves. `set_meta` assigns metadata (e.g.,POS tags, document embeddings) for each data record through user-defined functions. `get_status` returns the status of the project such as the number of annotated data records and detailed statistic about each label.

A critical feature of MEGAnno is to select interesting subsets of data to show in the widget. Subsets can be generated in a user-initiative way via our search engine or a data-driven way via automated suggestions.

Search for subsets MEGAnno supports sophisticated searches over data records, annotation, and user-defined metadata through the `Project.search` API. Users can search data records by keywords (e.g., documents mentioning "customer service") or regular expressions to express more complex patterns. The users can also search the database based on already assigned labels (e.g., records with a positive sentiment label). As will be explained later, MEGAnno acknowledges the value of auxiliary information for ML projects and provides advanced search functionalities over metadata. For example, users can query with patterns combining regex expressions and POS tags like `project.search("(best|amazing) <ADJ> <NOUN>", by="POS")`.

Automated subset suggestion Searches initiated by users can help users explore the dataset in a controlled way, but the quality of searches is only as good as users' knowledge or heuristic about the data and domain. MEGAnno provides an automated subset suggestion engine to assist the exploration. Users can customize the engine by plugging in external suggestion models as needed. Currently, the engine provides two types of techniques:

- **Embedding-based suggestions** makes suggestions based on data embedding vectors provided by the user. `Subset.suggest_similar` suggests neighbors of data in the querying subset. `Project.suggest_coverage` examines all the data records within the embedding space in an unsupervised way and suggests data points from the less annotated regions to improve annotation coverage of the corpus.
- **Active suggestions** utilizes active learning techniques to recommend the most informative data for the downstream model. With libraries like ModAL (Danka and Horvath), users can select from various selection strategies based on model uncertainty and entropy, etc. Since MEGAnno's seamless notebook experience covers the whole loop from annotation to model training and debugging, users

[2]Users can provide their aggregation function to resovle conflicts between annotators

can actively select a subset, annotate the subset, update the model, and test again in the same notebook without switching environments.

The output of selection engines are instances of the `Subset` class with the following methods: `show` returns a notebook widget for interactive exploration and annotation. `batch_annotation` sets the same record-level labels for all data records in the subset. `suggest_similar` returns a new subset of the database containing the most similar data for each record in the querying subset according to some metadata with valid distance functions.

3 Use Case: Sentiment Analysis

We present a use case to illustrate how MEGAnno can support data annotation in NLP researchers and practitioners' workflow. Meggie is a data scientist who wants to train a sentiment-related model for her project. She obtains a Twitter dataset[3]about US airlines and decides to label it using MEGAnno.

Import data In an empty notebook, Meggie starts by initializing the project named "Tweet Sentiment" using a MEGAnno Python API. She gets a copy of the data from the product manager who often uses Google spreadsheet and imports the data from its published link.

```
from meganno import Project
L = Project(<auth>, "Tweet Sentiment")
L.import_data(<doc_url>, format="csv")
```

Set up initial schema Without knowing much about the data, Meggie decides to start the project by collecting binary labels and setting up the project's schema. Knowing that MEGAnno supports flexible and editable schema, Meggie does not worry about getting the perfect schema in the first round and can start exploring and annotating.

```
label_schema = [{
    "label_name": "sentiment_label",
    "level": "record",
    "options": ["Positive", "Negative"]
}]
L.set_config(config1)
```

Explore and annotate She starts by exploring the first 300 data points in the widget's table view.

[3]The Kaggle dataset (for Everyone library) has ground-truth sentiment labels available. But for demonstration purposes, we ignore them and assume Meggie only gets the raw Tweets. The dataset contains 14K tweets about major US airlines scraped in February 2015.

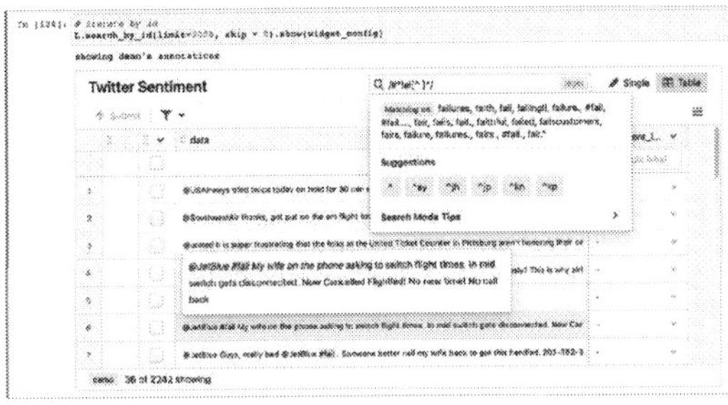

Figure 7: UI Search by regular expression. Matched keywords are highlighted.

Using the search box, she filters the subset with the keyword "amazing". As expected, most of the data records reflect a positive sentiment, so she assigns a positive label to multiple data items using the "Bulk label" button. Next, she wants to examine tweets with hashtags related to failing, so she tries regular expression search using `#fai[^ ]*` (Fig. 7). With better understanding of the dataset, Meggie chooses to perform more advanced exploration using part-of-speech metadata. She imports a POS tagger from spaCy (Honnibal and Montani, 2017) and retrieves tweets that match interesting patterns such as `best <NOUN> of <NOUN>`.

```
import spacy
tagger = spacy.load("en_core_web_sm")

pos1 = L.search("(best|amazing) <ADJ> <NOUN>", by="POS", tagger=tagger)
pos2 = L.search("best <NOUN> of <NOUN>", by="POS", tagger=tagger)
meganno.union(pos1, pos2).show()
```

With such an exploratory approach and the batch labeling feature, she can annotate much faster and in a more controlled way.

Candidate suggestion After a few more heuristics, she runs out of ideas, so she takes advantage of the suggestion feature. She selects the sentence bert (Reimers and Gurevych, 2019) encoder as the meta-data generation function. She first issues a query with strategy `similarity` to collect data points similar to the ones retrieved from the previous POS search. Finally, she wants to see samples from less covered areas in the embedding space to improve the diversity of the training data and issues a `coverage` query.

```
m = SentenceTransformer("all-MiniLM-L6")
# set metadata generation function
L.set_meta("bert", lambda x: list(m.encode(x)))
# get more data like the query result in the previous query(subset_pos)
```

```
subset_sim = pos2.suggest_similar(
    meta_name="bert")
# get data from less covered areas in
    the embedding space.
subset_cov = L.suggest_coverage(
    meta_name="bert")
```

Update the schema Meggie is now happy with the collected labels, but she aims to go one step further to understand which words or phrases lead to the sentiment judgment. So she updates her schema by adding a new span-level label called `sentiment_span` with label options being "happy" or "sad". Each data record can have arbitrary numbers of such span-level labels.

```
label_schema = [{
    "label_name": "sentiment_span",
    "level": "span",
    "options": ["Happy", "Sad"]
}, ... {# previous label options
}]
```

After updating the schema, she fetches all records with neutral labels in a widget. To highlight and annotate spans, she goes into the single view (as shown in Fig. 4). At any step of the iteration, she could refer to the dashboard widget to monitor the project progress. After several rounds of similar iterations, she feels good and concludes her exploration. Finally, Meggie can export the annotated data in JSON or CSV formats for training or plug in the model directly.

In conclusion, with MEGAnno, Meggie can explore her dataset using various heuristic-based or automated search functions and better understand the data corpus as she labels. She has the flexibility to iteratively update her schema as the project evolves. Using the widget, Meggie can finish the entire ML life cyle in the same Jupyter notebook.

4 Related Work

There exist numerous annotation tools that can support NLP tasks, which are extensively surveyed by Neves and Seva (2019, 2020). In this section, we focus on works that are closer to our flexible, exploratory, efficient, and seamless framework.

Flexible schema Unfortunately, most of existing tools are not designed for iterative schema development, and thus they are not flexible enough for evolving projects. Felix et al. (2018) and Kulesza et al. (2014) allow users to progressively define document classes by inspecting documents that are assigned to each class. But these works are more similar to interactive topic modeling or interactive classification, where users assign documents to classes, than document labeling, where users assign labels to documents. Our tool goes beyond document label refinement and supports a broader task of progressively defining annotation schema (e.g., additionally collecting span-level labels).

Exploratory labeling The concept of exploratory labeling is introduced by Felix et al. (2018) as using computational techniques to help users group documents into evolving labels. In our paper, we use the term "exploratory labeling" to refer to where exploratory data analysis and data annotation are iteratively conducted in the data understanding/exploration loop. Exploratory labeling can be beneficial because while labeling data, users gain insight into their dataset (Sun et al., 2017).

Efficient batch/bulk annotation A few tools offer a functionality to simultaneously assign labels to multiple spans within a record. For example, YEDDA (Yang et al., 2018) can annotate multiple span-level labels via command line. TALEN (Stephen Mayhew, 2018), a named entity tagging tool, has an entity propagation feature which annotates all mentions of an entity in a document at once. In contrast, users can annotate multiple records simultaneously using our Python API and a GUI widget.

Notebook widget Computational notebooks are frequently used by data analysts to iteratively write and edit code to understand data, test hypotheses, and build models (Head et al., 2019; Randles et al., 2017). Following the practice of mage (Kery et al., 2020) which extends Jupyter notebook with GUI widgets for specific tasks, our widget is designed to achieve flexible communication with the rest of ML development codes. Annotation tools which are implemented as Jupyter widgets include Pigeon (pig) and ipyannotate (ipy), but they only offer a simple label assignment feature.

5 Conclusion

In this paper, we present MEGAnno, an annotation framework designed for NLP researchers and practitioners. Through MEGAnno's programmatic interfaces and interactive widget, users can iteratively explore and search for interesting data subsets, annotate data, train models, evaluate and debug models within a Jupyter notebook without the overhead of context switch or data migration.

References

humanloop.com. `https://humanloop.com/`.

ipyannotate. `https://github.com/ipyannotate/ipyannotate`.

pigeon. `https://github.com/agermanidis/pigeon`.

Tivadar Danka and Peter Horvath. modAL: A modular active learning framework for Python. Available on arXiv at `https://arxiv.org/abs/1805.00979`.

Cristian Felix, Aritra Dasgupta, and Enrico Bertini. 2018. The exploratory labeling assistant: Mixed-initiative label curation with large document collections. In *Proceedings of the 31st Annual ACM Symposium on User Interface Software and Technology*, UIST '18, pages 153–164, New York, NY, USA. Association for Computing Machinery.

Crowdflower Data for Everyone library. Twitter US Airline Sentiment(Version 4).

R. Stuart Geiger, Dominique Cope, Jamie Ip, Marsha Lotosh, Aayush Shah, Jenny Weng, and Rebekah Tang. 2021. "garbage in, garbage out" revisited: What do machine learning application papers report about human-labeled training data? *Quantitative Science Studies*, pages 1–33.

Andrew Head, Fred Hohman, Titus Barik, Steven M. Drucker, and Robert DeLine. 2019. *Managing Messes in Computational Notebooks*, pages 1–12. Association for Computing Machinery, New York, NY, USA.

Fred Hohman, Kanit Wongsuphasawat, Mary Beth Kery, and Kayur Patel. 2020. Understanding and visualizing data iteration in machine learning. In *Proceedings of the 2020 CHI Conference on Human Factors in Computing Systems*, pages 1–13.

Matthew Honnibal and Ines Montani. 2017. spaCy 2: Natural language understanding with Bloom embeddings, convolutional neural networks and incremental parsing. To appear.

Mary Beth Kery, Donghao Ren, Fred Hohman, Dominik Moritz, Kanit Wongsuphasawat, and Kayur Patel. 2020. mage: Fluid moves between code and graphical work in computational notebooks.

Todd Kulesza, Saleema Amershi, Rich Caruana, Danyel Fisher, and Denis Charles. 2014. Structured labeling for facilitating concept evolution in machine learning. In *Proceedings of the SIGCHI Conference on Human Factors in Computing Systems*, CHI '14, pages 3075–3084, New York, NY, USA. Association for Computing Machinery.

Ines Montani and Matthew Honnibal. 2018. Prodigy: A new annotation tool for radically efficient machine teaching. *Artificial Intelligence*, to appear.

Mariana Neves and Jurica Seva. 2019. An extensive review of tools for manual annotation of documents. *Briefings in Bioinformatics*, 22(1):146–163.

Mariana Neves and Jurica Seva. 2020. Annotationsaurus: A searchable directory of annotation tools.

James Pustejovsky and Amber Stubbs. 2012. *Natural Language Annotation for Machine Learning: A guide to corpus-building for applications*. " O'Reilly Media, Inc.".

Sajjadur Rahman and Eser Kandogan. 2022. Characterizing practices, limitations, and opportunities related to text information extraction workflows: A human-in-the-loop perspective. CHI '22, New York, NY, USA. Association for Computing Machinery.

Bernadette M. Randles, Irene V. Pasquetto, Milena S. Golshan, and Christine L. Borgman. 2017. Using the jupyter notebook as a tool for open science: An empirical study. In *2017 ACM/IEEE Joint Conference on Digital Libraries (JCDL)*, pages 1–2.

Nils Reimers and Iryna Gurevych. 2019. Sentence-bert: Sentence embeddings using siamese bert-networks. In *Proceedings of the 2019 Conference on Empirical Methods in Natural Language Processing*. Association for Computational Linguistics.

Dan Roth Stephen Mayhew. 2018. Talen: Tool for annotation of low-resource entities. In *ACL System Demonstrations*.

Yunjia Sun, Edward Lank, and Michael Terry. 2017. Label-and-learn: Visualizing the likelihood of machine learning classifier's success during data labeling. In *Proceedings of the 22nd International Conference on Intelligent User Interfaces*, IUI '17, pages 523–534, New York, NY, USA. Association for Computing Machinery.

Laurens Van der Maaten and Geoffrey Hinton. 2008. Visualizing data using t-sne. *Journal of machine learning research*, 9(11).

Jie Yang, Yue Zhang, Linwei Li, and Xingxuan Li. 2018. YEDDA: A lightweight collaborative text span annotation tool. In *Proceedings of ACL 2018, System Demonstrations*, pages 31–36, Melbourne, Australia. Association for Computational Linguistics.

Cross-lingual Short-text Entity Linking: Generating Features for Neuro-Symbolic Methods

Qiuhao Lu[1], Sairam Gurajada[2], Prithviraj Sen[2], Lucian Popa[2], Dejing Dou[1,3], and Thien Huu Nguyen[1]
[1]Department of Computer Science, University of Oregon, Eugene, OR, USA
[2]IBM Research
[3]Baidu Research
{luqh, dou, thien}@cs.uoregon.edu
gu.sairam@gmail.com
{senp, lpopa}@us.ibm.com

Abstract

Entity linking (EL) on short text is crucial for a variety of industrial applications. Compared with general long-text EL, short-text EL poses particular challenges as the limited context restricts the clues one can leverage to disambiguate textual mentions. On the other hand, existing studies mostly focus on black-box neural methods and thus lack interpretability, which is critical to industrial applications in certain areas. In this study, we extend upon LNN-EL, a monolingual short-text EL method based on interpretable first-order logic (Jiang et al., 2021), by incorporating three sets of multilingual features to enable disambiguating mentions written in languages other than English. More specifically, we use multilingual autoencoding language models (i.e., mBERT) to capture the similarities between the mention with its context and the candidate entity; we use multilingual sequence-to-sequence language models (i.e., mBART and mT5) to represent the likelihood of the text given the candidate entity. We also propose a word-level context feature to capture the semantic evidence of the co-occurring mentions. We evaluate the proposed xLNN-EL approach on the QALD-9-multilingual dataset and demonstrate the cross-linguality of the model and the effectiveness of the features.

1 Introduction

Entity linking (EL), also known as entity disambiguation, is the task of linking textual mentions appearing in a document to the corresponding entities associated with a target knowledge base like DBpedia (Auer et al., 2007). As a fundamental task in natural language processing and information extraction, entity linking is crucial for a variety of applications such as semantic search, recommendation systems and chatbots (Tan et al., 2017).

Historically, relevant studies of entity linking mostly focus on long text scenario (i.e., documents) (Han et al., 2011; Gupta et al., 2017; Lu and Du, 2017; Cao et al., 2018; Kolitsas et al., 2018). Typically, such approaches mainly depend on specifically-designed features of candidates (e.g., priors), local context compatibility, and global coherence across the document (Shen et al., 2021).

With the rapidly growing short text on the web, e.g., search queries, social media posts, news headlines, etc., short-text entity linking has attracted increasing attention from researchers due to its potential for various industrial applications. However, long-text entity linking methods barely maintain the same level of performance on short text, as they heavily rely on document-level global coherence, i.e., the idea of *collective entity linking* (Cao et al., 2018), and short text (e.g., a single sentence or search query) cannot provide rich context and global signals for disambiguation (Chen et al., 2018).

To tackle the task of short-text entity linking, different methods are being proposed to exploit the short and limited context (Chen et al., 2018; Sakor et al., 2019; Gu et al., 2021). For example, Chen et al. (Chen et al., 2018) try to map the sparse short text to a topic space such that a topic coherence can be achieved through a specifically designed optimization objective, e.g., they aim to infer the topic is *literature* against *movie* from the word `read` in "read Harry Potter". Gu et al. (Gu et al., 2021) try to enhance the interactions between the local context and the candidate entity in multi-turn multiple-choice manner, so that global disambiguation can finally be achieved. More recently, autoregressive entity linking models, e.g., GENRE (De Cao et al., 2020) and mGENRE (De Cao et al., 2021b) demonstrate superior performance and are gaining a lot of attention. With the power of large pre-trained sequence-to-sequence language models (Lewis et al., 2020), GENRE and mGENRE are able to directly generate unique entity names conditioned on the context, yielding state-of-the-art

Proceedings of the Fourth Workshop on Data Science with Human-in-the-Loop (Language Advances), pages 8 - 14
December 8, 2022 ©2022 Association for Computational Linguistics

results on multiple datasets.

Recently, Jiang et al. propose LNN-EL, the first neuro-symbolic short-text entity linking method that combines first-order logic (FOL) rules with neural learning, and shows competitive performance against deep-learning-based black-box methods (Jiang et al., 2021). Essentially, LNN-EL uses FOL rules as a glue to combine different features into a final linking model, and demonstrates *interpretability* due to the interpretable nature of FOL. Nonetheless, LNN-EL is a monolingual model that only supports English, and does not meet the demands of modern industrial applications where enterprises need to establish effective cross-language interactions with users from all over the world.

To enable this approach to facilitate rapidly growing global business, in this study, we extend upon LNN-EL by incorporating three sets multilingual features to make it cross-lingual, i.e., xLNN-EL. First, we propose a word-level cross-lingual context feature that aims to capture the semantic evidence of co-occurring mentions. Second, we use multilingual autoencoding language models (i.e., mBERT (Pires et al., 2019)) to capture the similarities between the mention with its context and the candidate entity with a four-way feature. Third, we use multilingual sequence-to-sequence language models (i.e., mBART (Liu et al., 2020) and mT5 (Xue et al., 2021)) to represent the likelihood of the text given the candidate entity. More specifically, we try to reconstruct the text conditioned on the candidate's description, based on a fine-tuned generative language model, and it results in another two-way feature indicating the likelihood of the text. We evaluate xLNN-EL on the QALD-9-multilingual dataset with the state-of-the-art black-box method mGENRE (De Cao et al., 2021b), and the results demonstrate the effectiveness of the proposed features. Our contribution can thus be summarized as follows:

- We extend upon LNN-EL to facilitate disambiguating mentions appearing in non-English languages. To the best of our knowledge, xLNN-EL is the first neuro-symbolic method for cross-language short-text entity linking and performs competitively against state-of-the-art black-box method.

- We propose three sets of multilingual features that aim to capture the contextual semantic evidence of co-occurring mentions, the similarities between the mention with its context and the candidate, and the likelihood score of the context conditioned on the candidate. The experimental results show the effectiveness of the features.

2 xLNN-EL

We propose xLNN-EL, a cross-language extension of LNN-EL, where we seek to facilitate the model with better cross-linguality by incorporating a set of new features allowing it to link non-English mentions to the English knowledge base.

Following LNN-EL, we take the *English DBpedia* as the target knowledge base (Jiang et al., 2021). As to candidate retrieval, we adopt a hybrid method of PivotsCR (Liu et al., 2021) and mGENRE (De Cao et al., 2021b). Essentially, for each mention m_i, we take the union of their outputs and generate a set of $|C_i| = 250$ candidate entities, roughly reaching a 95% recall rate for each language[1].

Formally, given a single sentence or search query T containing a set of mentions $M = \{m_1, m_2, \ldots, m_p\}$, a triple m_i, C_i, L_i is generated for each mention m_i. L_i is a list of binary labels for the mention-candidate pair (m_i, e_{ij}) where $e_{ij} \in C_i$. The entity name and textual description of e_{ij} is denoted by $e_{ij}.name$ and $e_{ij}.desc$, respectively. For each candidate e_{ij}, a set of predefined features $f_w(m_i, e_{ij})$ is generated. In this section, we introduce the three cross-language features $f_w \in \mathcal{F}$ that we incorporate into the model.

2.1 Word-level Context Score

Given a mention, we introduce a word-level context score to capture the semantic evidence sustained by the similarity between the co-occurring mentions and the descriptions of the candidate entities, i.e., short abstracts[2]. The feature function f_{ctx} is defined as follows:

$$
\begin{aligned}
f_{\text{ctx}}(m_i, e_{ij}) &= \sum_{m_k \in M \setminus \{m_i\}} pr_{\text{word}}(m_k, e_{ij}) \\
pr_{\text{word}}(m_k, e_{ij}) &= \max_{s_k \in e_{ij}.desc} \cos(\mathbf{m_k}, \mathbf{s_k})
\end{aligned} \tag{1}
$$

[1]LNN-EL uses DBpedia lookup to retrieve top-100 candidates.

[2]http://downloads.dbpedia.org/wiki-archive/downloads-2016-10.html

Method	mono-lingual				multi-lingual				cross-lingual			
F1-score(%)	de	fr	en	it	de	fr	en	it	de	fr	en	it
mGENRE	47.50	47.50	62.50	50.83	57.50	54.17	56.67	54.17	55.00	57.50	50.83	52.50
base	58.82	62.61	83.76	58.82	58.82	60.92	83.76	57.14	61.34	60.50	80.08	57.14
base + ctx	61.34	62.61	83.76	57.14	60.50	61.34	84.60	57.14	60.50	63.03	83.05	55.46
base + mbert	61.34	62.61	84.60	56.72	59.66	61.76	83.76	56.30	60.50	60.92	80.08	56.30
base + generative	60.50	63.45	84.60	62.04	61.34	61.76	83.76	58.40	60.50	61.76	82.20	58.40
base + ctx + mbert	63.03	60.92	83.76	57.14	59.66	62.61	84.60	57.14	59.66	61.34	80.08	56.30
base + ctx + generative	**66.39**	62.61	84.60	59.66	60.78	61.34	84.60	57.14	60.08	63.03	82.63	57.56
base + mbert + generative	63.45	**69.75**	84.60	**63.03**	62.18	**63.87**	83.76	57.98	**64.99**	**63.87**	**83.47**	57.98
base + ctx + mbert + generative	65.13	64.29	**85.45**	60.50	**62.61**	62.18	**85.45**	**58.82**	61.34	62.18	83.05	**59.66**

Table 1: Performance of xLNN-EL on QALD-9-multilingual.

where pr_{word} is a word-level *Partial Ratio*[3] score. The idea is to find the maximum similarity between the mention m_k and any group of words of the same length s_k, i.e., a sliding window, in the candidate's textual description. We use fastText's pre-trained aligned word vectors[4] (Bojanowski et al., 2017; Joulin et al., 2018) to encode the mention and the entity description as they are in different languages in the cross-language setting, i.e., the vector representations $\mathbf{m_k}, \mathbf{s_k}$ are in the same embedding space though m_k are non-English and s_k are English. We then take the aggregated similarities as the feature indicating the semantic contextual relevance of the candidate.

2.2 Autoencoding-LM-based Scores

We also introduce a set of autoencoding-language-model-based features to encode the the overall similarities between the mention with its context and the candidate entity. In particular, autoencoding language models (e.g., BERT (Devlin et al., 2019)) create a bidirectional representation of the whole sentence which makes them a natural fit as text encoders, and the representations can be further facilitate discriminative downstream applications. Due to the *extensibility* of the framework in LNN-EL (Jiang et al., 2021), we are able to include various features to describe the relationship between the mention and the candidate from different levels and aspects. For this feature, we use the multilingual version of BERT, i.e., mBERT (Pires et al., 2019), as the language model, and the feature function f_{mbert} is defined as follows:

$$\begin{aligned} f_{\text{mbert}} &= \left[f_{\text{mbert}_1}, f_{\text{mbert}_2}, f_{\text{mbert}_3}, f_{\text{mbert}_4}\right] \\ &= \left[\cos(\mathbf{m_i}, \mathbf{e_{ij}.name}), \cos(\mathbf{T}, \mathbf{e_{ij}.name}),\right. \\ &\quad \left.\cos(\mathbf{m_i}, \mathbf{e_{ij}.desc}), \cos(\mathbf{T}, \mathbf{e_{ij}.desc})\right] \end{aligned} \tag{2}$$

where the bold fonts indicate the vector representations for the mention ($\mathbf{m_i}$), the input short text ($\mathbf{T}$), the candidate's name ($\mathbf{e_{ij}.name}$), and the candidate's description ($\mathbf{e_{ij}.desc}$), respectively. Essentially, the text is sent to mBERT and the vector representation for the `[CLS]` token is used. This four-way feature aims to explore the possibility of capturing the similarities between the input text and the candidate entity from different aspects, under the xLNN-EL framework. The experimental results in Section 3 show that they are useful and complementary.

2.3 Seq2Seq-LM-based Scores

Sequence-to-sequence language models (e.g., BART (Lewis et al., 2020)) are mostly adopted for tasks like translation, summarization and question answering. For short-text cross-lingual entity linking, however, this direction has been underexplored.

In this study, we propose to leverage seq2seq language models to reveal another aspect of similarity between the mention and the candidate entity, leveraging a set of features to reflect the likelihood of the context, given the candidate entity for each mention. Essentially, we first fine-tune multilingual generative models $\mathcal{G}$ (i.e., mBART (Liu et al., 2020) and mT5 (Xue et al., 2021) in this paper) on the training set of `<description, sentence>` pairs, where the `description` refers to the candidate entity's textual description and the `sentence` refers to the input short text, i.e., $< e_{ij}.desc, T >$. The idea is to enable the models to generate a short sentence conditioned on a textual description of a

[3] `pypi.org/project/py-stringmatching`

[4] `https://fasttext.cc/docs/en/aligned-vectors.html`

candidate entity. With a fine-tuned model $\mathcal{G}_{tuned}$, we assign a likelihood score to each candidate. The feature function $f_{\text{generative}}$ is defined as follows:

$$\begin{aligned} f_{\text{generative}} &= [f_{\text{mbart}}, f_{\text{mt5}}] \\ &= [\sum_{k}^{|T|} \log p_{\theta_{\text{mbart}}}(x_k | x_{<k}, e_{ij}.desc), \\ &\quad \sum_{k}^{|T|} \log p_{\theta_{\text{mt5}}}(x_k | x_{<k}, e_{ij}.desc)] \end{aligned} \tag{3}$$

where $T = (x_0, x_1, \ldots, x_{|T|})$ is the short text and $\log p_{\theta_{\text{mbart}}}(x_k|x_{<k})$, $\log p_{\theta_{\text{mt5}}}(x_k|x_{<k})$ are the log-likelihoods of the k-th token conditioned on the preceding tokens based on the fine-tuned models $\mathcal{G}_{\text{mbart}}$ and $\mathcal{G}_{\text{mt5}}$, respectively. This two-way generative feature serves to reflect the feasibility of the whole sentence given the candidate entity, without a special focus on the mention.

3 Experiment

3.1 Setup

We evaluate xLNN-EL on the QALD-9-multilingual dataset[5]. For a fair comparison, we take the German (de), French (fr), English (en), and Italian (it) versions of this dataset, as the other languages are incomplete comparing to the English version. The evaluation is conducted in three settings: **mono-lingual** refers to in-language training and testing; **multi-lingual** means training on the union of all languages and testing on individual languages; and **cross-lingual** means testing on one language while training on the other three. We compare the proposed model xLNN-EL with the state-of-the-art black-box method mGENRE (De Cao et al., 2021b) for entity linking. In addition, we also evaluate the adapted version of LNN-EL with basic features in the cross-language scenario, denoted by `base`.

3.2 Results

The results are shown in Table 1. We present different combinations of the proposed features in the table. xLNN-EL with the `base` feature set shows better performance than mGENRE, most likely due to the limitation that such methods (GENRE/mGENRE) need large amounts of data for adequate training (De Cao et al., 2021a). We

[5]https://github.com/ag-sc/QALD/tree/master/9/data

Method	mono-lingual				
F1-score(%)	de	fr	en	it	Δ
all	65.13	64.29	85.45	60.50	-
- mbert 1	65.55	62.61	84.60	57.56	-1.26
- mbert 2	63.03	62.61	82.91	58.82	-2.00
- mbert 3	60.50	61.34	84.60	57.98	-2.74
- mbert 4	60.50	60.92	84.60	57.98	-2.84
- mbart	64.29	61.76	86.30	58.82	-1.05
- mt5	63.87	62.18	84.60	57.14	-1.89

Table 2: Ablation study.

observe that with the three proposed sets of features, the performance gets boosted across all settings and languages and consistently outperforms mGENRE and `base`, the state-of-the-art neuro-symbolic short-text EL system, indicating the effectiveness of these features. We also notice that different languages have their own feature patterns, e.g., the context score seems more beneficial for German than for French, according to their performance in the mono-lingual and multi-lingual settings, and the language-specific feature patterns indicate a direction of future work. The impact of the language-model-based features, i.e., `mbert` and `generative`, is reflected in the last two rows of the table, where the performance reaches its peak when both features are included, thus demonstrating their importance as well as their complementary nature. Furthermore, the cross-lingual performance is on par with that in the multi-lingual setting, and that shows the transferability of the proposed features, reflecting a potential for real-world industrial cross-language scenarios.

3.3 Ablation Study

To better understand the contribution of each component in the `mbert` and `generative` feature, we present in Table 2 the results of the ablation results of the model `base + ctx + mbert + generative` in the mono-lingual setting, with their average performance change (Δ). As shown in the table, dropping each score of the LM-based features will cause the performance to decrease greatly, indicating the effectiveness and necessity of them.

4 Conclusion

In this study, we extend upon LNN-EL by incorporating three sets of multilingual features to enable disambiguating mentions written in languages other than English. This study also indicates directions of future work, as the results demonstrate language-specific patterns for the features and rules.

Acknowledgements

This research has been supported by the Army Research Office (ARO) grant W911NF-21-1-0112 and the NSF grant CNS-1747798 to the IUCRC Center for Big Learning. This research is also based upon work supported by the Office of the Director of National Intelligence (ODNI), Intelligence Advanced Research Projects Activity (IARPA), via IARPA Contract No. 2019-19051600006 under the Better Extraction from Text Towards Enhanced Retrieval (BETTER) Program. The views and conclusions contained herein are those of the authors and should not be interpreted as necessarily representing the official policies, either expressed or implied, of ARO, ODNI, IARPA, the Department of Defense, or the U.S. Government. The U.S. Government is authorized to reproduce and distribute reprints for governmental purposes notwithstanding any copyright annotation therein. We also would like to thank the IBM Research - Almaden team for their support in this work.

References

Sören Auer, Christian Bizer, Georgi Kobilarov, Jens Lehmann, Richard Cyganiak, and Zachary Ives. 2007. Dbpedia: A nucleus for a web of open data. In *Proceedings of the 6th International The Semantic Web and 2nd Asian Conference on Asian Semantic Web Conference*, ISWC'07/ASWC'07, page 722–735, Berlin, Heidelberg. Springer-Verlag.

Piotr Bojanowski, Edouard Grave, Armand Joulin, and Tomas Mikolov. 2017. Enriching word vectors with subword information. *Transactions of the Association for Computational Linguistics*, 5:135–146.

Yixin Cao, Lei Hou, Juanzi Li, and Zhiyuan Liu. 2018. Neural collective entity linking. In *Proceedings of the 27th International Conference on Computational Linguistics*, pages 675–686, Santa Fe, New Mexico, USA. Association for Computational Linguistics.

Lihan Chen, Jiaqing Liang, Chenhao Xie, and Yanghua Xiao. 2018. Short text entity linking with fine-grained topics. In *Proceedings of the 27th ACM International Conference on Information and Knowledge Management*, pages 457–466.

Marina Danilevsky, Kun Qian, Ranit Aharonov, Yannis Katsis, Ban Kawas, and Prithviraj Sen. 2020. A survey of the state of explainable AI for natural language processing. In *Proceedings of the 1st Conference of the Asia-Pacific Chapter of the Association for Computational Linguistics and the 10th International Joint Conference on Natural Language Processing*, pages 447–459, Suzhou, China. Association for Computational Linguistics.

Nicola De Cao, Wilker Aziz, and Ivan Titov. 2021a. Highly parallel autoregressive entity linking with discriminative correction. In *Proceedings of the 2021 Conference on Empirical Methods in Natural Language Processing*, pages 7662–7669, Online and Punta Cana, Dominican Republic. Association for Computational Linguistics.

Nicola De Cao, Gautier Izacard, Sebastian Riedel, and Fabio Petroni. 2020. Autoregressive entity retrieval. In *International Conference on Learning Representations*.

Nicola De Cao, Ledell Wu, Kashyap Popat, Mikel Artetxe, Naman Goyal, Mikhail Plekhanov, Luke Zettlemoyer, Nicola Cancedda, Sebastian Riedel, and Fabio Petroni. 2021b. Multilingual autoregressive entity linking. *arXiv preprint arXiv:2103.12528*.

Jacob Devlin, Ming-Wei Chang, Kenton Lee, and Kristina Toutanova. 2019. BERT: Pre-training of deep bidirectional transformers for language understanding. In *Proceedings of the 2019 Conference of the North American Chapter of the Association for Computational Linguistics: Human Language Technologies, Volume 1 (Long and Short Papers)*, pages 4171–4186, Minneapolis, Minnesota. Association for Computational Linguistics.

Francesc Esteva and Lluıs Godo. 2001. Monoidal t-norm based logic: towards a logic for left-continuous t-norms. *Fuzzy sets and systems*, 124(3):271–288.

Yingjie Gu, Xiaoye Qu, Zhefeng Wang, Baoxing Huai, Nicholas Jing Yuan, and Xiaolin Gui. 2021. Read, retrospect, select: An mrc framework to short text entity linking. In *Proceedings of the AAAI Conference on Artificial Intelligence*, pages 12920–12928.

Nitish Gupta, Sameer Singh, and Dan Roth. 2017. Entity linking via joint encoding of types, descriptions, and context. In *Proceedings of the 2017 Conference on Empirical Methods in Natural Language Processing*, pages 2681–2690, Copenhagen, Denmark. Association for Computational Linguistics.

Xianpei Han, Le Sun, and Jun Zhao. 2011. Collective entity linking in web text: a graph-based method. In *Proceedings of the 34th international ACM SIGIR conference on Research and development in Information Retrieval*, pages 765–774.

Hang Jiang, Sairam Gurajada, Qiuhao Lu, Sumit Neelam, Lucian Popa, Prithviraj Sen, Yunyao Li, and Alexander Gray. 2021. LNN-EL: A neuro-symbolic approach to short-text entity linking. In *Proceedings of the 59th Annual Meeting of the Association for Computational Linguistics and the 11th International Joint Conference on Natural Language Processing (Volume 1: Long Papers)*, pages 775–787, Online. Association for Computational Linguistics.

Armand Joulin, Piotr Bojanowski, Tomas Mikolov, Hervé Jégou, and Edouard Grave. 2018. Loss in translation: Learning bilingual word mapping with a retrieval criterion. In *Proceedings of the 2018 Conference on Empirical Methods in Natural Language Processing*.

Nikolaos Kolitsas, Octavian-Eugen Ganea, and Thomas Hofmann. 2018. End-to-end neural entity linking. In *Proceedings of the 22nd Conference on Computational Natural Language Learning*, pages 519–529, Brussels, Belgium. Association for Computational Linguistics.

Mike Lewis, Yinhan Liu, Naman Goyal, Marjan Ghazvininejad, Abdelrahman Mohamed, Omer Levy, Veselin Stoyanov, and Luke Zettlemoyer. 2020. BART: Denoising sequence-to-sequence pre-training for natural language generation, translation, and comprehension. In *Proceedings of the 58th Annual Meeting of the Association for Computational Linguistics*, pages 7871–7880, Online. Association for Computational Linguistics.

Qian Liu, Xiubo Geng, Jie Lu, and Daxin Jiang. 2021. Pivot-based candidate retrieval for cross-lingual entity linking. In *Proceedings of the Web Conference 2021*, pages 1076–1085.

Yinhan Liu, Jiatao Gu, Naman Goyal, Xian Li, Sergey Edunov, Marjan Ghazvininejad, Mike Lewis, and Luke Zettlemoyer. 2020. Multilingual denoising pre-training for neural machine translation. *Transactions of the Association for Computational Linguistics*, 8:726–742.

Qiuhao Lu and Youtian Du. 2017. Wikipedia-based entity semantifying in open information extraction. In *2017 14th IAPR International Conference on Document Analysis and Recognition (ICDAR)*, volume 1, pages 765–770. IEEE.

Telmo Pires, Eva Schlinger, and Dan Garrette. 2019. How multilingual is multilingual BERT? In *Proceedings of the 57th Annual Meeting of the Association for Computational Linguistics*, pages 4996–5001, Florence, Italy. Association for Computational Linguistics.

Ryan Riegel, Alexander Gray, Francois Luus, Naweed Khan, Ndivhuwo Makondo, Ismail Yunus Akhalwaya, Haifeng Qian, Ronald Fagin, Francisco Barahona, Udit Sharma, et al. 2020a. Logical neural networks. *arXiv preprint arXiv:2006.13155*.

Ryan Riegel, Francois Luus, and Alexander Gray. 2020b. Logical neural networks: From deep learning to deep thinking.

Ahmad Sakor, Isaiah Onando Mulang, Kuldeep Singh, Saeedeh Shekarpour, Maria Esther Vidal, Jens Lehmann, and Sören Auer. 2019. Old is gold: linguistic driven approach for entity and relation linking of short text. In *Proceedings of the 2019 Conference of the North American Chapter of the Association for Computational Linguistics: Human Language Technologies, Volume 1 (Long and Short Papers)*, pages 2336–2346.

Wei Shen, Yuhan Li, Yinan Liu, Jiawei Han, Jianyong Wang, and Xiaojie Yuan. 2021. Entity linking meets deep learning: Techniques and solutions. *IEEE Transactions on Knowledge and Data Engineering*, pages 1–1.

Chuanqi Tan, Furu Wei, Pengjie Ren, Weifeng Lv, and Ming Zhou. 2017. Entity linking for queries by searching Wikipedia sentences. In *Proceedings of the 2017 Conference on Empirical Methods in Natural Language Processing*, pages 68–77, Copenhagen, Denmark. Association for Computational Linguistics.

Linting Xue, Noah Constant, Adam Roberts, Mihir Kale, Rami Al-Rfou, Aditya Siddhant, Aditya Barua, and Colin Raffel. 2021. mT5: A massively multilingual pre-trained text-to-text transformer. In *Proceedings of the 2021 Conference of the North American Chapter of the Association for Computational Linguistics: Human Language Technologies*, pages 483–498, Online. Association for Computational Linguistics.

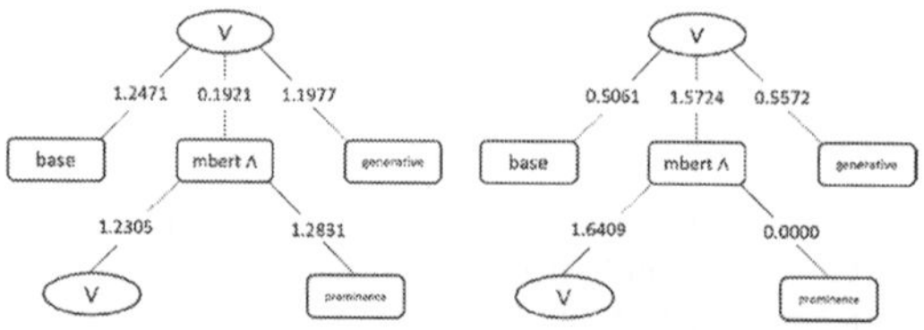

(a) German (b) French

Figure 1: Feature weights for German and French.

A Preliminaries and Interpretabiltiy

A.1 LNN-EL

First-order logic (FOL) rules form a closed language facilitating the expression of a variety of human interpretable models. To learn these rules, neuro-symbolic AI typically substitutes conjunctions with t-norms (Esteva and Godo, 2001) which actually limits their learning capacity as these norms do not have learnable parameters.

Recently, Riegel et al. propose Logical Neural Networks (LNN) (Riegel et al., 2020a), a modification of neural networks that can precisely model operations in real-valued logic, i.e., they construct logical operators conjunction ($\wedge$) and disjunction ($\vee$) and facilitate neural network-style learning with learnable parameters (Riegel et al., 2020b).

Subsequently, LNN-EL reformulates entity linking by mapping the Boolean-valued logic rules into the LNN formalism and the resulting model consists of parameterized LNN operators, i.e., conjunction ($\wedge$) and disjunction ($\vee$), along with learnable rule weights and feature weights. LNN-EL takes as input the pre-computed features of candidates and the definition for the features is the main focus of this study. We refer the readers to (Riegel et al., 2020a; Jiang et al., 2021) for more detailed treatment of the parameterized LNN opertors and the reformulation.

A.2 Interpretability of xLNN-EL

A common theme among existing EL methods is their lack of *interpretability*. Interpretability is an important and desirable property not only for machine learning research, but also for real-world downstream applications, especially for sensitive areas. In fact, there is a growing trend towards developing interpretable machine learning models (Danilevsky et al., 2020).

We show some learned feature weights of the `base + mbert + generative` model for German and French, in the mono-lingual setting, to illustrate the interpretability of xLNN-EL. The tree structure reflects the first-order logic (FOL) rule combination of the model, e.g., the three features `base`, `mbert` and `generative` are combined with a disjunction at the topmost level, the `mbert` feature is formed with a conjunction between a set of disjunct similarities and the `prominence` feature, the `generative` feature has the same substructure with `mbert` (not shown), etc. The rule combination part is beyond the scope of this paper and the reader is referred to the literature for further details (Jiang et al., 2021).

As shown in Figure 1, the feature `mbert` has a much higher relative feature weight for French than for German (1.5724 vs. 0.1921) in the disjunction, which might indicate a relative preference as to the `mbert` feature for French. This inspection provides clues for human experts to understand how these features impact performance, and further adjust features and rule combinations accordingly.

Crowdsourcing Preposition Sense Disambiguation with High Precision via a Priming Task

Shira Wein
Georgetown University
sw1158@georgetown.edu

Nathan Schneider
Georgetown University
nathan.schneider@georgetown.edu

Abstract

The careful design of a crowdsourcing protocol is critical to eliciting highly accurate annotations from untrained workers. In this work, we explore the development of crowdsourcing protocols for a challenging word sense disambiguation task. We find that (a) selecting a similar example usage can serve as a proxy for selecting an explicit definition of the sense, and (b) priming workers with an additional, related task within the HIT improves performance on the main proxy task. Ultimately, we demonstrate the usefulness of our crowdsourcing elicitation technique as an effective alternative to previously investigated training strategies, which can be used if agreement on a challenging task is low.

1 Introduction

Crowdsourcing work relies on effective protocol design in order to elicit meaningful and accurate annotations from lay workers. Traditional crowdsourcing protocols for challenging tasks train crowd workers, incentivize high quality work with bonuses, and filter out workers with pre-determined gold annotations.

In this work, we demonstrate a novel crowdsourcing technique which frames the task such that the worker is able to provide a high quality annotation for challenging tasks without extensive prior training. We consider the challenging task of English preposition supersense disambiguation.

Prepositions are difficult to disambiguate due to their extreme polysemy and frequency (Litkowski and Hargraves, 2007; Hovy et al., 2010; Gong et al., 2018). While some distinctions—such as the locative vs. temporal ambiguity of ***in** Seattle* vs. ***in** October*—are quite intuitive, the semantic range of English prepositions makes fully disambiguating them a daunting task. Consider the sentence "Nice and quiet place **with**$_{PartPortion}$ cosy living room just outside the city." Though **with** here denotes a part of a whole (a room in an abode), it is also describing a characteristic of the place/living room, suggesting that **with**$_{Characteristic}$ would also be a reasonable annotation. With this being a difficult task because of the inherently categorical nature of word sense disambiguation, we aim to develop simple linguistic tasks which elicit annotations by proxy.

Prepositions are critical to language understanding (Kim et al., 2019), which makes preposition sense disambiguation an important task, impacting a range of downstream applications, including: relation extraction (Elazar et al., 2021), paraphrasing of phrasal verbs (Gong et al., 2018) and noun compounds (Ponkiya et al., 2018; Hendrickx et al., 2013), machine translation (Parameswarappa and Narayana, 2012; Chiang et al., 2009; Chan et al., 2007), semantic role labelling (Ye and Baldwin, 2006; Srikumar and Roth, 2011), and more. Automatic supersense classifiers exist for preposition sense disambiguation (Liu et al., 2021), but are unable to achieve the precision levels of trained annotators.

In order to tackle the challenging aim of preposition sense annotation, we design linguistic tasks to enable the elicitation of high-quality annotations. We demonstrate that a weak form of guidance, which we call a *priming task*, improves performance on the main task.

In our case, the main task asks the worker to select the most similar usage to the prompt. However, the notion of meaning similarity between preposition usages may not be apparent to crowd workers. We find that first asking the worker to select an appropriate definition is an effective priming task: its mere presence enhances workers' ability to choose the correct exemplar in the second question. This related (priming) task serves as a high-precision, low-overhead alternative to training.

Finally, we compare the predictions of the crowd with those of a classifier, and find that they are largely complementary; for most prepositions

Proceedings of the Fourth Workshop on Data Science with Human-in-the-Loop (Language Advances), pages 15 - 22
December 8, 2022 ©2022 Association for Computational Linguistics

tested, combining the two predictions gives perfect or near-perfect precision.

Related work has proposed the ability to crowdsource supersenses and tested a pilot on trained in-house annotators (Gessler et al., 2020); in this work, we develop new formulations and collect actual crowdsourced annotations from Mechanical Turk to ascertain the suitability of our formulations.

Our contributions include:

- a **novel crowdsourcing elicitation technique** which primes implicit questions about lexical meaning with an explicit task
- a promising crowdsourcing **approach to preposition supersense annotation** to elicit high-precision labels for a subset of instances without prior annotator training
- a demonstration that the crowd and a supersense **classifier** give complementary signals conducive to ensembling.

2 Related Work on Crowdsourcing

The Amazon Mechanical Turk online crowdsourcing platform enables crowd workers from around the world to perform short tasks published by Requesters. Mechanical Turk has been used for a range of annotation tasks.

Mechanical Turk is used in many cases where a large amount of annotations are collected. If these many annotations are of lesser quality, it is not necessarily the case that having more data is better than having a small amount of expert annotations would have been (Bhardwaj et al., 2010).

Crowdsourcing Protocols. A variety of alternatives or additions to worker training have been employed in previous work. Notably, qualifying workers (filtering out who can and cannot complete the task) is a method akin to training which seeks to ensure higher quality annotations. Recent work evaluating crowdsourcing protocols for the development of natural language understanding datasets ask crowd workers to write a multiple choice question with one of four qualification follow ups; with the goal of making more difficult NLU questions, this work finds that training crowd workers, sending feedback, and qualifying crowd workers is an effective strategy (Nangia et al., 2021). Qualifying workers beforehand based on self-assessment is flawed due to bias in the self-assessment; leveraging a combination of self-assessment and performance on the task is a more useful filtering process (Gadiraju et al., 2017).

Lee et al. (2022) provides an ordering strategy for sentence-level annotation tasks such that the annotators learn and improve from task to task. Mikulová et al. (2022) considers the effect of pre-annotation and task design on dependency syntax annotation, finding that automatic pre-annotation is useful while other support tools are not as beneficial.

The *retainer method* has been developed for real-time crowdsourcing, using retainer pools (qualifying workers into a group of candidates who can be called upon quickly to complete the task), push notifications, and recruiting workers before the task is actually published (Bernstein et al., 2012). Vaughan (2017) put forward a set of best practices for Requesters, which includes providing clear instructions and iteratively piloting task designs.

The idea of "priming" a crowd worker to influence their performance (through the design of instructions, the order of items, etc.) has been explored in previous work. Jiang et al. (2017) investigated how the choice of provided examples and the phrasing of the prompt affect worker response. Federmann et al. (2019) further investigated the effect of prompt question on worker performance. Additional work also explored how providing surrounding text (Mitchell et al., 2014), drawings as prompts (Kumaran et al., 2014), lists of options (Wang et al., 2012), and diverse word suggestions (Yaghoub-Zadeh-Fard et al., 2020) improve worker performance. Jiang et al. (2018) suggests that workers are cognitively "primed" to replicate their own mistakes when completing numerous HITs in sequence. Colombini (2018) similarly investigates "inter-task effect" (effect from one HIT to the next), finding that consistency in task structure across HITs improves worker performance.

We introduce the concept of a *priming task*, an additional task designed to be completed first in order to improve performance on a related *main task*. The idea is that the priming task is a less ambiguous task not intended to collect data, but rather to frame the worker's thinking so as to draw attention to the relevant aspects of the main task.[1]

Word sense disambiguation is a difficult task (Artstein and Poesio, 2008), which is particularly true for prepositions, as they are widely polysemous (Gong et al., 2018; Hovy et al., 2010). Prior work has proposed, but not executed, the possibility

[1] The 2 tasks are questions that appear together on the same screen (in the same HIT), and the main task is actually a proxy task because it is an indirect form of labeling.

of crowdsourcing preposition sense disambiguation for the supersense schema—Gessler et al. (2020) proposed that, instead of training annotators to apply abstract labels, like STARTTIME, GESTALT, and AGENT, annotators could be asked to perform simpler *proxy tasks* from which the supersense labels could be inferred automatically. While Gessler et al. conducted a pilot with trained in-house annotators, we introduce a new definition-based formulation, which we combine with an exemplar-based approach, and collect annotations from Mechanical Turk to establish whether sense disambiguation of prepositions is able to be crowdsourced in practice.

3 Crowdsourcing Protocol

3.1 Task

Our crowdsourcing task is the challenging task of preposition sense disambiguation (§1), via the (indirect) annotation of *supersenses.* [2] We want to determine whether the most frequent senses of prepositions can be categorized by the crowd, such that the majority of prepositions could be annotated at a large scale, and any remaining long-tail cases could then by annotated by experts.

In this work, we ask: can we elicit preposition supersense data from crowd workers with high precision? Because the supersense training process is extensive and specialized, we leverage a *proxy task*, through which the crowd judgments can be converted into actual supersense labels. As a result of our study, we propose the technique of a *priming task*, which is designed to improve performance on the main task rather than to collect data.

The SNACS *supersense* annotation schema and corpus extensively document the senses of English prepositions and possessives, with 50 supersense classes categorizing the use of an adposition in context (Schneider et al., 2018). While some distinctions—such as the locative vs. temporal ambiguity of ***in** Seattle* (supersense label LOCUS) vs. ***in** October* (TIME)—are quite intuitive, the semantic versatility of prepositions requires extensive annotator training. Preposition supersenses form a subset of labels in the lexical semantic recognition task Liu et al. (2021).

From the STREUSLE corpus (Schneider and Smith, 2015), we use annotated tokens of 6 preposition types: **from**, **in**, **on**, **with**, **for**, and **of**, which we choose due to their high polysemy and frequency, collectively comprising more than 60% of all preposition tokens in the STREUSLE corpus. The gold annotations are used to evaluate our approach.

3.2 Two Task Designs

We evaluate crowd predictions with the aim of prioritizing precision over recall, because we want to ensure that any sense that receives an annotation by majority vote is very likely to be accurate. Our first task design provides definitions and examples of possible senses for the preposition, drawing from the traditional notion of word sense disambiguation being obtained by selecting a sense from a list of definitions as the *priming* task (cf. Ahlswede and Lorand, 1993; Jurgens, 2013; Tratz, 2011). The second design uses BERT (Devlin et al., 2019) to retrieve nearest neighbors from a gold-annotated seed corpus as the *proxy* task.

Definition-Based The Definition-Based approach presents the *target sentence* (the sentence to be annotated), and asks a question about the relationship between the governor and object of the preposition. The question presented to the crowd worker is "The word [preposition] expresses a relationship between two things. Which of the following options, if any, describes the kind of relationship?" The *definitions* include a simple, short description of what the preposition may be conveying in that sentence, as well as examples of that usage. We wrote a small number of definitions for each of the 6 prepositions, mindful to avoid jargon and to avoid imposing a high cognitive load with many options. These are presented as options along with "None of the above" and "Not sure/sentence is hard to understand". Since only a few of the possible senses receive definitions, annotators are encouraged to select "None of the above" if none is a good match. For example, for the relationship options included in figure 1, the four options provided cover 75% of the STREUSLE instances of the preposition **from**, corresponding respectively to the annotations: ORIGINATOR⇝SOURCE, SOURCE⇝SOURCE, LOCUS⇝SOURCE, and STARTTIME⇝STARTTIME, the last of which is the correct choice.

Exemplar Matching Our Exemplar Matching task utilizes contextualized embeddings from BERT (Devlin et al., 2019) to identify n nearest neighbors of the use of a preposition in a sentence. The intuition behind the exemplar-based approach is that annotators would have an easier time identi-

[2] Technically two supersense fields are annotated per token; they may be the same or different (Schneider et al., 2018).

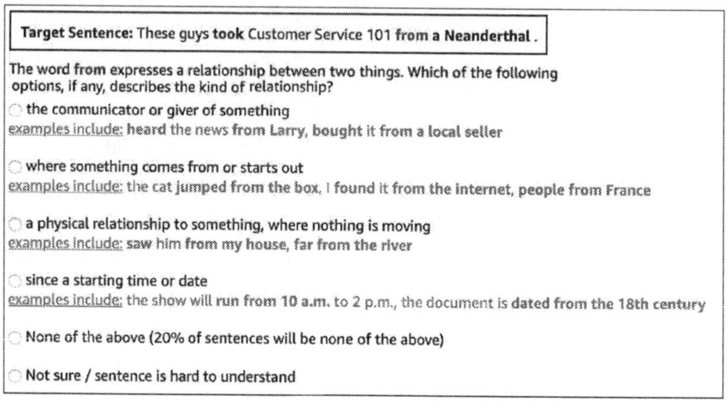

Target Sentence: These guys **took** Customer Service 101 **from a Neanderthal**.

The word **from** expresses a relationship between two things. Which of the following options, if any, describes the kind of relationship?

- the communicator or giver of something
  examples include: heard the news from Larry, bought it from a local seller
- where something comes from or starts out
  examples include: the cat jumped from the box, I found it from the internet, people from France
- a physical relationship to something, where nothing is moving
  examples include: saw him from my house, far from the river
- since a starting time or date
  examples include: the show will run from 10 a.m. to 2 p.m., the document is dated from the 18th century
- None of the above (20% of sentences will be none of the above)
- Not sure / sentence is hard to understand

Figure 1: Definition-Based approach for a sentence from the test set in the STREUSLE dataset.

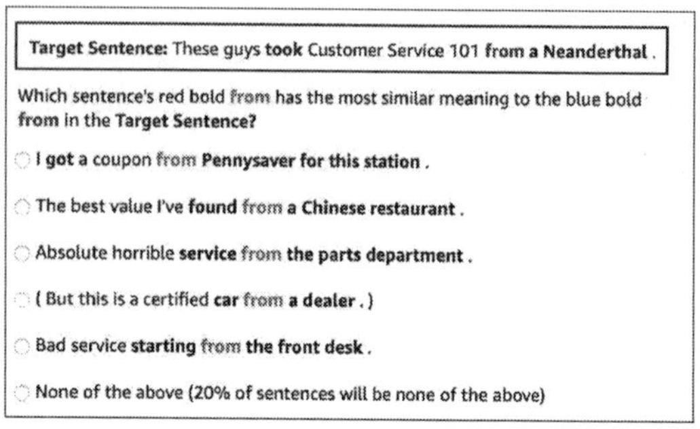

Target Sentence: These guys **took** Customer Service 101 **from a Neanderthal**.

Which sentence's red bold from has the most similar meaning to the blue bold from in the **Target Sentence?**

- **I got** a coupon **from Pennysaver for this station**.
- The best value I've **found from a Chinese restaurant**.
- Absolute horrible **service from the parts department**.
- (But this is a certified **car from a dealer**.)
- Bad service **starting from the front desk**.
- None of the above (20% of sentences will be none of the above)

Figure 2: Exemplar Matching approach for the same STREUSLE test set sentence as in figure 1, using the nearest neighbors from the STREUSLE train set as identified by BERT.

fying a similar use of a preposition in context than explicitly describing the use of the preposition.

STREUSLE is split into train, test, and dev sets. We use pre-trained (without any fine-tuning) BERT-base-uncased to collect a given test or dev sentence's 5 nearest unique neighbors in the train set, using cosine similarity. We concatenate the vectors from the last four layers, and only use the indexed embedding of the preposition in question to find nearest neighbors. We retrieve the 5 nearest neighbors with distinct supersenses, and present these 5 options plus a "None of the above" option.

Subject to the performance of the nearest neighbor retrieval metric, oracle recall of the crowd workers is therefore 87% overall, i.e. for our experiments, 87% of the retrieved nearest neighbors include a gold label in the 5 unique options. We also found that ensuring that the 5 options provided reflected unique supersenses did increase the likelihood that the majority consensus would match that of the gold label.

An example of this protocol can be seen in figure 2, which features the same sentence as figure 1. Figure 2 demonstrates the **Exemplar Matching** proxy task, with the 5 nearest neighbor preposition usages as well as a "None of the above" option being presented to the worker.

Combined In this design, we include in each HIT the Definition-Based task followed by the Exemplar Matching task, for the same sentence. Within the same HIT, the Definition-Based task is first presented and then below that (seen by the crowd worker by scrolling down) the Exemplar Matching task is shown.

3.3 Mechanical Turk Experimental Setup

Using the Mechanical Turk crowdsourcing platform, we have 5 crowd workers annotate each sentence. With there being 160 sentences (130 unique sentences, as the **for** experiment was performed twice with disjoint sets of annotators), we collect 1,650 judgments total. Consensus is established when 3 of 5 crowd workers select the same option—a simple majority balances precision and recall.

We filter the target and exemplar sentences to select instances of canonical phrase order between the syntactic governor, the preposition, and the object, such that the governor precedes (not necessarily immediately) the preposition, which also precedes the object (again, not necessarily immediately).[3] Target sentences were sampled randomly from this filtered set.

[3]This filtered set includes approximately 44% of the instances of the selected preposition types. We filter the data for simplicity of interpretation of results, and the filtered task would not be a more or less difficult task for annotation.

Prep.	n	Classifier P	*Exemplar Matching* P	R	O R	*Combined: EM* P	R	O R	*Combined: DB* P	R	O R	Ensemble P
for	30	0.70	0.76	0.53	0.90	**0.90**	0.63	0.90	0.74	0.57	0.57	18/19=0.95
for *(rpt.)*	30	0.70	0.71	0.50	0.90	**0.77**	0.57	0.90	0.74	0.57	0.57	15/15=1.00
of	20	**0.75**	0.33	0.20	0.90	0.42	0.25	0.90	0.29	0.10	0.40	4/4=1.00
from	10	0.50	0.60	0.30	0.80	0.67	0.40	0.80	**0.71**	0.50	0.80	2/2=1.00
in	30	0.73	**0.92**	0.77	0.87	0.88	0.73	0.87	0.88	0.73	0.80	22/22=1.00
on	15	0.60	0.83	0.33	0.93	**1.00**	0.60	0.93	0.92	0.80	0.87	6/6=1.00
with	30	0.43	0.30	0.10	0.80	0.47	0.27	0.80	**0.53**	0.30	0.43	7/10=0.70

Table 1: The results of the Exemplar Matching (EM) task alone, the Definition-Based (DB) task within the Combined approach, and the EM task within the Combined approach. For each preposition, the same n sentences are used in the EM and the Combined HITs, where n indicates the number of sentences tested for that preposition. Recall (R) is out of all n, not only the sentences which have gold options. This is also reflected in the Oracle Recall (O R) which indicates the best possible crowd performance given that not all tasks present a gold option. Precision is labeled as P. The rightmost column shows Ensemble results, discussed in §4.2.

4 Results & Analysis

Before coming to the task design presented in this work, we iterated over many approaches and techniques to crowdsourcing preposition sense disambiguation. In total, we elicited 4,080 annotations and developed 17 slight variations of the approach presented here, which primes the crowd workers by combining the definition-based and exemplar-based tasks. We saw consistent trends across these pre-study variations, resulting in the current approaches (presented in this work), which prime the crowd workers by combining the definition-based and exemplar-based tasks. For these results, we collect between 10 and 30 annotations for each of the 6 prepositions, via two methods: the Exemplar Matching design alone, and the Combined design.

4.1 Effect of Task Design

The precision and recall scores from the different task designs appear in table 1, accompanied by a classifier baseline. Precision is important for this task, because we want to have confidence that the annotations that are being produced are trustworthy. For 5 of the 6 prepositions tried, the best crowd design outperforms the classifier; notably, the precision for 3 prepositions—**for**, **in**, and **on**—is consistently high. The biggest exception is **of**, which is extremely polysemous, and the classifier picks up on the plethora of options with higher precision than the crowd workers (at least in our small sample). **With** achieves better precision from the Combined judgments than the classifier, though it barely scratches 50%.

We see that within the Combined design, the Exemplar Matching judgments are equal or superior to the Definition-Based judgments in all experiments except for **from**. The two-step process takes slightly longer for annotators and thus is slightly more expensive, but achieves very high precision, which is the aim here. Notably, the Exemplar Matching judgments are usually enhanced by the presence of the Definition-Based task in the HIT: Combined EM precision surpasses plain Exemplar Matching in all but the **in** experiment. This is surprising because the combined approach is useful even when the Definition-Based options do not include a correct definition, or when the annotator doesn't choose the correct definition—the presence of the task alone results in a statistically significant improvement in precision.The improved precision for Combined EM vs. plain EM is statistically significant per a t-test: Paired Two Sample for Means on precision resulting in a one-tailed p-value of 0.0083.

This suggests that the definitions are biasing crowd workers to attend to the preposition's meaning in context, *even if they don't actually choose the correct definition*. This insight may be useful for other kinds of crowdsourcing tasks, such as other word sense disambiguation tasks, which currently rely on only one annotation elicitation method, but could benefit from a combination of various methods. In particular, **if inter-annotator agreement is low on a more challenging task, a specialized protocol could be used to prime the crowd workers' thinking, without training.** While it is well-known that initial questions in a survey can bias answers to subsequent questions (Schuman, 2008), we are not aware of other crowdsourcing studies that have exploited this to improve workers' performance on a task by including another task first. We have demonstrated that this approach is successful on the challenging task of preposition sense disambiguation; future work should explore the utility of similar schemes for other tasks.

We ran the **for** experiment twice with the same instances to see how much randomness in the annotator sample would affect results. The absolute scores in some conditions were slightly affected, but in both cases the Combined: EM design was the best and all crowd designs outperformed the classifier.

4.2 Ensemble Results

In comparison to the highest performing supersense tagger (Liu et al., 2021), our crowdsourcing approach generally achieves higher precision. However, we find that ensembling (predicting only when the crowd workers via the Combined EM approach agrees with the supersense classifier) can give extremely high-precision predictions, showing that the two signals are complementary.

Specifically, we consider an ensemble where an annotation is produced only if the majority of crowd workers in the best design (Combined Exemplar Matching) and the classifier are in agreement. For the ensemble, the precision is perfect or near-perfect for 5 of 6 prepositions, as seen in the right-most column of table 1 (with the caveat that counts for some prepositions are too low to draw firm conclusions). The senses annotated via crowdsourcing alone are more varied than the senses annotated by the ensemble approach, but the ensemble approach is more reliable for more frequent senses. If we extrapolate the highly effective ensemble technique to the entirety of the relatively small STREUSLE corpus, the Combined Exemplar Matching approach would result in an estimated 808 annotations (approx. 606 of which would be correct), while the ensemble would produce an estimated 563 annotations (approx. 534 correct). This gives a sense of the potential for efficiency gains when applied on a larger scale.

Note that though the precision will be extremely high, to ensemble the crowdsourcing approach and classifier means that slightly fewer annotations will be produced. Of the 2,692 STREUSLE instances of the 6 prepositions used in this study, 1,191 of them meet the same filtering requirement we used (such that the governor precedes the preposition, which precedes the object). Extrapolating to these 1,191 tokens, the Combined Exemplar Matching approach would result in an estimated 808 annotations (an estimated 606 of which would be correct), while the ensemble would produce an estimated 563 annotations (an estimated 534 of which would be correct).

5 Conclusion

This paper outlined a promising approach to crowdsourcing preposition supersense annotation (a particularly challenging form of word sense disambiguation). The crowd workers outperformed automatic supersense tagging on 5 of the 6 prepositions studied. We compared multiple designs, finding that prompting annotators to reason both explicitly and implicitly about meaning is most effective, even when the explicit question does not elicit a correct annotation. The crowdsourcing approach achieves very high precision and acceptable recall for 3 prepositions.

6 Ethics

When using a crowdsourcing platform like Mechanical Turk, it is critical to ensure fair payment and treatment of crowd workers. For the Exemplar Matching tasks alone, we paid $0.15 per HIT, and for the combined Definition-Based and Exemplar Matching task, we paid $0.20 per HIT. Per reviews on the TurkerView website, which Turkers use to anonymously review Requesters, the reviews are positive, indicating that the payment is approved quickly, with Turkers never being rejected or blocked. The average hourly wage is reported on the site based on the payment for completion of the task and how long it takes to complete the task (as reported by the worker, rather than the time spent between accepting the task and submitting, as reported by Mechanical Turk), and reflects an average hourly wage of $20.66 based on 40 reports. IRB exemption was granted for this study. Intending to have this task primarily completed by native English speakers, we filtered crowd workers to require that the Location is United States and the number of approved HITS is greater than 5000.

Acknowledgements

Thank you to Vivek Srikumar and anonymous reviewers for their feedback. This work is supported by a Clare Boothe Luce Scholarship.

References

Thomas Ahlswede and David Lorand. 1993. Word sense disambiguation by human subjects: Computational and psycholinguistic applications. In *Acquisition of Lexical Knowledge from Text*.

Ron Artstein and Massimo Poesio. 2008. Survey article: Inter-coder agreement for computational linguistics. *Computational Linguistics*, 34(4):555–596.

Michael S. Bernstein, David R. Karger, Robert C. Miller, and Joel Brandt. 2012. Analytic methods for optimizing realtime crowdsourcing. *arXiv:1204.2995 [physics]*. ArXiv: 1204.2995.

Vikas Bhardwaj, Rebecca Passonneau, Ansaf Salleb-Aouissi, and Nancy Ide. 2010. Anveshan: A framework for analysis of multiple annotators' labeling behavior. In *Proceedings of the Fourth Linguistic Annotation Workshop*, pages 47–55, Uppsala, Sweden. Association for Computational Linguistics.

Yee Seng Chan, Hwee Tou Ng, and David Chiang. 2007. Word sense disambiguation improves statistical machine translation. In *Proceedings of the 45th Annual Meeting of the Association of Computational Linguistics*, pages 33–40, Prague, Czech Republic. Association for Computational Linguistics.

David Chiang, Kevin Knight, and Wei Wang. 2009. 11,001 new features for statistical machine translation. In *Proceedings of Human Language Technologies: The 2009 Annual Conference of the North American Chapter of the Association for Computational Linguistics*, pages 218–226, Boulder, Colorado. Association for Computational Linguistics.

Brian J Colombini. 2018. Worker retention, response quality, and diversity in microtask crowdsourcing: An experimental investigation of the potential for priming effects to promote project goals.

Jacob Devlin, Ming-Wei Chang, Kenton Lee, and Kristina Toutanova. 2019. BERT: Pre-training of deep bidirectional transformers for language understanding. In *Proceedings of the 2019 Conference of the North American Chapter of the Association for Computational Linguistics: Human Language Technologies, Volume 1 (Long and Short Papers)*, pages 4171–4186, Minneapolis, Minnesota. Association for Computational Linguistics.

Yanai Elazar, Victoria Basmov, Yoav Goldberg, and Reut Tsarfaty. 2021. Text-based np enrichment.

Christian Federmann, Oussama Elachqar, and Chris Quirk. 2019. Multilingual whispers: Generating paraphrases with translation. In *Proceedings of the 5th Workshop on Noisy User-generated Text (W-NUT 2019)*, pages 17–26, Hong Kong, China. Association for Computational Linguistics.

Ujwal Gadiraju, Besnik Fetahu, Ricardo Kawase, Patrick Siehndel, and Stefan Dietze. 2017. Using worker self-assessments for competence-based pre-selection in crowdsourcing microtasks. *ACM Transactions on Computer-Human Interaction*, 24:1–26.

Luke Gessler, Shira Wein, and Nathan Schneider. 2020. Supersense and sensibility: Proxy tasks for semantic annotation of prepositions. In *Proceedings of the 14th Linguistic Annotation Workshop*, pages 117–126, Barcelona, Spain. Association for Computational Linguistics.

Hongyu Gong, Jiaqi Mu, Suma Bhat, and Pramod Viswanath. 2018. Preposition sense disambiguation and representation. In *Proceedings of the 2018 Conference on Empirical Methods in Natural Language Processing*, pages 1510–1521, Brussels, Belgium. Association for Computational Linguistics.

Iris Hendrickx, Zornitsa Kozareva, Preslav Nakov, Diarmuid Ó Séaghdha, Stan Szpakowicz, and Tony Veale. 2013. SemEval-2013 task 4: Free paraphrases of noun compounds. In *Second Joint Conference on Lexical and Computational Semantics (*SEM), Volume 2: Proceedings of the Seventh International Workshop on Semantic Evaluation (SemEval 2013)*, pages 138–143, Atlanta, Georgia, USA. Association for Computational Linguistics.

Dirk Hovy, Stephen Tratz, and Eduard Hovy. 2010. What's in a preposition? dimensions of sense disambiguation for an interesting word class. In *Coling 2010: Posters*, pages 454–462, Beijing, China. Coling 2010 Organizing Committee.

Youxuan Jiang, Catherine Finegan-Dollak, Jonathan K. Kummerfeld, and Walter Lasecki. 2018. Effective crowdsourcing for a new type of summarization task. In *Proceedings of the 2018 Conference of the North American Chapter of the Association for Computational Linguistics: Human Language Technologies, Volume 2 (Short Papers)*, pages 628–633, New Orleans, Louisiana. Association for Computational Linguistics.

Youxuan Jiang, Jonathan K. Kummerfeld, and Walter S. Lasecki. 2017. Understanding task design trade-offs in crowdsourced paraphrase collection. In *Proceedings of the 55th Annual Meeting of the Association for Computational Linguistics (Volume 2: Short Papers)*, pages 103–109, Vancouver, Canada. Association for Computational Linguistics.

David Jurgens. 2013. Embracing ambiguity: A comparison of annotation methodologies for crowdsourcing word sense labels. In *Proceedings of the 2013 Conference of the North American Chapter of the Association for Computational Linguistics: Human Language Technologies*, pages 556–562, Atlanta, Georgia. Association for Computational Linguistics.

Najoung Kim, Roma Patel, Adam Poliak, Patrick Xia, Alex Wang, Tom McCoy, Ian Tenney, Alexis Ross, Tal Linzen, Benjamin Van Durme, Samuel R. Bowman, and Ellie Pavlick. 2019. Probing what different NLP tasks teach machines about function word comprehension. In *Proceedings of the Eighth Joint Conference on Lexical and Computational Semantics (*SEM 2019)*, pages 235–249, Minneapolis, Minnesota. Association for Computational Linguistics.

A. Kumaran, Melissa Densmore, and Shaishav Kumar. 2014. Online gaming for crowd-sourcing phrase-equivalents. In *Proceedings of COLING 2014, the 25th International Conference on Computational Linguistics: Technical Papers*, pages 1238–1247, Dublin, Ireland. Dublin City University and Association for Computational Linguistics.

Ji-Ung Lee, Jan-Christoph Klie, and Iryna Gurevych. 2022. Annotation curricula to implicitly train non-expert annotators. *Computational Linguistics*, 48(2):343–373.

Ken Litkowski and Orin Hargraves. 2007. SemEval-2007 Task 06: Word-Sense Disambiguation of Prepositions. In *Proceedings of the Fourth International Workshop on Semantic Evaluations (SemEval-2007)*, pages 24–29, Prague, Czech Republic. Association for Computational Linguistics.

Nelson F. Liu, Daniel Hershcovich, Michael Kranzlein, and Nathan Schneider. 2021. Lexical semantic recognition. In *Proceedings of the 17th Workshop on Multiword Expressions (MWE 2021)*, pages 49–56, Online. Association for Computational Linguistics.

Marie Mikulová, Milan Straka, Jan Štepánek, Barbora Štepánková, and Jan Hajic. 2022. Quality and efficiency of manual annotation: Pre-annotation bias.

Margaret Mitchell, Dan Bohus, and Ece Kamar. 2014. Crowdsourcing language generation templates for dialogue systems. In *Proceedings of the INLG and SIGDIAL 2014 Joint Session*, pages 172–180, Philadelphia, Pennsylvania, U.S.A. Association for Computational Linguistics.

Nikita Nangia, Saku Sugawara, Harsh Trivedi, Alex Warstadt, Clara Vania, and Samuel R. Bowman. 2021. What ingredients make for an effective crowdsourcing protocol for difficult nlu data collection tasks?

S. Parameswarappa and V.N. Narayana. 2012. Sense disambiguation of simple prepositions in english to kannada machine translation. In *2012 International Conference on Data Science Engineering (ICDSE)*, pages 203–208.

Girishkumar Ponkiya, Kevin Patel, Pushpak Bhattacharyya, and Girish Palshikar. 2018. Treat us like the sequences we are: Prepositional paraphrasing of noun compounds using LSTM. In *Proceedings of the 27th International Conference on Computational Linguistics*, pages 1827–1836, Santa Fe, New Mexico, USA. Association for Computational Linguistics.

Nathan Schneider, Jena D. Hwang, Vivek Srikumar, Jakob Prange, Austin Blodgett, Sarah R. Moeller, Aviram Stern, Adi Bitan, and Omri Abend. 2018. Comprehensive supersense disambiguation of English prepositions and possessives. In *Proceedings of the 56th Annual Meeting of the Association for Computational Linguistics (Volume 1: Long Papers)*, pages 185–196, Melbourne, Australia. Association for Computational Linguistics.

Nathan Schneider and Noah A. Smith. 2015. A corpus and model integrating multiword expressions and supersenses. In *Proceedings of the 2015 Conference of the North American Chapter of the Association for Computational Linguistics: Human Language Technologies*, pages 1537–1547, Denver, Colorado. Association for Computational Linguistics.

Howard Schuman. 2008. *Method and meaning in polls and surveys*. Harvard University Press.

Vivek Srikumar and Dan Roth. 2011. A joint model for extended semantic role labeling. In *Proceedings of the 2011 Conference on Empirical Methods in Natural Language Processing*, pages 129–139, Edinburgh, Scotland, UK. Association for Computational Linguistics.

Stephen Tratz. 2011. *Semantically-enriched parsing for natural language understanding*. Ph.D. dissertation, University of Southern California, Los Angeles, California.

Jennifer Wortman Vaughan. 2017. Making better use of the crowd: How crowdsourcing can advance machine learning research. *J. Mach. Learn. Res.*, 18:193:1–193:46.

William Yang Wang, Dan Bohus, Ece Kamar, and Eric Horvitz. 2012. Crowdsourcing the acquisition of natural language corpora: Methods and observations. In *2012 IEEE Spoken Language Technology Workshop (SLT)*, pages 73–78.

Mohammad-Ali Yaghoub-Zadeh-Fard, Boualem Benatallah, Fabio Casati, Moshe Chai Barukh, and Shayan Zamanirad. 2020. Dynamic word recommendation to obtain diverse crowdsourced paraphrases of user utterances. In *Proceedings of the 25th International Conference on Intelligent User Interfaces*, pages 55–66.

Patrick Ye and Timothy Baldwin. 2006. Semantic role labeling of prepositional phrases. *ACM Transactions on Asian Language Information Processing*, 5(3):228–244.

DoSA : A System to Accelerate Annotations on Business Documents with Human-in-the-Loop

Neelesh K Shukla and **MSP Raja** and **Raghu Katikeri** and **Amit Vaid**
State Street Corporation
Bengaluru, KA, India
{nshukla, smaddila1, rkatikeri, avaid}@statestreet.com

Abstract

Business documents come in a variety of structures, formats and information needs which makes information extraction a challenging task. Due to these variations, having a document generic model which can work well across all types of documents and for all the use cases seems far-fetched. For document-specific models, we would need customized document-specific labels. We introduce DoSA (**Do**cument **S**pecific **A**utomated Annotations), which helps annotators in generating initial annotations automatically using our novel bootstrap approach by leveraging document generic datasets and models. These initial annotations can further be reviewed by a human for correctness. An initial document-specific model can be trained and its inference can be used as feedback for generating more automated annotations. These automated annotations can be reviewed by human-in-the-loop for the correctness and a new improved model can be trained using the current model as pre-trained model before going for the next iteration. In this paper, our scope is limited to Form like documents due to limited availability of generic annotated datasets, but this idea can be extended to a variety of other documents as more datasets are built. An open-source ready-to-use implementation is made available on GitHub. [1]

1 Introduction

With the recent advancements in technology and increased adoption of digitization, almost all organizations maintain and exchange business documents in digitized formats like PDFs, scans, faxes, images etc. These documents come in all shape, sizes and format like invoices, emails, medical reports, contracts, scientific papers and many more. The majority of the research has concentrated on documents present on the web that do not adequately capture the complexity of analysis or comprehension required for business documents. These documents

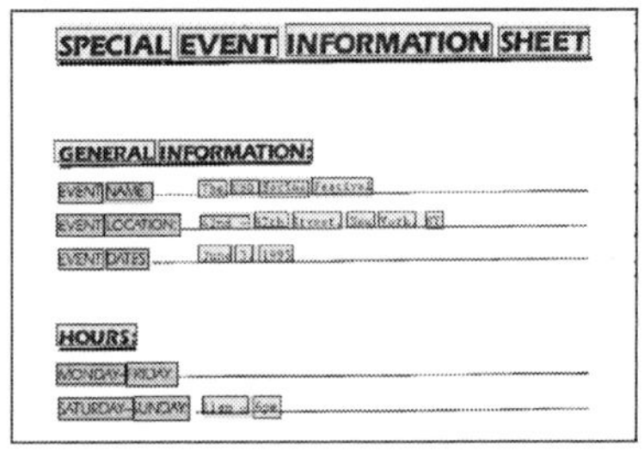

Figure 1: Form Example from FUNSD: Keys are represented in blue, headers in orange, and Values in green.

require a multidisciplinary approach that includes understanding of layout and structure, computer vision, natural language processing. Usually, organizations rely on humans to manually process these documents. The ability to read, understand and interpret these documents is referred as Document Intelligence (DI) or Document Understanding. There have been recent advancements in this area specifically with deep learning where many architectures (Huang et al., 2022; Appalaraju et al., 2021; Kim et al., 2021) and annotated datasets (Mathew et al., 2020; Zhong et al., 2019; Huang et al., 2019; Park et al., 2019) have been published for various DI tasks like Document Classification, Document Visual Q&A, Form Understanding etc. These publicly annotated datasets mostly capture only few document types like receipts, scientific articles etc. It becomes challenging & tedious to have annotated public datasets available for various document types which therefore brings in the very need of having customized annotated datasets for specific use cases and document types.

To limit our scope, in this paper we are focusing on information extraction from documents that follow a form-like structure. Forms are documents that have information usually present in Question-Answer or Key-Value format as shown in Figure 1. Documents like invoices, driving licenses, passports, medical records, financial statements, tax

[1] https://github.com/neeleshkshukla/DoSA

Proceedings of the Fourth Workshop on Data Science with Human-in-the-Loop (Language Advances), pages 23 - 27
December 8, 2022

forms, quotations, payment cards, etc. fall under this category.

There has been an effort in building a generic form dataset FUNSD[2] (Jaume et al., 2019). FUNSD is a dataset for form understanding in noisy scanned documents that aim at extracting and structuring the textual content of forms. It proposes an idea where a generic document can be represented via generic information and labels like question (or key), answer (or value), header and others. A model can consume this kind of generic representation to extract generic information. In most of the scenarios, users are interested in document-specific meaningful labels like document number, document date, etc and extracting a subset of information. Having a document generic labeling approach results in a noisy and verbose extraction. Therefore a need for document-specific annotations arises. Commercial solutions like Microsoft Form Recognizer[3] and Google Document AI [4] mostly support specific document type prebuilt models and provide a facility to custom train a model for specific documents[5] which require new annotations. The SOTA models of document intelligence use multimodality of the document: text, position and image. Due to a change in the format or layout of the document, these modalities might be affected and a new model needs to be trained which will need a new set of annotations. With these, manual annotation becomes repetitive, laborious, expensive and time-consuming.

To reduce the time and human effort, we are proposing an active learning based automated annotation system DoSA (**Do**cument **S**pecific **A**utomated Annotations), where the initial set of document-specific annotations are generated by the system which can be reviewed by human annotators for correctness. An initial model can be trained with these annotations and its inference can be taken by the system as feedback to generate annotations on new documents and improve the model incrementally with the human in the loop.

The main contribution of this paper is a novel bootstrapping approach to generate automated document-specific labels. To the best of our knowledge, this is the first attempt at generating automated annotations on business documents that contains visual and layout structure information along with the text. All other previous approaches have mostly focused on web or text (Dill et al., 2003; Wilson et al., 2018) or images (Yu et al., 2019). We have seen an attempt on research documents but the scope was limited to automatically annotating documents with topic (Singhal et al., 2013).

2 DoSA System

A high-level flow of the DoSA system is shown in Figure 2, where initial document-specific annotations are generated by document-generic model which is later reviewed by a human for correctness. With these initial annotations, a document-specific model is trained and its inference is taken as feedback to annotate further documents. A human will again review and correct the annotations and the reviewed documents can be added back to training for further improving the model. As the model matures, eventually the user would end up correcting a minimal number of annotated fields/documents. The journey for the model to get more precise with less human feedback is achieved by employing active learning strategies like uncertainty-based sampling which improve the document-specific model performance in very few iterations.

2.1 Bootstrapping: Generating Initial Document Specific Annotations with Document Generic Model

Here are the steps that are followed in generating annotations on the initial set of documents:

- A document is processed via an OCR engine to get the words and their respective bounding boxes. DoSA uses open source OCR engine pytesseract[6].
- As an intermediate step, the text areas are identified as 'Keys' and 'Values' in these documents (Section 2.1.1).
- Link respective Key and Values and form a key-value pair <K, V> (Section 2.1.2).
- Document-specific annotations can be generated by labeling the area identified as value V with the text of the area identified by the respective key K (Section 2.1.3).

[2]https://guillaumejaume.github.io/FUNSD/

[3]https://azure.microsoft.com/en-in/services/form-recognizer/

[4]https://cloud.google.com/document-ai

[5]https://docs.microsoft.com/en-us/azure/applied-ai-services/form-recognizer/concept-custom

[6]https://pypi.org/project/pytesseract/

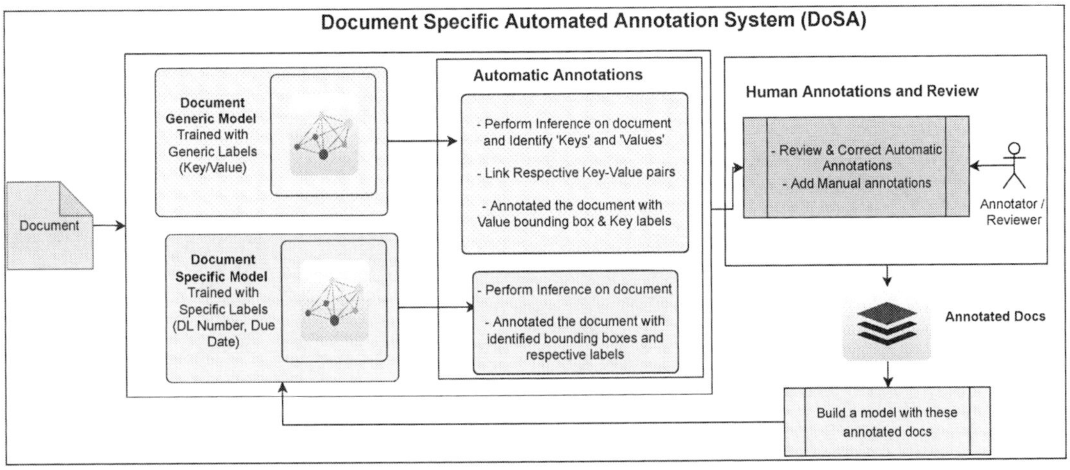

Figure 2: DoSA System Overview: Generating Annotations with Human in the Loop

2.1.1 Locating Keys and Values

As an intermediate step, text areas in a document are identified as 'Key' and 'Value'. DoSA uses LayoutLMv3(Huang et al., 2022) model for entity/token classification fine-tuned on generic FUNSD dataset[7]. This can classify the word/token/entity in 'Key (Question)', 'Value (Answer)', 'Header' and 'Others' with F1 0.9078. The areas are represented by bounding box coordinates <x1,y1, x2, y2> which are used for comparing the position and drawing rectangles in the next sections. In the fax cover example shown in figure 3, 'To', 'Fax Number', 'Phone Number', 'Date' has been identified as keys and 'George Baroody', '(336) 335-7392', '12/10/98' as values.

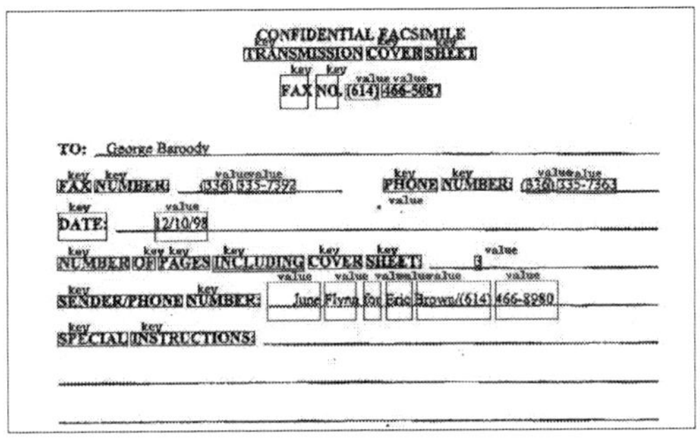

Figure 3: Areas marked with generic 'Key' and 'Value' labels as described in section 2.1.1

2.1.2 Key and Value Pair Linking

After identifying keys and values, DoSA links respective pairs <K, V>. There have been multiple recent works addressing this Form Entity Linking problem (Li et al., 2021; Zhang et al., 2021). These works have F1 0.4 and 0.64 respectively. These SOTA models are not good enough and were resulting in a lot of noisy pairs. Based on manual observations of a few documents, we designed the following heuristics to identify key-value pairs.

Given a list of values V ordered by their position in a document, Value Vj is linked to candidate key Ki if it satisfies the following conditions:
H1: Position of Ki is less than the position of Vj.
H2: Ki is not linked to any other Value Vk
H3: Ki is the closest to Vj compared to other candidate keys Km which satisfy H1 and H2.

If No such key is found for a Value Vj. Vj will be dropped else pair <Ki, Vj> is added to the output. For the document shown in figure 3, some of the examples are <Fax Number: (336) 335-7392> and <Date: 12/10/98>.

2.1.3 Document Specific Annotations and Review with Human-in-the-Loop

Once the <Key, value> pairs are identified, annotations can be generated by drawing the bounding boxes around 'value' and annotating it with the text of the respective 'key'. These automated annotations can be submitted for review and modifications with Human-in-the-loop.

An example is shown in Figure 4, once the key-value pair <Fax Number: (336) 335-7392> identified, the value (336) 335-7392 has been annotated with respective key 'Fax Number'.

[7] https://huggingface.co/nielsr/layoutlmv3-finetuned-funsd

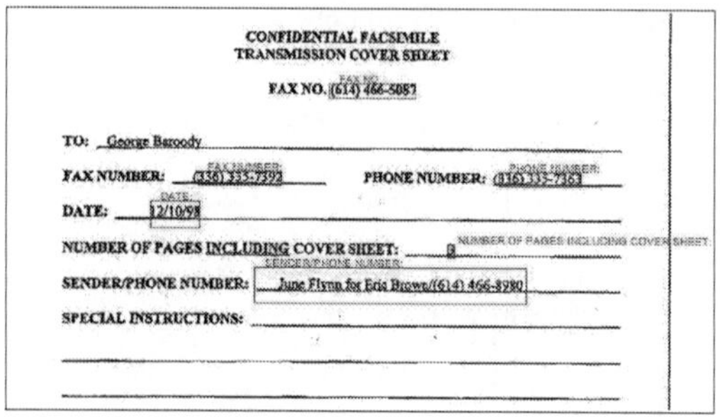

CONFIDENTIAL FACSIMILE
TRANSMISSION COVER SHEET

FAX NO. (614) 466-5087

TO: George Baroody

FAX NUMBER: (336) 335-7392 PHONE NUMBER: (336) 335-7363

DATE: 12/10/98

NUMBER OF PAGES INCLUDING COVER SHEET: 3

SENDER/PHONE NUMBER: June Flynn for Eric Brown/(614) 466-8980

SPECIAL INSTRUCTIONS:

Figure 4: Document specific annotations by labeling regions/texts identified as 'Value' with respective 'Key' in intermediate annotations as shown in figure 3.

2.2 Annotations with Document Specific Model

A custom initial model can be built by fine-tuning the generic model used in section 2.1.1 on these reviewed initial annotations which now have document-specific labels. This document-specific model can be used to generate annotations via inference feedback on new documents. As more documents and annotations are added and reviewed, the model will eventually get mature.

3 Conclusion and Future Work

In this work, we presented DoSA, a system to generate document specific annotations from model built on document generic datasets. Our scope was limited to Form like document which can be further enhanced with the availability of new type of generic datasets. This system in current state can only take one type of document to generate one set of annotations. In case the users have multiple type of documents, they have to group the documents by type beforehand and use this system for individual groups. A layer can be added on top of DoSA system to automatically classify the documents and use DoSA for individual groups. As this work is still in progress, in this paper we focused on proposing this idea. We are planning to discuss the effectiveness of our proposed approaches and overall system in the near future.

References

Srikar Appalaraju, Bhavan Jasani, Bhargava Urala Kota, Yusheng Xie, and R. Manmatha. 2021. Docformer: End-to-end transformer for document understanding. In *2021 IEEE/CVF International Conference on Computer Vision (ICCV)*, pages 973–983.

Stephen Dill, Nadav Eiron, David Gibson, Daniel Gruhl, R. Guha, Anant Jhingran, Tapas Kanungo, Sridhar Rajagopalan, Andrew Tomkins, John A. Tomlin, and Jason Y. Zien. 2003. Semtag and seeker: Bootstrapping the semantic web via automated semantic annotation. WWW '03, page 178–186, New York, NY, USA. Association for Computing Machinery.

Yupang Huang, Tengchao Lv, Lei Cui, Yutong Lu, and Furu Wei. 2022. Layoutlmv3: Pre-training for document ai with unified text and image masking. In *ACM Multimedia 2022*.

Zheng Huang, Kai Chen, Jianhua He, Xiang Bai, Dimosthenis Karatzas, Shijian Lu, and C. V. Jawahar. 2019. Icdar2019 competition on scanned receipt ocr and information extraction. In *2019 International Conference on Document Analysis and Recognition (ICDAR)*, pages 1516–1520.

Guillaume Jaume, Hazim Kemal Ekenel, and Jean-Philippe Thiran. 2019. Funsd: A dataset for form understanding in noisy scanned documents. In *2019 International Conference on Document Analysis and Recognition Workshops (ICDARW)*, volume 2, pages 1–6.

Geewook Kim, Teakgyu Hong, Moonbin Yim, Jinyoung Park, Jinyeong Yim, Wonseok Hwang, Sangdoo Yun, Dongyoon Han, and Seunghyun Park. 2021. Donut: Document understanding transformer without ocr. *CoRR*, abs/2111.15664.

Yulin Li, Yuxi Qian, Yuchen Yu, Xiameng Qin, Chengquan Zhang, Yan Liu, Kun Yao, Junyu Han, Jingtuo Liu, and Errui Ding. 2021. Structext: Structured text understanding with multi-modal transformers. *CoRR*, abs/2108.02923.

Minesh Mathew, Dimosthenis Karatzas, R. Manmatha, and C. V. Jawahar. 2020. Docvqa: A dataset for VQA on document images. *CoRR*, abs/2007.00398.

Seunghyun Park, Seung Shin, Bado Lee, Junyeop Lee, Jaeheung Surh, Minjoon Seo, and Hwalsuk Lee. 2019. {CORD}: A consolidated receipt dataset for post-{ocr} parsing. In *Workshop on Document Intelligence at NeurIPS 2019*.

Ayush Singhal, Ravindra Kasturi, and Jaideep Srivastava. 2013. Automating document annotation using open source knowledge. In *2013 IEEE/WIC/ACM International Joint Conferences on Web Intelligence (WI) and Intelligent Agent Technologies (IAT)*, volume 1, pages 199–204.

Shomir Wilson, Florian Schaub, Frederick Liu, Kanthashree Mysore Sathyendra, Daniel Smullen, Sebastian Zimmeck, Rohan Ramanath, Peter Story, Fei Liu, Norman Sadeh, and Noah A. Smith. 2018. Analyzing privacy policies at scale: From crowdsourcing to automated annotations. *ACM Trans. Web*, 13(1).

Chao-Wei Yu, Yen-Lin Chen, Ko-Feng Lee, Chen-Hsiang Chen, and Chia-Yu Hsiao. 2019. Efficient intelligent automatic image annotation method based on machine learning techniques. In *2019 IEEE International Conference on Consumer Electronics - Taiwan (ICCE-TW)*, pages 1–2.

Yue Zhang, Zhang Bo, Rui Wang, Junjie Cao, Chen Li, and Zuyi Bao. 2021. Entity relation extraction as dependency parsing in visually rich documents. In *Proceedings of the 2021 Conference on Empirical Methods in Natural Language Processing*, pages 2759–2768, Online and Punta Cana, Dominican Republic. Association for Computational Linguistics.

Xu Zhong, Jianbin Tang, and Antonio Jimeno Yepes. 2019. Publaynet: largest dataset ever for document layout analysis. In *2019 International Conference on Document Analysis and Recognition (ICDAR)*, pages 1015–1022. IEEE.

Execution-based Evaluation for Data Science Code Generation Models

Junjie Huang[1*], Chenglong Wang[3], Jipeng Zhang[5*], Cong Yan[3], Haotian Cui[6*], Jeevana Priya Inala[3], Colin Clement[4], Nan Duan[2], Jianfeng Gao[3]

[1] Beihang University [2] Microsoft Research Asia [3]Microsoft Research Redmond
[4] Microsoft [5] Hong Kong University of Science and Technology [6] Toronto University

[1]huangjunjie@buaa.edu.cn,
[2,3,4]{chenwang,coyan,janala,coclemen,nanduan,jfgao}@microsoft.com
[5]jzhanggr@connect.ust.hk, [6]ht.cui@mail.utoronto.ca

Abstract

Code generation models can benefit data scientists' productivity by automatically generating code from context and text descriptions. An important measure of the modeling progress is whether a model can generate code that can correctly execute to solve the task. However, due to the lack of an evaluation dataset that directly supports execution-based model evaluation, existing work relies on code surface form similarity metrics (e.g., BLEU, CodeBLEU) for model selection, which can be inaccurate.

To remedy this, we introduce ExeDS, an evaluation dataset for execution evaluation for data science code generation tasks. ExeDS contains a set of 534 problems from Jupyter Notebooks, each consisting of code context, task description, reference program, and the desired execution output. With ExeDS, we evaluate the execution performance of five state-of-the-art code generation models that have achieved high surface-form evaluation scores. Our experiments show that models with high surface-form scores do not necessarily perform well on execution metrics, and execution-based metrics can better capture model code generation errors.
[1]

1 Introduction

Code generation models (Chen et al., 2021a; Tunstall et al., 2022) have shown promising results to improve developer productivity by generating code from natural specifications (Le et al., 2020; Al-Hossami and Shaikh, 2022). These promising results also bring interest to code generation for data scientists, who program data analysis scripts in interactive notebook environments like Jupyter Notebooks (Kluyver et al., 2016) where programs are written interactively in loosely organized program cells (Figure 1 (1)). This domain and style

```
Context:                                                        (1)
  d.columns = []
  # split data. input column & column to be predicted
  X = d.values[:,:-1]
  y = d.values[:,-1]
  # now create an estimator, train and predict
  from sklearn.naive_bayes import GaussianNB
  from sklearn.model_selection import cross_val_score
  from sklearn.metrics import *
  est = GaussianNB()
  est.fit(X,y)
  predictions = est.predict(X)
Intent: Compute the accuracy of predictions compared with y
-----------------------------------------------------------------
Target:
  accuracy_score(predictions, y)

Ground truth code cell:                                         (2)
  In [ ]: accuracy_score(predictions, y)
  Out [ ]: 0.8410769068020736
Generated code cell:
  In [ ]: print("Accuracy: ",cross_val_score(est,X,y,cv=10).mean())
  Out [ ]: Accuracy: 0.8410769068020736
```

Figure 1: An example from ExeDS. The first block describes the task of data science code generation with code context and NL intents. The second block compares the code and output of reference and generation.

differences motivates new modeling resources, e.g., new datasets (e.g. JuiCe (Agashe et al., 2019)) and models (e.g. JuPyT5 (Chandel et al., 2022)) specific to data science tasks.

However, we still lack a good methodology to evaluate data science (DS) code generation models. JuiCe dataset uses the BLEU (Papineni et al., 2002) and Exact Match (EM), the prevailing metrics in code generation, to measure semantic similarity between the generated and reference code. However, these two surface-form metrics have limitations: the former neglects code syntactic features and the latter is too strict (Ren et al., 2020). Execution-based metrics are another widely accepted line of metrics in general software engineering (SE) domain, where the correctness of generated functions is determined by whether the outputs are consistent with oracle input-output data/unit tests. For DS problems, however, collecting an executable dataset and performing execution-based evaluation are challenging. DS notebooks usually do not come with their own set of unit tests and existing datasets like JuiCe do not track the input data (such as tables) needed to run the notebooks. In addition, the outputs from notebook cells are often not "pure"

*Work done during internship at Microsoft Research Asia.

[1]Source code and data can be found at https://github.com/Jun-jie-Huang/ExeDS.

Proceedings of the Fourth Workshop on Data Science with Human-in-the-Loop (Language Advances), pages 28 - 36
December 8, 2022 ©2022 Association for Computational Linguistics

values (e.g., numbers, strings, or lists) like the outputs of the functions in SE problems. The DS notebook cell outputs are meant for human understanding and hence, may contain complex data structures (e.g., data frames, plots) accompanied with texts; thus simply checking whether outputs are the same is too strict to capture cases when the generated cell output is semantically correct but formatted differently from the reference (Figure 1-(2)).

In this paper, we provide a dataset for evaluating DS code generation models, dubbed ExeDS, which contains 534 data science problems built on JuiCe (Agashe et al., 2019). We collect ExeDS by first crawling data dependencies from original GitHub repositories for the notebooks and filtering out notebooks with runtime errors; then, we curated 534 high-quality problems with sufficient code context and human-written natural language (NL) to describe tasks as the testset. With ExeDS, we can evaluate execution correctness by comparing outputs from generated code with desirable outputs.

We experiment with 5 existing code generation models on ExeDS to identify their execution performance. Experiment results show that (1) models with high/low surface-form scores do not necessarily generate execution-correct code – for example, while Codex (Chen et al., 2021a) is low in BLEU, it achieves high execution scores. (2) Execution-based metrics can better capture code errors which might be helpful for model improvements.

2 Related Works

Data science (DS) refers to the practice of analyzing data and acquiring insights with computational methods (Donoho, 2017). With the goal to improve productivity, there are increasing interests in building systems to solve a variety of DS tasks, including code synthesis (Agashe et al., 2019), code synthesis for visualization (Chen et al., 2021b) and data preparation (Yan and He, 2020), documentation (Liu et al., 2021; Wang et al., 2021), etc. In our work, we focus on code generation in DS, which generates code with code, NL and data context.

Code generation benchmarks are predominantly evaluated by matching code surface forms(Papineni et al., 2002; Lin, 2004; Ren et al., 2020). These datasets evaluate explicit code generation with different input specifications, including natural language (Wang et al., 2015; Oda et al., 2015; Zhong et al., 2017; Yin et al., 2018; Yu et al., 2018; Lin et al., 2018), unfinished code (Iyer et al., 2018; Lu et al., 2021), and input-output examples (Polosukhin and Skidanov, 2018; Zavershynskyi et al., 2018). However, surface form metrics are unable to assess code as programmers, who focus on the functionality and execution correctness in practice.

Dataset	#	Domain	Evaluation
APPS (Hendrycks et al., 2021)	10,000	SE	Unit Test
MBPP (Austin et al., 2021)	974	SE	Unit Test
HumanEval (Chen et al., 2021a)	164	SE	Unit Test
DSP (Chandel et al., 2022)	1,139	DS	Unit Test
JuiCe (Agashe et al., 2019)	1,981	DS	Surface Form
PlotCoder (Chen et al., 2021b)	894	DS	Surface Form
ExeDS (ours)	534	DS	Output Match

Table 1: Comparisons of code generation testsets.

Consequently, recent works turn to execution-based metrics instead, where the code would be correct if it passes a set of unit tests defined by humans (Roziere et al., 2020; Kulal et al., 2019; Austin et al., 2021; Chen et al., 2021a; Hendrycks et al., 2021). However, the complex output data and scarcity of units tests in DS limit its application in DS code generation. Chandel et al. (2022) explore applying unit tests in DS, but they only focus on educational problems. Table 1 compares ExeDS with various related datasets.

3 ExeDS for Execution Evaluation

As mentioned in Section 1, the lack of executable environments for notebooks is a key limiting factor of execution-based model evaluation for data science tasks. Thus we first construct an evaluation dataset ExeDS and analyze its characteristics. Then describe the methods for execution evaluation.

Dataset Collection ExeDS contains 534 problems with code context, NL task description, reference code and target execution output, which is built upon JuiCe (Agashe et al., 2019) with 659K publicly available Python Jupyter notebooks from GitHub. We create ExeDS in the following steps.

Step1: Crawling Data Context and Execution. Programming problems in DS often deal with data, which are often stored in files (e.g., `.csv`) and loaded by code. Executing notebooks needs such data dependencies, which are not provided in JuiCe. Thus, we first crawl dependent data for notebooks from their GitHub repositories. Notebooks with inaccessible data or using libraries not present in Python standard library and default DS environment are removed. With data dependency, we execute notebooks with a time limit of 1000 sec-

Function Type	%	Examples
Data statistic	40	Avg., var., p-value, ...
Explore data value	19	Min/max value, ...
Explore data property	10	Dtype, shape, ...
Machine learning	16	Loss, train, predict, ...
Simple math	6	Arithmetic, ...
Data changing	5	Sort, sample, ...
Data displaying	4	Head/tail columns, ...

Table 2: Function types of target code in ExeDS.

onds per cell. After execution, code cells have three types of outputs: (1) *displaying data* with a figure; (2) *execute result* with a textual execution output; and (3) *stream output* with a printed textual output through streams. Since it's hard to compute figure similarities, in this paper, we only evaluate execution correctness on textual outputs and construct ExeDS with *execute result* and *stream output*.

Step 2: Dataset Filtering and Intent Curation. As some cells are overly complex for code generation, for simplicity, we remove examples with more than 5 lines or using customized methods in target code cells. To keep diversity, we downsample cells with frequent outputs, e.g. `df.summary()`, `df.info()`, `df.shape`, etc. To ensure sufficient context is provided, we remove the target code whose variables are absent in the previous 5 cells.

Since some cells lack sufficient descriptions for the problems, for clarity, we recruit two university students with Python and notebook experience to manually write NL descriptions for each example. After viewing the context, target code and output, they are asked to write descriptions containing information in two aspects: (1) the functions of target code; (2) the instructions to print outputs. We discard examples that annotators feel hard to describe.

Finally, we obtain 534 problems from 278 notebooks for ExeDS, each with code context, NL description, target code, and desired execution output.

Dataset Statistics Table 2 shows the function types in ExeDS. We found the majority of target codes are computing statistics (40%), exploring data value (19%) or property (10%), and for machine learning (16%), which are popular DS tasks.

Table 4 presents the types of execution output in all 534 problems. We find the majority of execution output are numbers, which is not surprising considering the fraction of data statistics and exploring data value in code functions. Also comparing numbers is less complicated than comparing other types of data like strings or data frames, which helps easier evaluation of execution outputs.

Library	# problems
pandas	534
numpy	473
matplotlib	431
sklearn	287
seaborn	211
scipy	135
statsmodels	57
math	46
datetime	42
re	39

Table 3: Frequency of most common 10 libraries used in 534 examples of ExeDS.

Table 3 displays the most common libraries used in ExeDS. We find the majority of them use data science libraries and all of them use `pandas`, which indicates our focus on data science code generation.

Evaluation Metrics In ExeDS, we measure the execution correctness by comparing the reference outputs with outputs from generated code, which is called output exact match (OutputEM). However, as a variety of examples produce outputs in numbers, we convert all numbers in `string` type to the `float` type with two decimal spaces to better match numbers. Similarly, we remove the explanation string when printing outputs for better comparison.

4 Evaluating Code Generation on ExeDS

Based on ExeDS, we evaluate the models' performance on data science code generation and compare both surface-form code and execution output.

DS Code Generation We investigate the task of target code cell generation in notebooks with context. Figure 1 presents an example of the task. For each target code cell, we prepare a source-target example, conditioned on prior multimodal context and natural language intent. The context includes: (1) the closest three cells prior to the target cell, regardless of code or markdown; (2) a code state-

Output Type	%	Examples
Single number	55	0.841076906802073; 68
List/tuple/array	34	(256, 10); ['UserID', 'Gender']
Dataframe	11	Weight 26.25 Speed 36.70 dtype: float64

Table 4: Types of ground truth outputs in ExeDS.

	BLEU	CodeBLEU	EM	OutputEM
GPT-style framework				
GPT-neo-125M	3.4	17.2	0.0	1.5
GPT-neo-1.3B	9.2	26.2	0.0	10.7
GPT-neo-2.7B	9.1	28.8	0.4	13.3
CodeGPT	26.4	28.6	1.5	12.7
CodeGPT-adapted	25.1	26.8	3.3	13.1
Codex*	3.9	23.5	0.0	27.7
encoder-decoder framework				
PyMT5	25.7	35.8	2.8	19.7
JuPyT5	**35.3**	**41.1**	**6.2**	**31.6**

Table 5: Evaluation results of surface form metrics and execution metric. * denotes a zero-shot setting.

ment to define the columns names of data in the format of `df.columns=['a', 'b']`.

Baseline Models We test five code generation models: (1) PyMT5 (Clement et al., 2020) is an encode-decoder transformer (Vaswani et al., 2017) pretrained on Python corpus. (2) JuPyT5 (Chandel et al., 2022) is an encoder-decoder transformer pretrained on Jupyter notebooks with the code-infilling objective. (3) CodeGPT and CodeGPT-adapted (Lu et al., 2021) are two GPT-style models (Solaiman et al., 2019) pretrained on CodeSearchNet Python functions (Husain et al., 2019), where the former is trained from scratch and the latter is trained from GPT-2 checkpoint. (4) GPT-neo (Black et al., 2021) is a GPT-style model pretrained on The Pile (Gao et al., 2021), a dataset with a variety of text sources including 8% GitHub code. We evaluate three GPT-neo models with different parameters, including 125M, 1.3B, and 2.7B. (5) Codex (Chen et al., 2021a) is the state-of-the-art model trained on 159G GitHub Python files from GPT-3 (Brown et al., 2020). We test its zero-shot performance due to the inaccessibility of model weights.

Finetuning For training and validation, we filter a set of 123K source-target examples from JuiCe with data dependencies, where the target is any code cell and the source is the prior multimodal context as in ExeDS. We randomly select 4K examples for validation and leave the rest for finetuning. More details can be found in Appendix A.

Metrics We report results with OutputEM, which is the proportion of examples with correct output, and surface-form metrics, i.e. BLEU, CodeBLEU (Ren et al., 2020), and Exact Match (EM).

Error Category	%	Exception Examples
Use undefined variable	45	NameError...
Use undefined API	16	AttributeError...
Use wrong schema	22	KeyError, ValueError, IndexError...
Wrong Syntax	8	IndentationError, SyntaxError ...
Other errors	9	No message, ImportError, ...

Table 6: Qualitative error analysis on examples that raise exceptions during execution. Some representative exception types for each error category are listed.

5 Evaluation Results

In this section, we show and analyze evaluation results to show the advantages of our ExeDS dataset.

5.1 Main Results

Table 5 shows the results of different baseline models in surface form metrics and execution correctness. We have the following main observations.

(1) For all models, the surface form EM is close to zero while the OutputEM is in a normal range. This suggests that surface form EM often fails to evaluate code correctness, while the execution metric is better which covers more correct cases and shows correctness beyond matching code strings.

(2) Surprisingly, zero-shot Codex achieves compatible results with finetuned JuPyT5 in OutputEM, but it performs badly with surface-form metrics. This finding suggests the strength of Codex to generate correct code and understand the multimodal context. In addition, the difference between surface-form scores and OutputEM again shows the superiority of measuring code with execution correctness.

(3) Encoder-decoder models perform better than GPT-style models with all metrics, which indicates their strength in generating code. Also, JuPyT5 achieves the best performance with all metrics. One possible reason is that JuPyT5 is pretrained on a large corpus of notebooks, which learns the necessary knowledge from the notebook context.

5.2 Error Analysis

We give two error analyses of execution results to investigate examples with raised execution exceptions and erroneous outputs. The code examples are produced by our top-performing model JuPyT5. Detailed examples can be found in Appendix B.

Exception Types Table 6 shows five exception types from 154 examples. We find for 45% cases, the model fails to capture data-flow and uses undefined variables in context. For 16% cases, the

Error Category	%	Examples
Incorrect Code	56	Figure 3 & 4
No Output	8	Figure 5
Partially Correct	12	Figure 6
To Many Output	24	Figure 7 & 8

Table 7: Analysis of 50 examples with wrong outputs.

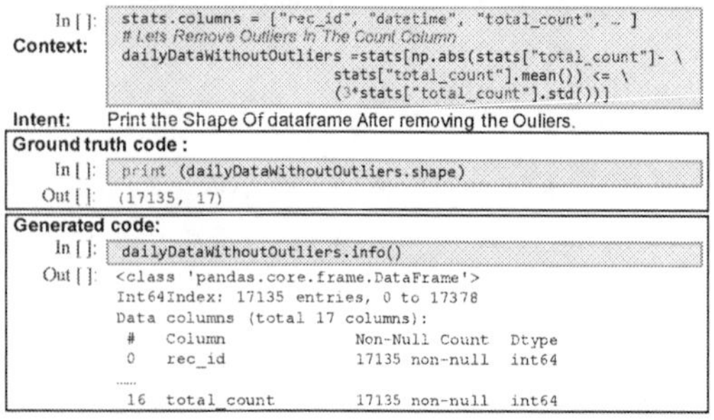

Figure 2: An incorrect example with high surface form metrics scores but low execution metrics scores. Surface form metrics are deficient to evaluate code correctness.

model misuses API methods and often leads to `AttributeError` , possibly due to version differences and calling methods without import. 22% cases misuse the data schema of dataframes, which indicates the need to improve code generation models with such multimodal context, especially how to incorporate the data schema context. Only 8% cases have syntax problems, suggesting the model's strong ability to generate syntax-correct code.

Output Errors Table 7 shows four types of output errors from 50 examples. We find 56% cases have incorrect code. The challenging NL description and context might be hard for models to understand and generate correct code. 8% cases complete the correct functions but do not call `print()` to output. 12% of cases are partially correct, where the output mismatch is caused due to some missing details, for example, the absence of some parameters. Finally, 24% cases produce too many outputs.

6 Case Study

We give an example predicted by JuPyT5 with a high BLEU score but erroneous outputs in Figure 2, to show the advantages of execution evaluation for DS code generation. The example is a typical DS task which intends to explore the shape of a dataframe. But the model misunderstands the intents and generates code to display all dataframe information. Although we can find the expected shapes from the output, i.e., 17135 entries and 17 columns, the output is not exactly correct. However, as the code is short while the variable name is long, which leads to a high overlap between prediction and ground truth, the generated code obtains above average BLEU and CodeBLEU scores. This example reveals the deficiency of surface form metrics to evaluate code correctness.

7 Conclusion

In this paper, we propose an evaluation dataset to support execution correctness evaluation for data science code generation dubbed ExeDS, which consists of 534 typical data science problems from Jupyter Notebooks, each with code context, task description, target code, and desired execution output. By performing experiments with five strong code generation models on ExeDS, we find models that achieve high surface-form scores do not necessarily produce execution correct code, and execution-based metrics could capture more detailed code generation errors. We expect our efforts to attract more attention to code execution correctness and generating executable code.

Limitations

Firstly, only the test set examples have high quality of human annotation and verification. Thus the training set might be too noising to train a robust code generation model. Secondly, the execution metric is insufficient to show other information like semantic relatedness, variable naming, and API usages, which are also important in evaluating a good code. Thirdly, our datasets and metrics focus on Python code in data science domain. It's unclear whether is applicable to general software code. Fourth, our execution-based automatic evaluation is more time-consuming to compute and evaluate than other surface-form metrics like EM, BLEU. At last, evaluating generated code is far different from evaluating natural languages. The final goal of code generation is to generate execution and functional correct code. Though with many limitation, our work could be a pilot study which provides insights and possible solutions on how to better evaluate code generation models.

References

Rajas Agashe, Srinivasan Iyer, and Luke Zettlemoyer. 2019. JuICe: A large scale distantly supervised dataset for open domain context-based code generation. In *Proceedings of the 2019 Conference on Empirical Methods in Natural Language Processing and the 9th International Joint Conference on Natural Language Processing (EMNLP-IJCNLP)*, pages 5436–5446, Hong Kong, China. Association for Computational Linguistics.

Erfan Al-Hossami and Samira Shaikh. 2022. A survey on artificial intelligence for source code: A dialogue systems perspective. *ArXiv*, abs/2202.04847.

Jacob Austin, Augustus Odena, Maxwell Nye, Maarten Bosma, Henryk Michalewski, David Dohan, Ellen Jiang, Carrie J. Cai, Michael Terry, Quoc V. Le, and Charles Sutton. 2021. Program synthesis with large language models. *ArXiv*, abs/2108.07732.

Sid Black, Leo Gao, Phil Wang, Connor Leahy, and Stella Biderman. 2021. GPT-Neo: Large Scale Autoregressive Language Modeling with Mesh-Tensorflow.

Tom Brown, Benjamin Mann, Nick Ryder, Melanie Subbiah, Jared D Kaplan, Prafulla Dhariwal, Arvind Neelakantan, Pranav Shyam, Girish Sastry, Amanda Askell, Sandhini Agarwal, Ariel Herbert-Voss, Gretchen Krueger, Tom Henighan, Rewon Child, Aditya Ramesh, Daniel Ziegler, Jeffrey Wu, Clemens Winter, Chris Hesse, Mark Chen, Eric Sigler, Mateusz Litwin, Scott Gray, Benjamin Chess, Jack Clark, Christopher Berner, Sam McCandlish, Alec Radford, Ilya Sutskever, and Dario Amodei. 2020. Language models are few-shot learners. In *Advances in Neural Information Processing Systems*, volume 33, pages 1877–1901. Curran Associates, Inc.

Shubham Chandel, Colin B. Clement, Guillermo Serrato, and Neel Sundaresan. 2022. Training and evaluating a jupyter notebook data science assistant. *ArXiv*, abs/2201.12901.

Mark Chen, Jerry Tworek, Heewoo Jun, Qiming Yuan, Henrique Ponde, Jared Kaplan, Harrison Edwards, Yura Burda, Nicholas Joseph, Greg Brockman, Alex Ray, Raul Puri, Gretchen Krueger, Michael Petrov, Heidy Khlaaf, Girish Sastry, Pamela Mishkin, Brooke Chan, Scott Gray, Nick Ryder, Mikhail Pavlov, Alethea Power, Lukasz Kaiser, Mohammad Bavarian, Clemens Winter, Philippe Tillet, Felipe Petroski Such, David W. Cummings, Matthias Plappert, Fotios Chantzis, Elizabeth Barnes, Ariel Herbert-Voss, William H. Guss, Alex Nichol, Igor Babuschkin, S. Arun Balaji, Shantanu Jain, Andrew Carr, Jan Leike, Joshua Achiam, Vedant Misra, Evan Morikawa, Alec Radford, Matthew M. Knight, Miles Brundage, Mira Murati, Katie Mayer, Peter Welinder, Bob McGrew, Dario Amodei, Sam McCandlish, Ilya Sutskever, and Wojciech Zaremba. 2021a. Evaluating large language models trained on code. *ArXiv*, abs/2107.03374.

Xinyun Chen, Linyuan Gong, Alvin Cheung, and Dawn Song. 2021b. PlotCoder: Hierarchical decoding for synthesizing visualization code in programmatic context. In *Proceedings of the 59th Annual Meeting of the Association for Computational Linguistics and the 11th International Joint Conference on Natural Language Processing (Volume 1: Long Papers)*, pages 2169–2181, Online. Association for Computational Linguistics.

Colin Clement, Dawn Drain, Jonathan Timcheck, Alexey Svyatkovskiy, and Neel Sundaresan. 2020. PyMT5: multi-mode translation of natural language and python code with transformers. In *Proceedings of the 2020 Conference on Empirical Methods in Natural Language Processing (EMNLP)*, pages 9052–9065, Online. Association for Computational Linguistics.

David L. Donoho. 2017. 50 years of data science. *Journal of Computational and Graphical Statistics*, 26:745 – 766.

Leo Gao, Stella Rose Biderman, Sid Black, Laurence Golding, Travis Hoppe, Charles Foster, Jason Phang, Horace He, Anish Thite, Noa Nabeshima, Shawn Presser, and Connor Leahy. 2021. The pile: An 800gb dataset of diverse text for language modeling. *ArXiv*, abs/2101.00027.

Dan Hendrycks, Steven Basart, Saurav Kadavath, Mantas Mazeika, Akul Arora, Ethan Guo, Collin Burns, Samir Puranik, Horace He, Dawn Song, and Jacob Steinhardt. 2021. Measuring coding challenge competence with apps. *NeurIPS*.

Hamel Husain, Hongqi Wu, Tiferet Gazit, Miltiadis Allamanis, and Marc Brockschmidt. 2019. Codesearchnet challenge: Evaluating the state of semantic code search. *ArXiv*, abs/1909.09436.

Srinivasan Iyer, Ioannis Konstas, Alvin Cheung, and Luke Zettlemoyer. 2018. Mapping language to code in programmatic context. In *Proceedings of the 2018 Conference on Empirical Methods in Natural Language Processing*, pages 1643–1652, Brussels, Belgium. Association for Computational Linguistics.

Thomas Kluyver, Benjamin Ragan-Kelley, Fernando Pérez, Brian E. Granger, Matthias Bussonnier, Jonathan Frederic, Kyle Kelley, Jessica B. Hamrick, Jason Grout, Sylvain Corlay, Paul Ivanov, Damián Avila, Safia Abdalla, Carol Willing, and Jupyter Development Team. 2016. Jupyter notebooks - a publishing format for reproducible computational workflows. In *ELPUB*.

Sumith Kulal, Panupong Pasupat, Kartik Chandra, Mina Lee, Oded Padon, Alexander Aiken, and Percy Liang. 2019. Spoc: Search-based pseudocode to code. In *NeurIPS*.

Triet Huynh Minh Le, Hao Chen, and Muhammad Ali Babar. 2020. Deep learning for source code modeling and generation. *ACM Computing Surveys (CSUR)*, 53:1 - 38.

Chin-Yew Lin. 2004. ROUGE: A package for automatic evaluation of summaries. In *Text Summarization Branches Out*, pages 74–81, Barcelona, Spain. Association for Computational Linguistics.

Xi Victoria Lin, Chenglong Wang, Luke Zettlemoyer, and Michael D. Ernst. 2018. NL2Bash: A corpus and semantic parser for natural language interface to the linux operating system. In *Proceedings of the Eleventh International Conference on Language Resources and Evaluation (LREC 2018)*, Miyazaki, Japan. European Language Resources Association (ELRA).

Xuye Liu, Dakuo Wang, April Wang, Yufang Hou, and Lingfei Wu. 2021. HAConvGNN: Hierarchical attention based convolutional graph neural network for code documentation generation in Jupyter notebooks. In *Findings of the Association for Computational Linguistics: EMNLP 2021*, pages 4473–4485, Punta Cana, Dominican Republic. Association for Computational Linguistics.

Shuai Lu, Daya Guo, Shuo Ren, Junjie Huang, Alexey Svyatkovskiy, Ambrosio Blanco, Colin Clement, Dawn Drain, Daxin Jiang, Duyu Tang, Ge Li, Lidong Zhou, Linjun Shou, Long Zhou, Michele Tufano, MING GONG, Ming Zhou, Nan Duan, Neel Sundaresan, Shao Kun Deng, Shengyu Fu, and Shujie LIU. 2021. CodeXGLUE: A machine learning benchmark dataset for code understanding and generation. In *Thirty-fifth Conference on Neural Information Processing Systems Datasets and Benchmarks Track*.

Yusuke Oda, Hiroyuki Fudaba, Graham Neubig, Hideaki Hata, Sakriani Sakti, Tomoki Toda, and Satoshi Nakamura. 2015. Learning to generate pseudo-code from source code using statistical machine translation (t). *2015 30th IEEE/ACM International Conference on Automated Software Engineering (ASE)*, pages 574–584.

Kishore Papineni, Salim Roukos, Todd Ward, and Wei-Jing Zhu. 2002. Bleu: a method for automatic evaluation of machine translation. In *ACL*.

Illia Polosukhin and Alexander Skidanov. 2018. Neural program search: Solving data processing tasks from description and examples. In *ICLR 2018*.

Shuo Ren, Daya Guo, Shuai Lu, Long Zhou, Shujie Liu, Duyu Tang, M. Zhou, Ambrosio Blanco, and Shuai Ma. 2020. Codebleu: a method for automatic evaluation of code synthesis. *ArXiv*, abs/2009.10297.

Baptiste Roziere, Marie-Anne Lachaux, Lowik Chanussot, and Guillaume Lample. 2020. Unsupervised translation of programming languages. In *Advances in Neural Information Processing Systems*, volume 33, pages 20601–20611. Curran Associates, Inc.

Irene Solaiman, Miles Brundage, Jack Clark, Amanda Askell, Ariel Herbert-Voss, Jeff Wu, Alec Radford, and Jasmine Wang. 2019. Release strategies and the social impacts of language models. *ArXiv*, abs/1908.09203.

Lewis Tunstall, Leandro von Werra, and Thomas Wolf. 2022. *Natural Language Processing with Transformers: Building Language Applications with Hugging Face*. O'Reilly Media, Incorporated.

Ashish Vaswani, Noam Shazeer, Niki Parmar, Jakob Uszkoreit, Llion Jones, Aidan N Gomez, Ł ukasz Kaiser, and Illia Polosukhin. 2017. Attention is all you need. In *Advances in Neural Information Processing Systems*, volume 30. Curran Associates, Inc.

April Yi Wang, Dakuo Wang, Xuye Liu, and Lingfei Wu. 2021. Graph-augmented code summarization in computational notebooks. In *IJCAI*.

Yushi Wang, Jonathan Berant, and Percy Liang. 2015. Building a semantic parser overnight. In *ACL*.

Cong Yan and Yeye He. 2020. Auto-suggest: Learning-to-recommend data preparation steps using data science notebooks. *Proceedings of the 2020 ACM SIGMOD International Conference on Management of Data*.

Pengcheng Yin, Bowen Deng, Edgar Chen, Bogdan Vasilescu, and Graham Neubig. 2018. Learning to mine aligned code and natural language pairs from stack overflow. *2018 IEEE/ACM 15th International Conference on Mining Software Repositories (MSR)*, pages 476–486.

Tao Yu, Rui Zhang, Kai-Chou Yang, Michihiro Yasunaga, Dongxu Wang, Zifan Li, James Ma, Irene Z Li, Qingning Yao, Shanelle Roman, Zilin Zhang, and Dragomir R. Radev. 2018. Spider: A large-scale human-labeled dataset for complex and cross-domain semantic parsing and text-to-sql task. In *EMNLP*.

Maksym Zavershynskyi, Alexander Skidanov, and Illia Polosukhin. 2018. Naps: Natural program synthesis dataset. *ArXiv*, abs/1807.03168.

Victor Zhong, Caiming Xiong, and Richard Socher. 2017. Seq2sql: Generating structured queries from natural language using reinforcement learning. *ArXiv*, abs/1709.00103.

A Finetuning Details

We finetune all the baseline models, except Codex, on our cleaned training set and select the best checkpoint with the perplexity score on dev set for testing. All models are trained on 16 Tesla V100 32GB GPUs. The hyper parameter are presented in Table 8.

At inference time, we use beam search decoding with a beam size of 5.

B More Examples

In this section, we present 6 examples to show the typical types of errors with erroneous outputs in Figure 3 - Figure 8. We also give an example with a typical type of errors causing exceptions in Figure 9.

Context:

In [ ]:
```
train_data.columns =  ["price", "bedrooms", "bathrooms", …]
# 3 - Building a regression model with several more features
x_train = train_data[features].values.reshape(-1,len(features))
y_train = train_data['price'].values.reshape(-1, 1)
mult_model = linear_model.LinearRegression()
mult_model.fit(x_train, y_train)
x_test = test_data[features].values.reshape(-1, len(features))
y_test = test_data['price'].values.reshape(-1, 1)
y_pred = mult_model.predict(x_test)
```

Intent: Compute and print the rooted mean squared error of test data

Ground truth code :

In [ ]:
```
features_rmse = rmse(y_pred, y_test)
print(features_rmse)
```
Out [ ]: `249311.90032627754`

Generated code:

In [ ]:
```
mse=((y_test-y_pred)**2).mean()
print(mse)
```
Out [ ]: `62156423644.29977`

Figure 3: An example with incorrect code. The NL intent is too challenging and the generated code misses the key information to compute the (rooted) error. More powerful models to understand NL intent are required.

Context:

In [ ]:
```
data_pd.columns =  ["Verbal", "State", "Rate", "age", … ]
# How many states are above the mean? What does this tell you about the
distribution of Verbal scores?
sns.set(rc={"figure.figsize": (8, 8)})
ax_v = sns.distplot(data_pd.Verbal,kde=False,bins=20,color='y')
ax_v.set(ylabel='Counts', title='Distribution of Verbal')
mean = plt.plot([data_pd.Verbal.mean(), data_pd.Verbal.mean()],
                [0, 5], linewidth=2)
```

Intent: Print a list of states whose `Verbal` scores above the mean `Verbal` score:

Ground truth code :

In [ ]:
```
data_mask = data_pd.Verbal > data_pd.Verbal.mean()
list_states = data_pd[data_mask]['State']
print(list(list_states))
```
Out [ ]: `['CO', 'OH', 'MT', 'ID', 'TN', 'NM', 'IL', 'KY', 'LA']`

Generated code:

In [ ]:
```
mean=plt.plot([data_pd.Verbal.mean(),data_pd.Verbal.mean()],
              [0,5],linewidth=2)
```
Out [ ]:

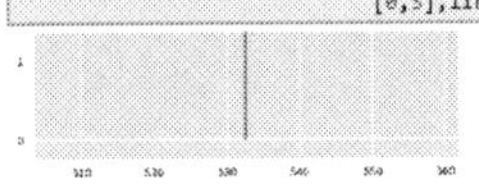

Figure 4: An example with incorrect code. The model fails to perform contextual reasoning over such multimodal context.

Context:

In [ ]:
```
dftouse.columns =  ["RESP", "AXSPEND", "MAILED", …]
# 1.2 Standardize the data
from sklearn import preprocessing
std = preprocessing.StandardScaler().fit(dftouse[mask==True])
df_std = std.transform(dftouse[mask==True])
dftouse.set_value(mask==True, 0, df_std)
std2 = preprocessing.StandardScaler().fit(dftouse[mask==False])
df_std2 = std2.transform(dftouse[mask==False][0])
dftouse.set_value(mask==False, 0, df_std2)
```

Intent: Create a list `lcols` of the columns in the dataframe `dftouse`. This list should not contain the response `RESP` so we should remove the `RESP` item. After that how many features do we have?

Ground truth code :

In [ ]:
```
lcols = list(dftouse.columns)
lcols.remove(u'RESP')
print (len(lcols))
```
Out [ ]: `68`

Generated code:

In [ ]:
```
lcols=list(dftouse.columns)
lcols.remove('RESP')
```
Out [ ]:

Figure 5: An example with a no output error. the generated code satisfies the intent to create a list and remove the item. But it fails to produce the output, i.e., the length of the feature list.

Context:

In [ ]:
```
data.columns =  []
from sklearn import preprocessing
print("Mean Cross Validation Score of Kernalized SVC:", '%.4f'
   %cross_val_score(SVC(kernel='poly',degree=2,C=1,gamma=0.05),
     x_train, y_train, cv = 10).mean())
svcpa = SVC(kernel='poly', degree=3, C=0.5, gamma=0.05)
svc = svcpa.fit(x_trainscaled,z_train)
print("The best Train score is :", svc.score(x_trains,z_train))
print("The best Test Score is :", svc.score(x_test, z_test))
svcp = svc.predict(x_test)
```

Intent: Compute the Mean Cross Validation Score of Kernalized SVC Classifier using `x_train` and `z_train`

Ground truth code :

In [ ]:
```
print(cross_val_score(SVC(kernel='poly',degree=3,C=0.5,
        gamma=0.05), x_train, z_train, cv = 10).mean())
```
Out [ ]: `0.778698752228164`

Generated code:

In [ ]:
```
svcscores=cross_val_score(svc,x_train,z_train,cv=5)
svcscores.mean()
```
Out [ ]: `0.7729148375768217`

Figure 6: An example with a partially correct error. The code is actually correct but the parameter for cv is different, resulting in the difference between the ground truth and execution outputs.

Context:

In [ ]:
```
df.columns =  ["label", "text", "v1", "v2", … ]
# Converting words to vectors
## Counting how many times a word appears in the dataset
from collections import Counter
counts = Counter()
for i in range(len(text)):
    for word in text.values[i][0].split(" "):
        counts[word] += 1
print("Total words in data set: ", len(counts))
```

Intent: Sorting the `counts` in decreasing order (Word with highest frequency appears first). Print the first 10 items in the sorted list.

Ground truth code :

In [ ]:
```
vocab = sorted(counts, key=counts.get,reverse=True)
print(vocab[:10])
```
Out [ ]: `['to', 'you', 'I', 'a', 'the', 'and', 'in', 'is', 'i', 'u']`

Generated code:

In [ ]:
```
vocab=sorted(counts.items(), key=lambda x:x[1], reverse=True)
vocab[:10]
```
Out [ ]:
```
[('to', 2134), ('you', 1622), ('I', 1466), ('a', 1327),
('the', 1197), ('and', 857), ('in', 798), ('is', 781),
('i', 742), ('u', 692)]
```

Figure 7: An example with too many output. The correct output actually exists in the execution output, but the excessive output causes the inexact match and decline in ExeF1.

Hyperparameter	CodeGPT	CodeGPT-adapted	GPT-neo 125M	GPT-neo 1.3B	GPT-neo 2.7B	PyMT5	JuPyT5
# vocab size	50001	50260	50257	50257	50257	50337	50340
# parameters	124M	124M	125M	1.3B	2.7B	374M	374M
# hidden size	768	768	768	2048	2560	1472	1472
# layers	12	12	12	16	20	12	12
# heads	12	12	12	24	32	12	12
dropout	0.1	0.1	0.1	0.1	0.1	0.1	0.1
optimizer	AdamW	AdamW	AdamW	AdamW	AdamW	Adam	Adam
learning rate	5e-05	5e-05	5e-05	5e-05	5e-05	1e-4	1e-4
batch size	16	16	3	1	1	1	1
epochs	30	30	10	10	10	10	10
max tokens	512	512	2048	2048	1536	3600	3600

Table 8: Details of the hyperparameters used during fine-tuning for the code generation task in this paper.

Context:

In [ ]:
```
X.columns =  ["Horse", "Tipster", "Date", "ID", …]
# Random Forest
from sklearn.ensemble import RandomForestClassifier
rf = RandomForestClassifier()
classifier3 = rf.fit(X_train, y_train)
prediction3 = classifier3.predict(X_test)
print("Acc of Random Forest:", classifier3.score(X_test,y_test))
print("Kappa:", cohen_kappa_score(y_test, prediction3))
```

Intent: Removing `horse` attribute in the dataframe `X`. Split the dataset into training set and text set with a `test_size` of `0.2`. Then print the shapes of `X` training data and test data.

Ground truth code :

In [ ]:
```
del X['horse']
X_train,X_test,y_train,y_test=train_test_split(X,y,test_size=0.2)
print(X_train.shape, X_test.shape)
```

Out [ ]: `(30598, 5) (7650, 5)`

Generated code:

In [ ]:
```
X=X.drop('horse', axis=1)
X_train,X_test,y_train,y_test=train_test_split(X,y,test_size=0.2)
print(X_train.shape,X_test.shape,y_train.shape,y_test.shape)
```

Out [ ] `(30598, 5) (7650, 5) (30598,) (7650,)`

Figure 8: Another example with too many output.

Context:

In [ ]:
```
df.columns =  ["CO2 ppm", "Global Temp", "Year"  ]
# Performing the regression. We will use scipy's built in regression analysis here. There are quite a number of options out there, e.g., statsmodels, scikit-learn, etc , that you can explore
res = stats.linregress(df["CO2 ppm"], df["Global Temp"])
```

Intent: Print the slope, intercept, R value, std error of the regression model

Ground truth code :

In [ ]:
```
print(res.slope, res.intercept, res.rvalue, res.stderr)
```

Out [ ]: `0.927802179 -298.243887005 0.90607748814 0.065315887945`

Generated code:

In [ ]:
```
print(res.slope)
print(res.intercept)
print(res.rvalue)
print(res.std_error)
```

Out [ ]: `AttributeError:'LinregressResult' has no attribute 'std_error'`

Figure 9: An example running with exceptions. The model misuses the attribute to call the standard errors.

A Gamified Approach to Frame Semantic Role Labeling

Emily Amspoker
Carnegie Mellon University
eamspoke@andrew.cmu.edu

Miriam R. L. Petruck
International Computer Science Institute
miriamp@icsi.berkeley.edu

Abstract

Much research has investigated the possibility of creating **games with a purpose (GWAPs)**, i.e., online games whose purpose is gathering information to address the insufficient amount of data for training and testing of large language models (Von Ahn and Dabbish, 2008). Based on such work, this paper reports on the development of a game for **frame semantic role labeling**, where players have **fun** while using **semantic frames as prompts for short story writing**. This game will generate additional annotation for FrameNet and original content for annotation, **supporting FrameNet's goal of characterizing the English language in terms of Frame Semantics.**

1 Introduction

To create large-scale linguistic resources, linguistic database development projects have turned to crowd-sourcing. **Games with a purpose** (GWAPs), games whose purpose is to gather information, are a common approach to crowd-sourcing. GWAPs have been used for various tasks in computational linguistics, from anaphoric co-reference identification (Poesio et al., 2013) to word sense disambiguation (Lafourcade and Brun, 2017) to ontology population (Lafourcade et al., 2018). Informed by both the successes and shortcomings of previous games, this paper reports on the development of a game for frame semantic role labeling, ultimately for the FrameNet project, where players use semantic frames as prompts for short story writing. Upon completion of their stories, they also must provide semantic role annotation of their stories.

2 Background

This project focuses on the crowd-sourcing of frame semantic role labeling in FrameNet. This section provides background information about Frame Semantics (Fillmore, 1985) FrameNet, and crowd-sourcing to understand designing the game.

2.1 Frame Semantics

Frame Semantics (Fillmore, 1985), holds that each word or phrase in a text evokes a **semantic frame**, or structured background knowledge, that helps language users understand the text based on their experience (as a human, of a nationality, culture, etc). FrameNet calls a word or phrase that evokes a frame a **lexical unit** (**LU**), a pairing of a lemma and a frame. FrameNet treats each sense of a word or phrase with multiple meanings as different LUs based on their meaning in context.

For each LU, FrameNet records information about its dependents, the words or phrases that supply additional information about the participants in the frame, i.e., **frame elements** (**FE**s).

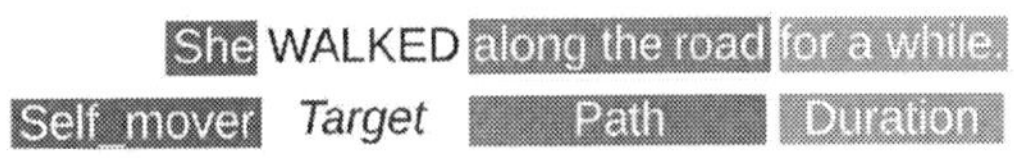

Figure 1: Semantic Role Annotation: `Self_Motion`

Consider the sentence *She walked along the road for a while.* in Figure 1. The LU **walk** evokes the `Self_Motion` frame, while the other parts of the sentence fill roles that give details about self-motion, including who is moving, how they are moving, and for how long they are moving.[1]

2.2 FrameNet

FrameNet (Ruppenhofer et al., 2016) is a research and resource development project based on the principles of Frame Semantics that provides information about the mapping between form and meaning for English, and documents its findings with corpus-based research. The FrameNet database holds frames, their descriptions, FEs, LUs, lexical entries with valence descriptions, and annotations of sentences that illustrate the use of each LU.

[1]By convention, FrameNet frames appear in `teletype font`, frame element names appear in SMALL CAPS; and in the prose, *italicized text* are example sentences.

Proceedings of the Fourth Workshop on Data Science with Human-in-the-Loop (Language Advances), pages 37 - 42
December 8, 2022 ©2022 Association for Computational Linguistics

FrameNet analysts create annotations in a two-step process. The first step is **frame disambiguation**. Polysemous words can exist in multiple frames; determining which frame a word evokes is critical. For example, the word **about** exists in the `Topic` frame, as in *This book is mostly* ***about*** *particle physics*, and the `Proportional_quantity` frame, as in *It took* ***about*** *three hours*.

FrameNet analysts determine which frame a word evokes, then label the FEs of that frame on the parts of the sentence (i.e., syntactic constituents) to which they correspond. Labeling is annotating; doing so automatically is **semantic role labeling** (**SRL**). The example in Figure 1 requires labeling *she* as the SELF_MOVER FE, *along the road* as the PATH FE, and *for a while* as the DURATION FE.

To date, FrameNet lexicographers have annotated example sentences **manually**, a resource-intensive activity that necessarily limits the amount of training data that the project has produced. Gamifying frame semantic SRL is but one effort to incorporate automatically produced annotation for the project. See (Pancholy et al., 2021) for another potential approach to automate annotation in FrameNet.

2.3 Crowdsourcing

Since large language models require massive amounts of data, which do not exist for FrameNet, the project has sought a variety of different ways to bolster the number of gold-standard annotated example sentences.

For example, Hong and Baker (2011) used crowdsourcing for frame disambiguation. On Amazon Mechanical Turk, a platform where *Turkers*, crowd-workers, perform small tasks (Human Intelligence Tasks) for a small amount of money. Workers had to choose the frame for a given target word based on its use in context. After filtering based on agreement, this method of collecting data yielded results that were approximately 86%-96% accurate.

While the crowd work approach works well for a multiple-choice task like frame disambiguation, semantic role labeling is more complex and requires a different approach, for example, that of **GWAPs**. Crowdsourcing efforts using GWAPs began in the early 2000s and mostly included simple labeling and image recognition tasks. For example, the ESP Game attracted over 200K players and created over 50 million labels four years after its release (Von Ahn and Dabbish, 2008).

Other GWAPs have completed linguistic annotation tasks: PackPlay, developed for semantic annotation, focused on Named Entity Recognition (Green et al., 2010). Similarly, Phrase Detectives, another successful GWAP used a reading comprehension game to identify anaphoric co-reference (Poesio et al., 2013). These games were successful in creating resources of a similar quality to traditionally generated data. However, many of these examples and others such as JeuxDesMots (Lafourcade et al., 2018), OntoGalaxy (Krause et al., 2010), and Zombilingo (Fort et al., 2014), focused on tasks less challenging than frame-semantic role labeling.

QANom (Klein et al., 2020) illustrates crowdsourcing for SRL, which gathered data for NomBank (Meyers et al., 2004) as microworkers answered questions about filling semantic roles via a question-and-answer format. Similarly, VerbCorner (Hartshorne et al., 2013), a game to crowdsource SRL for VerbNet (Kipper et al., 2000) had users read sentences with a sci-fi backstory and answer multiple-choice questions about the sentence. This approach required choosing specific verbs and crafting stories around them. If applied to SRL for FrameNet, the question-and-answer format would limit the ability to crowdsource data for numerous frames because rephrasing FrameNet data into comprehensible questions for the average player is terribly time-consuming.

Other fields boast examples of more complex tasks through gamification, such as *Foldit*, where players fold three-dimensional protein chains. This game generated enough high-quality data that players received credit as authors on several papers about the structure of various proteins (Khatib et al., 2011). Since online micro-working services can perform mechanical tasks, researchers have called for the creation of a new generation of GWAPs, where players complete complex tasks for a meaningful cause (Tuite, 2014).

3 The FrameGame

3.1 Principles

A literature review on designing GWAPs helped to establish four principles to guide our design.

1. The game's purpose must be **transparent** so players connect to its cause (Krause, 2013).
2. The game must have **skilled** tasks that highlight player creativity (Tuite, 2014).
3. The game must be **social** with an active community of members (Lafourcade et al., 2018).

4. If the game has orthogonal game elements, they must be **specifically aligned** with a stated goal (Bonetti and Tonelli, 2021).

3.2 Game Format

Given these core ideas, we created the FrameGame, where players use semantic frames as writing prompts. Along with creating annotated data for FrameNet, the game makes players brainstorm, think critically, and receive feedback on stories inspired by the frames that serve as prompts.

The game begins with a **start screen**. Players log in using the Facebook Gaming API, as FrameNet collects annotations through Facebook's unique player identifier. Once logged in, players can choose to read information about the game and FrameNet. Upon agreeing, players must agree to the terms and conditions, which state that they retain the rights to their creative work and allow FrameNet to use their text and annotation.

Next, players can navigate away from this page or read more about the FrameNet project. Also, the description of the project includes links to FrameNet's website,[2] as shown in Figure 2. The start screen is key for transparency about the purpose of the game and gives players the opportunity to engage with FrameNet further.

Figure 2: FrameNet Information Screen

If players choose to click on the coffee cup icon in the cafe in the left corner, they see the **story creation screen**, which makes up most of the gameplay. Likely players are already familiar with the concept of practicing their writing via social platforms that provided prompts for writing, e.g. Reddit's Writing Prompts. The FrameGame uses a single textbox where users enter one or more sentences to create a story, based on the LUs of the frame under consideration.

While writing, players view a list of frames using LUs from those frames (Figure 3). Also, they read further information about each frame by clicking on the **Info** tab; doing so displays annotated example sentences, lists of LUs that evoke the frame, and definitions of both the frame itself and FEs.

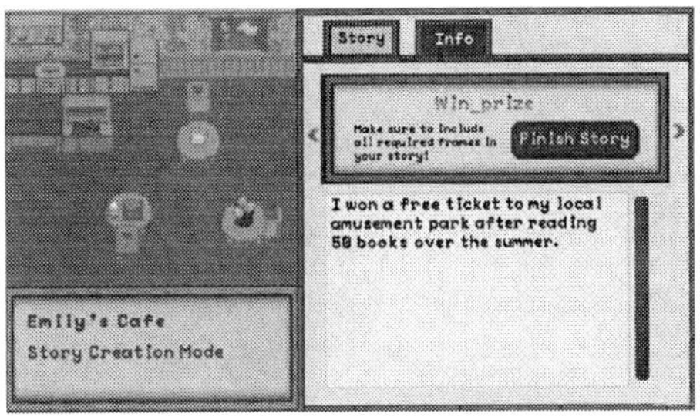

Figure 3: Writing Screen

These annotated example sentences, LUs. etc., exemplify how annotation for a given frame actually works. Similarly, players can take advantage of the opportunity to study and internalize the frame definition, including its FEs and their definitions.

After successfully completing their stories, players press a button to lock the text and begin the annotation part of the gameplay (Figure 4). Players must highlight the frame-evoking LU and the FEs of the given frame.

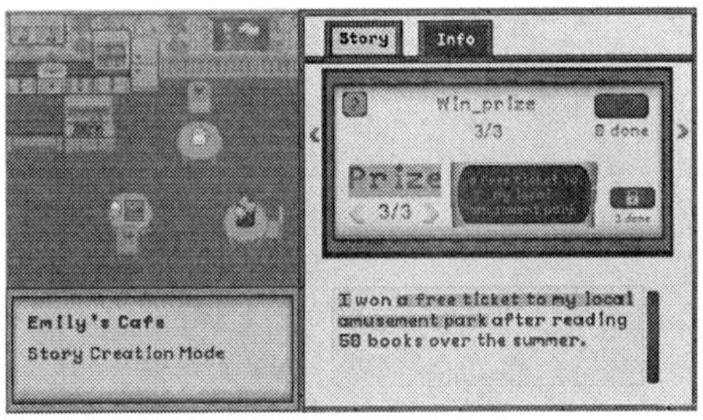

Figure 4: Annotation Screen

To ensure consistent annotation, the game places some restrictions on players during the annotation process: players must select a lexical unit from the list via the Info tab (available for reference during annotation), and they must label the FEs in the phrase or sentence under consideration.

Players can also access a screen for **viewing other players' work** (Figure 5) by clicking on the computer icon in the café. At present, this screen shows individual annotated sentences, their author, the frame, and its FEs.

3.3 Unexpected Findings

The FrameGame has not yet been deployed; the collection of player stories and sentence annota-

[2]https://framenet.icsi.berkeley.edu/fndrupal/

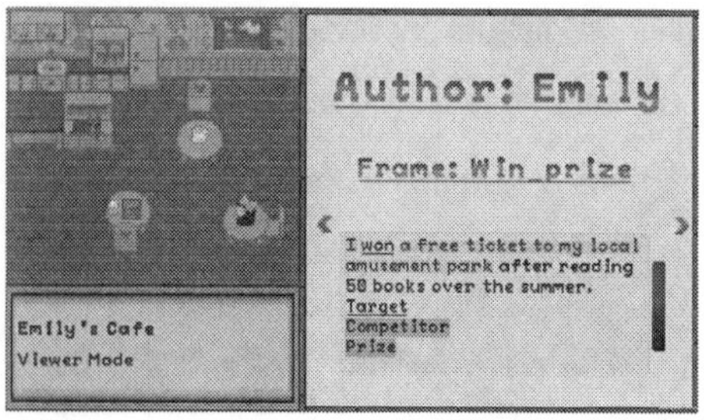

Figure 5: Viewing Others' Work Screen

Issue	Frame(s)
Incorrect Exemplars	`Transition_to_a_state`
Incorrect FE Labels	`Arraignment` `Expensiveness`
Missing all LUs	`Influencing_potential`

Table 1: Problematic Issues and Frames

tion can only begin after the release of the game. However, even in the development phase, the game contributed to improving the FrameNet database. During the testing of gameplay (in the development phase), the game parsed the XML for a given frame to JSON format for display. Whenever the code threw an error, it provided a link to FrameNet's frame index, and sent FrameNet an error report.

Parse errors originating from the game become an issue in the game's open access Github repository[3] and later corrected. Such parsing also detects and facilitates the correction of errors in FrameNet data. Importantly, the game will parse FrameNet's XML when anyone plays the game, i.e., not only during the development of the game.

The restrictions on gameplay (Section 3.2) also highlight issues with missing targets or confusing examples. Table 1 displays these issues and their respective frames. The subsections that follow here discuss the errors.

3.3.1 Incorrect Exemplars

FrameNet includes exemplar sentences in the definitions of FEs in a frame.[4] Although the exemplar sentences in the FE definitions for `Transition_to_a_state` included *become*.v, that lemma is not listed as such in the frame itself. Actually, FrameNet characterizes *become.v* in the `Becoming` frame, which inherits from `Transition_to_a_state`. The investigation of the frame determined the exemplar sentence error, which the FrameNet team has since corrected.

[3] `https://github.com/eamspoker/FrameGameAssets`

[4] See, for example, the FE definitions for `Becoming`.

3.3.2 Incorrect FE Labels

In both the `Arraignment` and `Expensiveness` frames, annotations for the example sentences included incorrectly placed tags or missing Frame Element names. As a result, the game could not correctly parse the examples to display to the player. FrameNet corrected these FE tags.

3.3.3 Missing all LUs

The `Influencing_potential` frame had no LUs listed, leaving no possibility for players to create annotated sentences based on the frame. While FrameNet holds valid **non-lexical** frames to maintain the integrity of the frame hierarchy, `Influencing_potential` is not one of them; the frame must have LUs in its XML file.

The unexpected exposure of errors and the need for corrections to the FrameNet database during the testing of the game showcase the potential of the game both to identify and facilitate the correction of pre-existing errors in the FrameNet database.

4 Conclusion and Future Work

4.1 Game Improvements

We must implement several features before deploying the game, including the following: (1) adding an interactive tutorial to ensure that players fully understand how to write stories and annotate sentences before beginning to play the game, (2) building a separate database to store player data and these crowd-sourced annotations, (3) implementing a points system, and (4) creating a system for verification and correction of annotations. We will detail these steps in the following paragraphs.

In its current unfinished state, the game only includes written instructions. We plan to add an interactive tutorial where users annotate an example sentence and receive feedback on the accuracy of their annotations.

Before declaring the game available to the general public, we also must ensure that the player-produced data remains separate from FrameNet's existing data. Game players do not possess the same expertise as highly-trained FrameNet annotators; mixing the two types of data before checking the quality of player-produced annotations is not desirable. We must store player-annotated sentences and player points to provide an accurate record of players' achievements, as well as other data too, such as average annotation time and quality, descriptions of which appear below.

We will implement a points system based on the number of frames for which players provide annotation. The goal of this points system is to motivate players to produce more annotations. As a result, players will receive a small number of points each time they annotate a sentence. Based on previous game theoretic approaches to GWAP design (Ghosh, 2013), this choice might cause players to create rushed or incorrect annotations simply to earn points. To prevent this scenario from occurring, players will receive a greater point reward than their initial reward once their annotation is deemed correct.[5]

Finally, numerous GWAPs, such as PackPlay (Green et al., 2010), Phrase Detectives (Poesio et al., 2013), and Jeux Des Mots (Lafourcade et al., 2018), include verification and correction measures in the game itself, or in the form of another game. We would filter out user annotations by drawing from the user data collected in the FrameGame database. Additionally, we want players to read each others' stories and to suggest revisions or corrections for others' annotations. Combining these recommendations and the original annotation may result in a more accurate final annotation.

4.2 User Study

After deploying the game, we will advertise its availability to several different groups, including the FrameNet mailing list, and online writing communities, like Reddit's r/WritingPrompts, and indie game enthusiasts on websites, such as Itch.io. After collecting these data, we will use a combination of agreement based on both the in-game verification methods (section 4.1) and formal analyses of the player-generated sentences for FrameNet analysts to determine the quality of the annotations.

Since the envisioned user study will only occur after the game has been deployed, we will determine the methods for filtering annotations and the strategy for evaluating the quality of annotations as the start of the study draws near.

We believe that this game has much potential to contribute to FrameNet. By crowd-sourcing both the creation of new example sentences and their annotation, the game will help FrameNet to capture language as it exists "in the wild" through the lens of frame semantics.

[5]We envision involving a highly trained member of the FrameNet team to make such decisions.

Acknowledgements

The authors acknowledge the contributions of Collin F. Baker to this work; he advised the lead author during the development of the game. Additionally, the International Computer Science Institute (**ICSI**) hosted Amspoker during her stay in Berkeley. The authors also thank the NSF and the Summer Undergraduate Program in Engineering Research at Berkeley (SUPERB) for their generous support of this research.

References

Federico Bonetti and Sara Tonelli. 2021. Measuring orthogonal mechanics in linguistic annotation games. *Proc. ACM Hum.-Comput. Interact.*, 5(CHI PLAY).

Charles J Fillmore. 1985. Frames and the semantics of understanding. *Quaderni di semantica*, 6(2):222–254.

Karën Fort, Bruno Guillaume, and Hadrien Chastant. 2014. Creating zombilingo, a game with a purpose for dependency syntax annotation. In *Proceedings of the First International Workshop on Gamification for Information Retrieval*, GamifIR '14, page 2–6, New York, NY, USA. Association for Computing Machinery.

Arpita Ghosh. 2013. Game theory and incentives in human computation systems. In Pietro Michelucci and Peng Dai, editors, *Handbook of Human Computation*, pages 725–742. Springer.

Nathan Green, Paul Breimyer, Vinay Kumar, and Nagiza Samatova. 2010. PackPlay: Mining semantic data in collaborative games. In *Proceedings of the Fourth Linguistic Annotation Workshop*, pages 227–234, Uppsala, Sweden. Association for Computational Linguistics.

Joshua K. Hartshorne, Claire Bonial, and Martha Palmer. 2013. The VerbCorner project: Toward an empirically-based semantic decomposition of verbs. In *Proceedings of the 2013 Conference on Empirical Methods in Natural Language Processing*, pages 1438–1442, Seattle, Washington, USA. Association for Computational Linguistics.

Jisup Hong and Collin F. Baker. 2011. How good is the crowd at "real" WSD? In *Proceedings of the 5th Linguistic Annotation Workshop*, pages 30–37, Portland, Oregon, USA. Association for Computational Linguistics.

Firas Khatib, Seth Cooper, Michael D. Tyka, Kefan Xu, Ilya Makedon, Zoran Popović, David Baker, and Foldit Players. 2011. Algorithm discovery by protein folding game players. *Proceedings of the National Academy of Sciences*, 108(47):18949–18953.

Karin Kipper, Hoa Trang Dang, and Martha Palmer. 2000. Class-based construction of a verb lexicon. In *Proceedings of the Seventeenth National Conference on Artificial Intelligence and Twelfth Conference on Innovative Applications of Artificial Intelligence*, pages 691–696. AAAI Press.

Ayal Klein, Jonathan Mamou, Valentina Pyatkin, Daniela Stepanov, Hangfeng He, Dan Roth, Luke Zettlemoyer, and Ido Dagan. 2020. QANom: Question-answer driven SRL for nominalizations. In *Proceedings of the 28th International Conference on Computational Linguistics*, pages 3069–3083, Barcelona, Spain (Online). International Committee on Computational Linguistics.

Markus Krause. 2013. Designing systems with homo ludens in the loop. In *Handbook of Human Computation*, pages 393–409. Springer.

Markus Krause, Aneta Takhtamysheva, Marion Wittstock, and Rainer Malaka. 2010. Frontiers of a paradigm: Exploring human computation with digital games. In *Proceedings of the ACM SIGKDD Workshop on Human Computation*, HCOMP '10, page 22–25, New York, NY, USA. Association for Computing Machinery.

Mathieu Lafourcade and Nathalie Le Brun. 2017. Ambiguss, a game for building a sense annotated corpus for French. In *IWCS 2017 — 12th International Conference on Computational Semantics — Short papers*.

Mathieu Lafourcade, Alain Joubert, and Nathalie Brun. 2018. The jeuxdemots project is 10 years old: What we have learned. In *Proceedings of the LREC 2018 Workshop "Games and Gamification for Natural Language Processing (Games4NLP)*, Miyazaki (Japan).

Adam Meyers, Ruth Reeves, Catherine Macleod, Rachel Szekely, Veronika Zielinska, Brian Young, and Ralph Grishman. 2004. The NomBank project: An interim report. In *Proceedings of the Workshop Frontiers in Corpus Annotation at HLT-NAACL 2004*, pages 24–31, Boston, Massachusetts, USA. Association for Computational Linguistics.

Ayush Pancholy, Miriam R L Petruck, and Swabha Swayamdipta. 2021. Sister help: Data augmentation for frame-semantic role labeling. In *Proceedings of the Joint 15th Linguistic Annotation Workshop (LAW) and 3rd Designing Meaning Representations (DMR) Workshop*, pages 78–84, Punta Cana, Dominican Republic. Association for Computational Linguistics.

Massimo Poesio, Jon Chamberlain, Udo Kruschwitz, Livio Robaldo, and Luca Ducceschi. 2013. Phrase detectives: Utilizing collective intelligence for internet-scale language resource creation. *ACM Trans. Interact. Intell. Syst.*, 3(1).

Josef Ruppenhofer, Michael Ellsworth, Miriam R. L. Petruck, Christopher R. Johnson, Collin F. Baker, and Jan Scheffczyk. 2016. *FrameNet II: Extended Theory and Practice*. ICSI: Berkeley.

Kathleen Tuite. 2014. Gwaps: Games with a problem. In *FDG*.

Luis Von Ahn and Laura Dabbish. 2008. Designing games with a purpose. *Commun. ACM*, 51(8):58–67.

A Comparative Analysis between Human-in-the-loop Systems and Large Language Models for Pattern Extraction Tasks

Maeda F. Hanafi, Yannis Katsis, Ishan Jindal, Lucian Popa
IBM Research
{maeda.hanafi, yannis.katsis, ishan.jindal}@ibm.com, lpopa@us.ibm.com

Abstract

Building a natural language processing (NLP) model can be challenging for end-users such as analysts, journalists, investigators, etc., especially given that they will likely apply existing tools *out of the box*. In this article, we take a closer look at how two complementary approaches, a state-of-the-art human-in-the-loop (HITL) tool and a generative language model (GPT-3) perform out of the box, that is, without fine-tuning. Concretely, we compare these approaches when end-users with little technical background are given pattern extraction tasks from text. We discover that the HITL tool performs with higher precision, while GPT-3 requires some level of engineering in its input prompts as well as post-processing on its output before it can achieve comparable results. Future work in this space should look further into the advantages and disadvantages of the two approaches, HITL and generative language model, as well as into ways to optimally combine them.

1 Introduction

Creating custom AI models for natural language processing (NLP) tasks is not an easy feat: it typically involves labeling large datasets, selecting appropriate ML architectures/models, and training them. To lower the barrier of entry in NLP model creation, the scientific and industrial community has proposed human-in-the-loop (HITL) systems (Wu et al., 2022; Hanafi et al., 2017; Monarch, 2021). While they differ in the NLP tasks they target (e.g., classification, extraction, question answering) and the techniques they employ (e.g., active learning, custom algorithms), their operation from the perspective of the end user is similar: The user labels a few examples, which are then used by the system to build a first version of the model and then to ask back the user for additional targeted feedback. This feedback is in turn used to iteratively refine the model and continue the loop by asking for further feedback. By asking for targeted feedback at each iteration, the goal is to lower the effort required to build a model, enabling fast convergence to a performant model while using a small number of labeled examples.

While such tools are gaining popularity, the NLP community has also recently proposed several pretrained generative language models, such as GPT-3. The largest versions of such models have shown incredible few-shot performance on several tasks (Brown et al., 2020). Thus the question arises: Given the out-of-the-box performance of such models, is it possible to feed them with a few examples and get similar performance to that of more complex HITL systems?

In this paper, we answer this question for the task of text pattern extraction. In this task, the goal is to extract text instances that follow a similar pattern. Examples include extracting crime incidents from crime reports, e.g. 4,556,123 incidents or 5,193,927 incidents, or revenue from financial press releases, e.g. revenue was $5.5 billion or revenue of $1.3 million.

To answer the question, we compare *Pattern Induction* (Hanafi et al., 2022), an HITL tool tailored to pattern extraction tasks, against *GPT-3* (Brown et al., 2020). We evaluate the two approaches based on how an *end-user*, who does not necessarily have a technical background, would use these tools to accomplish an NLP task, in this case pattern extraction. Unlike NLP experts, end-users typically use tools out-of-the-box, that is, without writing code and without fine-tuning parameters or modifying and re-training the layers of the AI model. Our preliminary results show that the use of simple techniques to prompt GPT-3 does not yet lead to the same performance as that of the tailored HITL tool. In this work, we describe these results and present further research directions on the relationship of models such as GPT-3 to HITL tools.

Proceedings of the Fourth Workshop on Data Science with Human-in-the-Loop (Language Advances), pages 43 - 50
December 8, 2022 ©2022 Association for Computational Linguistics

The following summarizes the contributions of this paper:

- A preliminary comparative analysis between an HITL system and large language model (GPT-3) in an information extraction (IE) context and a discussion of the pros and cons of the two approaches.
- A description of different techniques to leverage GPT-3 in this setting and evaluation of their impact on model performance.
- A discussion of interesting future directions that emanate from this preliminary study.

We start with literature review in Section 2, provide empirical study in Section 3, discuss each approach pros and cons in Section 4, and conclude in Section 5.

2 Related Works

In this work, we focus on few-shot learning systems (FSL) (Lake et al., 2016; Wang et al., 2020), which can learn from a handful of examples. This paradigm appeals to non-technical users given the small number of required examples to fine-tune a system, thus removing the need to label and maintain large labeled training datasets.

2.1 Human-In-The-Loop (HITL) Systems

HITL systems utilize human-interaction as opposed to systems that are fully automated, e.g. distant supervision, unsupervised, or semi-supervised methods (Ratner et al., 2017; Rühling Cachay et al., 2021). Automated methods leverage external data sources or seed inputs or rely on patterns or structures present in the dataset. They prove to be quite popular due to their ability to cover cases that a human would otherwise overlook. On the other hand, HITL systems integrate a human component in the relevant target task, and in this case an HITL information extraction would extract relevant texts with a human more involved in the process compared to a fully automated method (Monarch, 2021; Wu et al., 2022).

One such HITL tool for IE is Pattern Induction (Hanafi et al., 2017), and given an IE task, a user would do the following: (1) Highlights a minimum of two examples of text to extract, (2) The system learns a rule-based model, where each rule captures all of the examples, (3) The user provides "Yes" and "No" feedbacks to candidate extractions,

```
Prompt:
[ISO 9001 is probably the most well
recognized ISO number in the world.]

ISO numbers:
|ISO 18788|
|ISO 223000|

GPT-3's Completion:  |ISO 9001|
```

Figure 1: A naive way of prompting GPT-3 to complete the text pattern extraction task.

which in turn refines the rules, i.e. saying "No" to revenue of 2013 would inform Pattern Induction to filter out rules capturing such extractions, (4) The user is either satisfied with the set of extractions or further refines the rule-based model with additional highlights of positive examples on the document. Additional examples and feedbacks further refines the learned rule-based model. Pattern Induction showcases an HITL system that provides the human interactions the IE tasks needs to ensure accuracy in the underlying learned model.

2.2 Generative Language Models

Unlike HITL models, large language models (LLMs), e.g. BERT (Devlin et al., 2019) and GPT (Brown et al., 2020), are pre-trained with large unlabeled datasets, which enables the LLMs to understand contextual information in the input text. While both BERT and GPT are transformer-based models, enabling their few-shot abilities is done in different ways; templates with masking are built to take advantage of BERT while one has to prompt GPT with text, such that it generates relevant text (Wang et al., 2021). GPT falls under the category of generative language models, and GPT-3 has a larger number of parameters (175 billion parameters in its largest *davinci* version), making it one of the most powerful generative language models compared to its predecessors. Performing IE with GPT often entails constructing and engineering well-structured *prompts* (Schick and Schütze, 2021a). Prompts contain examples of extractions where a desired extracted text is paired with the sentence where it occurs.

3 Experiments

Since HITL models help end-users with little to no technical background perform IE tasks, we want to understand how they compare against popular generative language models out of the box.

Since Pattern Induction is an HITL system, its output depends on the sequence of user actions. To

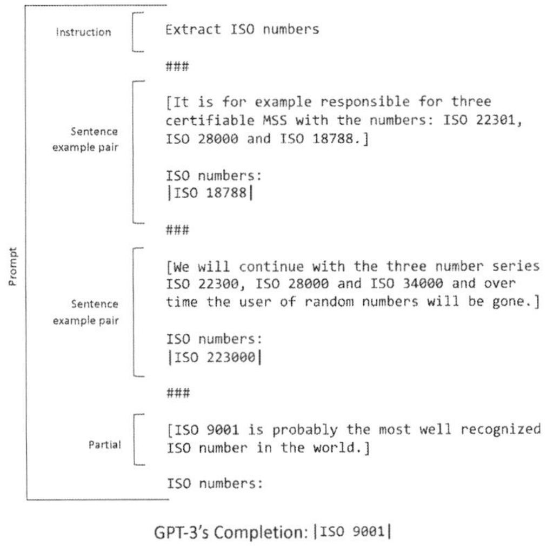

Figure 2: Structured Prompts containing an instruction, sentence example pairs, and a partial of the document to extract texts from. For some sentence example pairs, not all of the desired extractions will appear in the example extractions, e.g. ISO 22301 , ISO 28000 (to mimic how an end-user might prompt GPT-3).

evaluate the system at scale, we perform user simulation in lieu of a real user that interacts directly with the system. As an added benefit, the user simulation also automates the manual aspects of evaluating the underlying model, namely recording the performance of the underlying models.

We recreate the use cases and user simulation framework described in (Hanafi et al., 2022). The use cases are shown in Table 1. The 7 pattern extraction use cases are based on 5 collections of unstructured texts documents covering a variety of topics, such as food recipes (Recipes), reports on the financial performance of a particular company (Financial Press Releases), and crime statistics (FBI Press Releases). Each dataset contains no more than 10 documents, where each document varies in length. Each use case has no more than 100 extractions in the groundtruth. We then compare how a generative language model, specifically GPT-3, performs on the same set of use cases.

The use cases supported in Pattern Induction can be described as syntactic text patterns. How well does a generative language model extract text patterns such as the ones in Pattern Induction?

3.1 User Simulation of an HITL System

Evaluating Pattern Induction for the IE use cases involves running a user simulation, constructed by the core *user actions* it supports: (a) highlighting examples and (b) providing "Yes" or "No" feedbacks to *candidate extractions* generated by Pattern Induction. Specifically, a user simulation, r_i, provides 2 seed examples, $E = \{e_1, e_2\}$, and provides answers to all of Pattern Induction's candidate extractions, $F = \{f_1, ..., f_n\}$. The user simulation's answers to the candidate extractions are determined by the groundtruth, which is provided as input to the user simulation framework. We ran the user simulation 100 times, $R = \{r_1, ..., r_{100}\}$. In each run r_i, $e \in E$ was randomly selected from the ground truth. At the end of each run, the precision (P), recall (R), and F1 (F1) score of the model learned by Pattern Induction was evaluated on the same set of ground truth. The final P/R/F1 of Pattern Induction for each use case was computed as the average value of the respective metric over all 100 runs. The resulting performance of Pattern Induction for each of the seven use cases in Table 1, is shown in Figure 3 (see HITL line).

3.2 Prompting GPT-3 for IE with Example Extractions

We performed a similar set of experiments using GPT-3, where we prompted GPT-3 using OpenAI's completion API, which is recommended for entity extraction [1].

The prompts were constructed with the same 2 seed examples, E, from the user simulation in Pattern Induction. While Pattern Induction does not require any sort of prompting, constructing a prompt requires some level of engineering in order for GPT-3 to understand the intent of our extraction task. GPT-3 is sensitive to the context and the structure of the prompt's text (Shin et al., 2020; Gao et al., 2021; Jiang et al., 2020; Schick and Schütze, 2021b). Moreover, GPT-3 has a limit of about 4,000 tokens for its most powerful model, the *davinci*. We thus split the documents d in the dataset D into *partials*, $p \subset d, d \in D$.

We experimented with the following prompt structures:

- Baseline, Naive Prompts, $GPT3_E$: We experimented with a rather naive approach to the prompt's structure, where the example extractions E are appended to the document's partial p (see Figure 1). This prompt structure aims to mimic an end-user's intuition when using Pattern Induction: directly highlighting

[1] https://beta.openai.com/docs/api-reference/completions

ID	Use Cases	Dataset	Representative Examples
U1	Covid Cases by Country	Disease Fatality Reports	Spain (239 932) , Malta (620)
U2	Crime Incident Count	FBI Press Releases	4,927,535 incidents , 6,572,870 incidents
U3	Crime Percentages by Type	FBI Press Releases	62.9 percent involved crimes against property , 24.6% were crimes against persons
U4	Cups Multiple Forms	Recipes	2 cup , 1/4 cup , 1 1/2 cup
U5	Earnings Time Period Multiple Forms	Financial Press Releases	2014 First-Quarter , fourth-quarter of 2013
U6	ISO Numbers	ISO Number Articles	ISO 639 , ISO 22300
U7	ISO Numbers Multiple Forms	ISO Number Articles	ISO 639 , TC 292 , ISO/IEC 40180 , ISO/TC 28

Table 1: Summary of Text Pattern Extraction Tasks in the Experiments.

or specifying example extractions in the document itself.

- Structured Prompts, $GPT3_{C(E)}$: We experimented with a more *structured* format of prompting. For each example e, we paired it with a sentence $s \in D$ that e appears in. When multiple examples, e.g. e_i and e_j, appear in the same sentence s, we combined the multiple examples with the same s in the prompt. Any additional desired extractions in s that are not in the example set E were not indicated in the prompt (to mimic how an end-user might prompt GPT-3). Moreover, to provide GPT-3 with a better contextual understanding of the pattern extraction task, we prepended each prompt with an instruction describing the task, such as "Extract crime percentages by type". We then added the sentence example pairs and appended the partial p that GPT-3 must extract text patterns from (see Figure 2). Note that in baseline prompting, an example e may not appear in the partial p, but in structured prompting, each e will appear in its paired sentence s.

The above methods of prompting GPT-3 may not be enough to take advantage of the contextual understanding capabilities of GPT-3. But the focus of our study is to use methods similar to how an end-user might prompt GPT-3, assuming the end-user does not have much technical background.

Given a prompt, GPT-3 returns a string containing a *completion*. The completion is usually delimited by the characters it learns from the prompt, e.g. "|". To calculate the precision and recall scores of what GPT-3 extracts, we split the completion text according to the delimiters.

Given the 100 runs along with each run's associated seed examples E from the user simulation on Pattern Induction, we constructed a prompt with each E as described above and fed the prompts into GPT-3. The results of prompting GPT-3 for text pattern extraction are shown in Figure 3, along with the results for HITL. Our preliminary investigation seems to suggest that GPT-3 is not a right choice. However, we believe that extensive experiments to find more suitable prompts will need to be conducted.

The results for $GPT3_E$ and $GPT3_{C(E)}$ have lower precision scores compared to Pattern Induction's precision scores. We observed that low-precision runs are due to the fact that GPT-3's extracted text is not always a part of the document dataset. We thus added a post-processing step over a set of runs, R:

- $Post(R)$: removes outputs that are not part of the document. So $Post(GPT3_E)$ indicates that the post-processing step is applied to the set of runs in $GPT3_E$.

3.2.1 Insights: Better-Structured Prompts Improve Recall

As we move from naive prompting, $GPT3_E$, to structured prompting, $GPT3_{C(E)}$, the recall scores improve. Constructing well-structured prompts poses a limitation when using GPT, whereas Pattern Induction has no such requirement for an end-user.

The post-processing step improved the precision scores, but not the recall scores, as the lines in the chart (see Figure 3b) of the post-processing step's

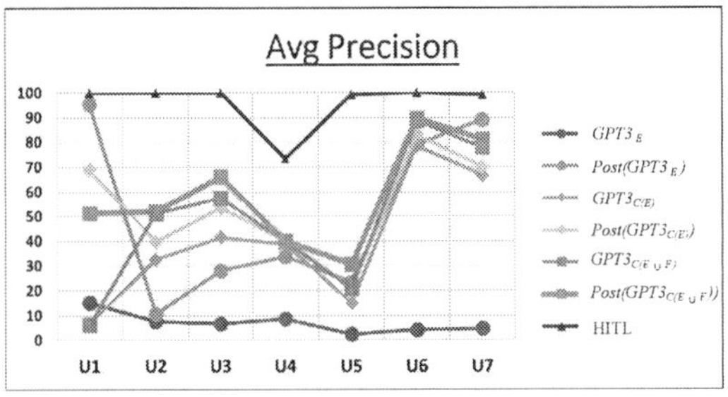

(a) Precision

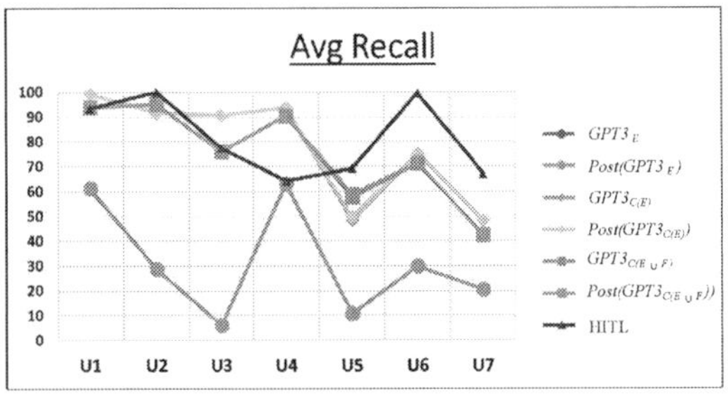

(b) Recall

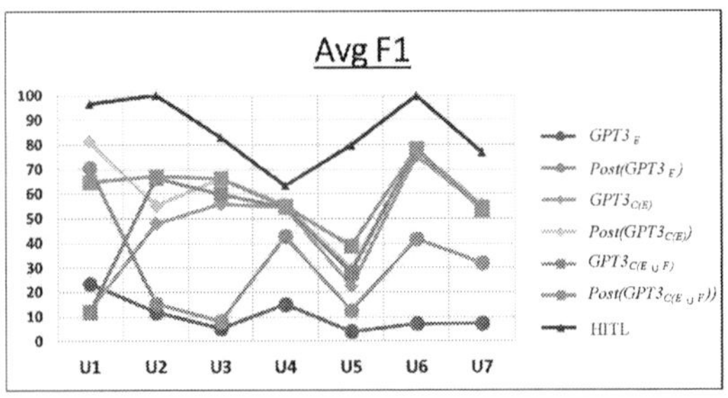

(c) F1

Figure 3: Experimental Results: HITL refers to Pattern Induction's user simulation results.

recall scores do not deviate much from the lines of the corresponding recall scores of raw output extractions.

The recall scores for U1, U3, and U4 (see task descriptions in Table 1) were higher with $GPT3_{C(E)}$ than in Pattern Induction (HITL). These tasks also happen to have *variations* in their extractions. For instance U1 requires the extraction of a country, U3 requires extraction regarding different crime types, e.g. "crimes against property", "crimes against persons", and U4 requires extractions of measuring cups of both integer and fractional types. GPT-3 seems to be able to understand that some of the words refers to countries, crime types, or integer and fractional quantities, where all the expected extractions may not necessarily abide to some syntactic pattern. In contrast, for the other tasks U2, U5, U6, U7 (see Table 1), the extractions follow

Substring of the prompt with F_N

```
###

[Part 1]

ISO numbers:
|###|

###
```

Figure 4: Substring of a prompt that demonstrates Part 1 should not be extracted, since Part 1 was rejected by the user simulation in Pattern Induction..

strict pattern extractions, e.g. in U2, the literal "incidents" constantly appears at the end of a 6 digit integer for all expected extractions, and in U5, the literal "quarter" and a 4 digit year appears in all extractions.

3.3 Prompting GPT-3 for IE with Additional Example Extractions

One may argue that the above method for prompting GPT-3 did not include the same set of inputs we provided to Pattern Induction. Namely, in Pattern Induction, the evaluation method also allows the user to provide feedback to candidate extractions, F, to further refine Pattern Induction's model, but no such additional inputs were added to the prompt for GPT-3. In this round, we reran the experiments with additional extraction examples:

- Prompts with Additional Extraction Examples, $GPT3_{C(E \cup F)}$: The structured prompts include the same set of candidate extractions F in addition to the set of highlighted seed examples E from the Pattern Induction user simulation.

We denote the set of extractions the user simulation accepted, i.e. answered "Yes" to fourth-quarter of 2012 , as $F_Y \subseteq F$, and the set of extractions the user simulation rejected, i.e. answered "No" to revenue of 2013 , as $F_N \subseteq F$. We integrated accepted extractions to the prompt in the same structured format as the seed examples (see Figure 2). Integrating rejected extractions to the prompt was done in a slightly different manner: for each $n \in F_N$, we append an end of sequence token in between the extraction delimiters (see Figure 4). While we have explored different ways of adding rejected extractions to the prompt such as using empty strings in between extraction delimiters, we found better performance with the end of sequence token.

3.3.1 Insights: Additional Examples in GPT-3 Improve Recall

The results of prompting GPT-3 with additional extraction examples are shown in Figure 3.

The precision scores are lower for $Post(GPT3_{C(E \cup F)})$ in comparison to HITL, with the exception of U6 and U7. The recall scores for both raw $GPT3_{C(E \cup F)}$ and post-processed $Post(GPT3_{C(E \cup F)})$ results are on par with HITL (U1, U2, U3), and they both even beat HITL in U4. Oddly enough $GPT3_{C(E)}$'s recall scores are very similar to $GPT3_{C(E \cup F)}$, except in U3 where the additional examples counter-intuitively dropped the recall scores by more than 10 points.

We observed that GPT-3 outputs creative texts regardless of whether there are additional examples or not ($GPT3_{C(E)}$ and $GPT3_{C(E \cup F)}$). Creative text outputs include "The race was unknown for 15.3 percent of reported known offenders." when given the U3 task. In addition to creative outputs, GPT-3, prompted with and without additional examples, also generates texts that are somewhat similar to the context in the examples but not exactly found in the text. In the U3 task, incorrect generated outputs would often contain percentage phrases that refer to statistics of other topics aside from crimes such as gender or race, e.g. "0.6 percent were American Indian or Alaska Native".

While the current set of experiments are only seeded with 2 examples, future experiments should look into the impact of increasing seed examples.

4 Discussion

Our experiments show that the HITL method for IE results in higher precision while in the large generative model, given a structured prompting and post-processing step, GPT-3 gives higher recall. GPT-3 is able to contextualize the prompts and learns a more general model.

Yet, the downside of GPT-3 for IE is that in of itself does not perform the IE tasks. To get comparable results to the HITL model, we had to (1) engineer and design the structure of the prompts to leverage GPT-3's powerful language abilities and (2) post-process the string output from GPT-3.

Additionally, the HITL model (1) elicits targeted user feedback and (2) allows for an iterative approach to building the underlying rule-based model. These two aspects are not found in GPT-3.

In light of these results, how do we then combine the advantages of each approach, human-in-the-loop and traditional AI models? How do we leverage the human-machine interactions to help increase both metrics? We leave these questions for future work.

5 Conclusions & Future Work

In this short work, we evaluate information extraction tasks on a human-in-the-loop, rule-based approach against a state-of-the-art generative language model, GPT-3. Our results show that the rule-based model outperforms GPT-3, when used out-of-the-box similar to how an end-user might use it to perform an NLP task. There are potentially better ways of constructing the prompts for GPT-3, but we wanted to better understand the performance of both the rule-based models and generative language model out-of-the-box.

Future work in this area should look into enabling end-users with little to no technical expertise to accurately and quickly build NLP models. For instance, one possibility is to go beyond user simulations and study how actual end-users create prompts. Another possibility is to leverage previous works in automatically generating prompts and then designing ways to elicit user input to craft better prompts (Shin et al., 2020; Jiang et al., 2020). An important future direction is to identify disadvantages and advantages of each approach, traditional large language models and rule-based models, and look into how combining such approaches would better enable end-users in NLP.

References

Tom Brown, Benjamin Mann, Nick Ryder, Melanie Subbiah, Jared D Kaplan, Prafulla Dhariwal, Arvind Neelakantan, Pranav Shyam, Girish Sastry, Amanda Askell, et al. 2020. Language models are few-shot learners. *Advances in neural information processing systems*, 33:1877–1901.

Jacob Devlin, Ming-Wei Chang, Kenton Lee, and Kristina Toutanova. 2019. BERT: Pre-training of deep bidirectional transformers for language understanding. In *Proceedings of the 2019 Conference of the North American Chapter of the Association for Computational Linguistics: Human Language Technologies, Volume 1 (Long and Short Papers)*, pages 4171–4186, Minneapolis, Minnesota. Association for Computational Linguistics.

Tianyu Gao, Adam Fisch, and Danqi Chen. 2021. Making pre-trained language models better few-shot learners. In *Proceedings of the 59th Annual Meeting of the Association for Computational Linguistics and the 11th International Joint Conference on Natural Language Processing (Volume 1: Long Papers)*, pages 3816–3830, Online. Association for Computational Linguistics.

Maeda F. Hanafi, Azza Abouzied, Laura Chiticariu, and Yunyao Li. 2017. Seer: Auto-generating information extraction rules from user-specified examples. CHI '17, page 6672–6682, New York, NY, USA. Association for Computing Machinery.

Maeda F. Hanafi, Yannis Katsis, Martín Santillán Cooper, and Yunyao Li. 2022. A simulation-based evaluation framework for interactive ai systems and its application. 36:12658–12664.

Zhengbao Jiang, Frank F. Xu, Jun Araki, and Graham Neubig. 2020. How can we know what language models know? *Transactions of the Association for Computational Linguistics*, 8:423–438.

Brenden M. Lake, Tomer David Ullman, Joshua B. Tenenbaum, and Samuel J. Gershman. 2016. Building machines that learn and think like people. *Behavioral and Brain Sciences*, 40.

Robert Munro Monarch. 2021. *Human-in-the-Loop Machine Learning: Active learning and annotation for human-centered AI*. Simon and Schuster.

Alexander Ratner, Stephen H Bach, Henry Ehrenberg, Jason Fries, Sen Wu, and Christopher Ré. 2017. Snorkel: Rapid training data creation with weak supervision. In *Proceedings of the VLDB Endowment. International Conference on Very Large Data Bases*, volume 11, page 269. NIH Public Access.

Salva Rühling Cachay, Benedikt Boecking, and Artur Dubrawski. 2021. End-to-end weak supervision. In *Advances in Neural Information Processing Systems*, volume 34, pages 1845–1857. Curran Associates, Inc.

Timo Schick and Hinrich Schütze. 2021a. Exploiting cloze-questions for few-shot text classification and natural language inference. In *Proceedings of the 16th Conference of the European Chapter of the Association for Computational Linguistics: Main Volume*, pages 255–269, Online. Association for Computational Linguistics.

Timo Schick and Hinrich Schütze. 2021b. It's not just size that matters: Small language models are also few-shot learners. In *Proceedings of the 2021 Conference of the North American Chapter of the Association for Computational Linguistics: Human Language Technologies*, pages 2339–2352, Online. Association for Computational Linguistics.

Taylor Shin, Yasaman Razeghi, Robert L. Logan IV, Eric Wallace, and Sameer Singh. 2020. AutoPrompt: Eliciting Knowledge from Language Models with Automatically Generated Prompts. In *Proceedings of the 2020 Conference on Empirical Methods in Natural Language Processing (EMNLP)*, pages 4222–4235, Online. Association for Computational Linguistics.

Chenguang Wang, Xiao Liu, Zui Chen, Haoyun Hong, Jie Tang, and Dawn Song. 2021. Zero-shot information extraction as a unified text-to-triple translation. In *Proceedings of the 2021 Conference on Empirical Methods in Natural Language Processing*, pages 1225–1238, Online and Punta Cana, Dominican Republic. Association for Computational Linguistics.

Yaqing Wang, Quanming Yao, James T. Kwok, and Lionel M. Ni. 2020. Generalizing from a few examples: A survey on few-shot learning. *ACM Comput. Surv.*, 53(3).

Xingjiao Wu, Luwei Xiao, Yixuan Sun, Junhang Zhang, Tianlong Ma, and Liang He. 2022. A survey of human-in-the-loop for machine learning. *Future Generation Computer Systems*.

A Appendix

Table 2 shows the exact numbers for the average precision, recall, and F1 scores across the different experiments.

ID	Tool	Avg Precision	Avg Recall	Avg F1
U1	$GPT3_E$	15.3	61.1	23.5
	$Post(GPT3_E)$	95.4	61.3	70.7
	$GPT3_{C(E)}$	6.7	99.2	12.5
	$Post(GPT3_{C(E)})$	69.1	**99.2**	81.2
	$GPT3_{C(E \cup F)}$	6.3	93.8	11.9
	$Post(GPT3_{C(E \cup F)})$	51.4	93.8	64.8
	HITL	**100.0**	93.4	**96.5**
U2	$GPT3_E$	7.6	28.6	11.7
	$Post(GPT3_E)$	10.7	28.6	15.3
	$GPT3_{C(E)}$	32.6	91.7	47.9
	$Post(GPT3_{C(E)})$	39.8	91.7	55.2
	$GPT3_{C(E \cup F)}$	51.2	95.1	66.4
	$Post(GPT3_{C(E \cup F)})$	52.0	95.1	67.1
	HITL	**100.0**	**100.0**	**100.0**
U3	$GPT3_E$	6.7	6.1	5.2
	$Post(GPT3_E)$	28.0	6.1	8.1
	$GPT3_{C(E)}$	41.5	90.7	55.9
	$Post(GPT3_{C(E)})$	53.5	**90.7**	66.1
	$GPT3_{C(E \cup F)}$	57.4	75.9	59.8
	$Post(GPT3_{C(E \cup F)})$	66.1	75.9	66.2
	HITL	**100.0**	77.3	**83.0**
U4	$GPT3_E$	8.6	63.0	14.9
	$Post(GPT3_E)$	33.7	62.9	42.7
	$GPT3_{C(E)}$	38.8	93.5	54.5
	$Post(GPT3_{C(E)})$	40.1	**93.5**	55.7
	$GPT3_{C(E \cup F)}$	39.8	90.4	54.6
	$Post(GPT3_{C(E \cup F)})$	40.1	90.4	54.9
	HITL	**73.4**	64.2	**63.4**
U5	$GPT3_E$	2.4	10.8	3.9
	$Post(GPT3_E)$	23.5	10.9	12.4
	$GPT3_{C(E)}$	15.0	48.4	22.6
	$Post(GPT3_{C(E)})$	21.2	49.6	29.4
	$GPT3_{C(E \cup F)}$	20.9	57.6	28.2
	$Post(GPT3_{C(E \cup F)})$	30.6	58.9	38.8
	HITL	**99.2**	**69.1**	**79.7**
U6	$GPT3_E$	4.2	29.8	7.1
	$Post(GPT3_E)$	79.1	29.8	41.6
	$GPT3_{C(E)}$	78.5	75.1	75.2
	$Post(GPT3_{C(E)})$	82.9	75.1	77.6
	$GPT3_{C(E \cup F)}$	88.7	71.1	77.9
	$Post(GPT3_{C(E \cup F)})$	89.6	71.1	78.3
	HITL	**100.0**	**99.5**	**99.7**
U7	$GPT3_E$	4.6	20.4	7.2
	$Post(GPT3_E)$	89.1	20.4	31.9
	$GPT3_{C(E)}$	66.6	48.0	54.5
	$Post(GPT3_{C(E)})$	70.0	48.0	55.7
	$GPT3_{C(E \cup F)}$	77.8	42.5	53.5
	$Post(GPT3_{C(E \cup F)})$	81.2	42.5	54.5
	HITL	**99.1**	**67.0**	**76.9**

Table 2: Experimental Results: ID refers to the use case ID. HITL refers to Pattern Induction's user simulation results.

Guiding Generative Language Models for Data Augmentation in Few-Shot Text Classification

Aleksandra Edwards† **Asahi Ushio**† **Jose Camacho-Collados**†
Hélène de Ribaupierre† **Alun Preece**‡
†School of Computer Science and Informatics, Cardiff University, United Kingdom
‡Crime and Security Research Institute, Cardiff University, United Kingdom
{edwardsai,ushioa,camachocolladosj,deribaupierreh,preecead}@cardiff.ac.uk

Abstract

Data augmentation techniques are widely used for enhancing the performance of machine learning models by tackling class imbalance issues and data sparsity. State-of-the-art generative language models have been shown to provide significant gains across different NLP tasks. However, their applicability to data augmentation for text classification tasks in few-shot settings have not been fully explored, especially for specialised domains. In this paper, we leverage GPT-2 (Radford et al., 2019) for generating artificial training instances in order to improve classification performance. Our aim is to analyse the impact the selection process of seed training examples has over the quality of GPT-generated samples and consequently the classifier performance. We propose a human-in-the-loop approach for selecting seed samples. Further, we compare the approach to other seed selection strategies that exploit the characteristics of specialised domains such as human-created class hierarchical structure and the presence of noun phrases. Our results show that fine-tuning GPT-2 in a handful of label instances leads to consistent classification improvements and outperform competitive baselines. The seed selection strategies developed in this work lead to significant improvements over random seed selection for specialised domains. We show that guiding text generation through domain expert selection can lead to further improvements, which opens up interesting research avenues for combining generative models and active learning.

1 Introduction

Data sparsity and class imbalance are common problems in text classification tasks (Türker et al., 2019; Zhang and Wu, 2015; Shams, 2014; Kumar et al., 2020), especially when the text to be labelled is from a highly-specialised domain where only scarce domain experts can perform the labelling task (Türker et al., 2019; Ali, 2019; Lu et al., 2021). Data Augmentation (DA) is a widely used method for tackling such issues (Anaby-Tavor et al., 2020; Kumar et al., 2020; Papanikolaou and Pierleoni, 2019). However, the well-established DA methods in domains such as computer vision and speech recognition (Anaby-Tavor et al., 2020; Giridhara et al., 2019; Krizhevsky et al., 2017; Cui et al., 2015; Ko et al., 2015; Szegedy et al., 2015), relying on simple transformations of existing samples, cannot be easily transferred to textual data as they can lead to syntactic and semantic distortions to text (Giridhara et al., 2019; Anaby-Tavor et al., 2020).

Recent advances in text generation models, such as GPT and subsequent releases (Radford et al., 2018), have led to the development of new DA approaches which generate additional training data from original samples, rather than perform only local changes to the text. Related studies use text generation models for improving relation extraction (Papanikolaou and Pierleoni, 2019; Kumar et al., 2020), tackle class imbalance problems for extreme multi-label classification tasks (Zhang et al., 2020), and augment domain-specific datasets in order to improve performance in various domain-specific classification tasks (Amin-Nejad et al., 2020). Specifically, Kumar et al. (2020) and Anaby-Tavor et al. (2020) explore different fine-tuning approaches for pre-trained models for data augmentation in order to preserve class-label information. Results showed the potential of generative models such as GPT-2 (Radford et al., 2019) and BART (Lewis et al., 2019) to augment small collections of labelled data. Further, an important problem with text generation techniques is the possibility of generating noise which decreases the performance of classification models rather than improving it (Yang et al., 2020). However, this problem is ignored in the aforementioned studies.

The most similar study to ours is that of Yang

Proceedings of the Fourth Workshop on Data Science with Human-in-the-Loop (Language Advances), pages 51 - 63
December 8, 2022

et al. (2020) in the context of commonsense reasoning. They proposed an approach based on the use of influence functions and heuristics for selecting the most diverse and informative artificial samples from an already-generated artificial dataset. Instead, we focus on the previous step of selecting the most informative samples (or *seeds*) from the original data. We show that a careful selection of class representative samples from the original data in the first place can already lead to improvements and has an important efficiency advantage, as it prevents an unnecessary waste of resources and time of generating unused generated documents, especially considering how resource expensive generative language models are (Strubell et al., 2019; Schwartz et al., 2019). Finally, there is no research on exploiting the use of experts knowledge for improving the performance of generative language models for specialised domains.

Therefore, our aim is to improve the quality of generated artificial instances used for text classification training by developing seed selection strategies to guide the generation process. Specifically, we propose three DA methods in order to improve few-shot text classification performance using GPT-2 — 1) a human-in-the-loop method that involves a domain expert choosing class representative samples; 2) a method that leverages the expert-generated classification hierarchy of a dataset in order to improve the classification of the top hierarchy classes; 3) a method that selects the seeds with the maximum occurrence of nouns. We chose these seed selection strategies because they exploit characteristics associated with specialised domains such as high number of terms, annotation performed by experts, and hierarchical class structure (common for social science and medical domains which require thematic analysis).

Our contributions are summarised as follows.

- We advocate an important but not-well-studied problem of exploring how the quality of generated data and consequently few-shot classification can be improved using text generation-based DA strategies. We perform analysis for more specialised domain requiring domain experts for annotation.
- We propose novel seed selection strategies and analyse their impact on the performance of text generation-based data augmentation methods for few-shot text classification — We show that classification performance can be improved significantly for specialised domains with limited labelled data using seed selection strategies and label preservation techniques. The human-in-the-loop seed selection proved to be the most suitable method for improving the quality of the generated data for specialised domains.
- We analyse how different approaches of fine-tuning GPT-2 model affect the quality of generated data and consequently the classification performance.

2 Methodology

We experiment with two fine-tuning techniques for GPT in order to identify optimal ways for adapting GPT-2 model for DA for classification. Further, our analysis focus on few-shot classification because of the demand for approaches which can perform well for only a handful of training instances especially in specialised domains where experts are sparse and data access is limited. However, our methodology can be easily extended for classification problems with more labelled data and it can also be used to generate more artificial training data.

2.1 Seed Selection Strategies

We implement four seed selection strategies, which we describe below.

Human-in-the-loop Seed Selection. The highly specialised nature of some domains where the manual annotation of documents is performed by experts show that identifying class representative samples might require more implicit knowledge that is hard to be captured by statistical approaches. Therefore, we conducted a study asking experts to select the class representative samples from the original training data. The chosen seeds are then used to generate additional training data. We explain the approach in Section 3.5.

Maximum Nouns-guided Seed Selection. Many specialised domains are rich of domain-specific terminology and thus we believe that noun-rich instances might be more indicative for the classes compared to the other training samples. Therefore, we use this strategy to select the seeds with the maximum occurrence of nouns. We identify single word nouns and compound nouns within data using NLTK (Bird and Loper, 2004).

Subclass-guided Seed Selection. In this strategy, we leverage the human-generated classification hierarchy of a dataset in order to improve the classification of the top classes. Specifically, we select a roughly balanced number of seeds from each subclass belonging to a given label. In this way, we diversify the vocabulary for each overall class by ensuring the equal participation of representative samples from even the most underrepresented subclasses.

Random Seed Selection. For this strategy we simply select a fixed number of instances in a random manner. We use random selection to evaluate whether the rest of the seed selection strategies lead to improvements in classification.

2.2 Text Generation

We generate artificial data using the generative pre-trained model, GPT-2 (Radford et al., 2019). We use GPT-2 model as it gives a state-of-the-art performance for many text generation tasks and also have been designed with the objective to fit scenarios with few-shot and even zero-shot settings. We use two methods for fine-tuning the GPT-2 model — we fine-tune the model on the entire dataset and we also fine-tune a specific GPT-2 model for each given class to ensure label-preservation for the generated sequences. Fine-tuning a separate GPT-2 model per label ensures that each model has been exposed to text associated with a single class. We also perform experiments using a pre-trained GPT-2 model. We compare three models in order to assess the need of fine-tuning and the use of additional methods for label-preservation when using TG-based DA for classification tasks. These models are then leveraged to generate new documents given a labeled instance. These analyses help identify whether fine-tuning a separate model per label is a suitable method for ensuring label-preservation of the generated data.

Ensuring Robustness To ensure robustness, the text generation step is performed for three iterations and the results are averaged. Additionally, we perform statistical analysis to check overall whether text generation-based methods are suitable for improving the performance of classifiers or they tend to add more noise versus using no augmentation approaches.

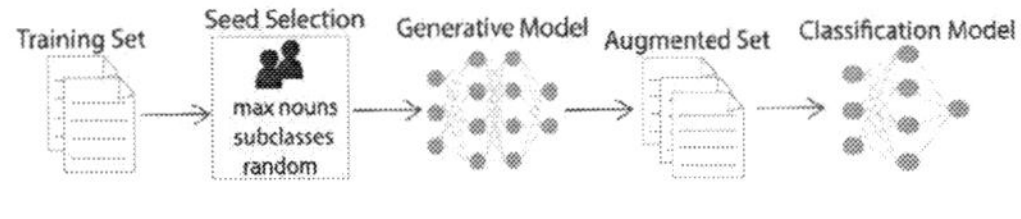

Figure 1: Overview of the methodology

2.3 Text Classification

In this final step, we use the augmented training data to train a fastText classifier (Joulin et al., 2017) coupled with domain-trained fastText word embeddings. The reason to use a simple model such as fastText is its efficiency and that transformer-based models tend to not perform well with limited data in document classification and in general tasks that do not require a fine granularity (Joshi et al., 2020). Indeed, fastText has been shown to perform equally or better with limited labeled data in document classification, compared to more sophisticated models such as BERT (Edwards et al., 2020).

3 Experimental Setting

In the following we describe our few-shot text classification experimental setting.[1]

3.1 Safeguarding Domain

For our experiments, we selected the *Safeguarding reports* dataset (Edwards et al., 2021). The purpose of the safeguarding reports is to identify and describe related events that precede a serious safeguarding incident and to reflect on agencies' roles. As a special trait of this dataset, the reports contain domain-specific terminology which makes them hard to analyse with existing text analysis tools (Edwards et al., 2019). Further, safeguarding is a multi-disciplinary domain involving terminology and issues from various other disciplines such as criminology, healthcare, and law. Thus, approaches conducted for the safeguarding documents should be applicable for wider range of domains. Additionally, we perform comparison for two additional datasets which do not require domain expert for annotation. These are: *20 Newsgroups* (Lang, 1995) and *Toxic comments* (Hosseini et al., 2017) (more information is given in the Appendix). However, we conducted the human-in-the-loop, i.e., expert-guided seed selection strategy only for the safeguarding domain where the class framework is created by subject-matter experts. While the manual annotation of the documents is performed on

[1]Code and data are available.

passage level [2], we include experiments on sentence level in order to evaluate performance of text generation methods for generating both short and long sequences. We perform prediction for the top classes of the dataset. However, as mentioned in Section 2, we use the sub-classes to select seed instances. For providing clarity and transparency into the sample generation process, we convert the multi-label classification task of the *Safeguarding* and *Toxic comments* dataset to multi-class problem, removing the few instances that were labeled with more than one class in the original dataset. Focusing on samples with a single label can further help generate stronger class representatives and thus can help both multi-class and multi-label classification. The main features and statistics for the datasets are summarized in Table 1.

Dataset	Domain	Task	Class	Subclass	Avg len	# Test
Safeguarding (passages)	Social reports	Theme detection	5	34	45	284
Safeguarding (sentences)	Social reports	Theme detection	5	34	18	284
20 Newsgroups	Newsgroups	285	6	20	285	6,728
Toxic comments	Wikipedia	46	2	5	46	63,978

Table 1: Overview of the datasets used for text classification: Average number of tokens per instance (Av len), number of classes (Class), number of subclasses (Subc) and number of test instances (Test)

Filtering training data. We focus on few-shot scenarios where the dataset is balanced. We start experiments with 5 and 10 instances per label, extracted randomly from the original data ('base' instances), with at least one instance per subclass. Then, we add 5, 10, and 20 artificially generated instances to the 'base' instances ('add' instances) in order to evaluate the effect of methods over different sized training data (consisting of both original and artificially generated samples).

Domain data. In addition to the datasets with a limited amount of labels, we also leverage domain-specific corpora (in the form of the original training sets for each dataset, without making use of the labels) with two purposes: (1) analyzing the effect on GPT-2 fine-tuned on more data for generating new instances, and (2) recreating a usual scenario in practice, which is having a relatively large unlabeled corpus but a small number of annotations. The corresponding domain corpus were also used by fastText (Bojanowski et al., 2017) to learn domain-specific embeddings.

[2]Passages in the safeguarding reports are a list of a few sentences which could be viewed as short paragraphs. The labels for the classification remain unchanged.

3.2 Text Generation

As mentioned in Section 2, we use the GPT-2 language model (Radford et al., 2019) for generating additional training instances. We fine-tuned the GPT-2 model using the GPT-2 Hugging Face default transformers implementation (Wolf et al., 2019). In addition to the pre-trained general-domain model, we fine-tune GPT-2 in each training set as well as per label using causal language model technique where the model predicts the next token in a sequence. We fine-tune the model for 4 epochs and learning rate 5e-5. For generating additional training sequences we use the sampling method of Holtzman et al. (2019).

3.3 Classification

As mentioned in Section 2.3, we use fastText[3] as our text classifier (Joulin et al., 2017, FT) where we use 'softmax', 2 grams, and domain-trained word embeddings. In order to learn domain-specific word embedding models we used the corresponding training sets for each dataset by using fastText's skipgram model (Bojanowski et al., 2017). We use fastText word embeddings rather than other word embedding models as they tend to deal with OOV words better than Glove and word2vec approaches. Also, fastText embeddings are the default using the fastText classifier. We report results based on the standard micro- and macro- averaged F1 (Yang, 1999).

3.4 Data Augmentation Baselines

For our baselines, we employ synonym, word embedding and language model based strategies for word replacement, and back-translation for sentence replacement (see Section A in the Appendix for more details on DA techniques). As implementations, we rely on *TextAttack* (Morris et al., 2020) for the synonym and word embedding approaches, and *nlpaug* (Ma, 2019) for the language model and back-translation. We follow the default configurations for both libraries, where WordNet (Miller, 1998) is used as a thesaurus for synonym replacement, BERT (Devlin et al., 2019) (*bert-uncased-large*) as the language model, and Transformer NMT models (Vaswani et al., 2017) trained over WMT19 English/Germany corpus for back-translation.

[3]We provide classification results based on fastText trained on the entire non-augmented training sets in the appendix.

3.5 Human-in-the-loop Approach

For the purpose of the experiments, we randomly selected two samples from the original data, one consisting of sentences ('sentence sample') and another one consisting of passages ('passages sample'). Each sample contained 20 instances per label or 100 instances in total. The 'sentence sample' and the 'passage sample' were distributed among two experts. Participants were asked for each sentence/passage to choose whether it is a *good* or *bad* representative of the class, or to indicate whether they are unsure. We use only a sample of the original data and involve two experts in order to evaluate whether expert-guided seed selection strategy work in a real case scenario in which the selection process is time- and cost- consuming for larger datasets. The experts followed standard procedures in thematic analysis for completing the task, similar to those used for annotating the safeguarding reports (Robinson et al., 2019). Specifically, participants arrived to the final selection of the good theme representative samples through discussion. The participants are practitioners in the safeguarding domain working for Welsh Government, performing qualitative analysis for safeguarding documents. The results from the experiments (see Table 2) show that experts selected more than 10 instances per theme for both samples as 'good representatives'. To select 10 and 5 seeds from the 'good representatives' we use random selection and max-noun selection strategies. An example of the process is given in Figure 2.

Theme	passages		sentences	
	#good rep	#bad rep	#good rep	#bad rep
Contact with Agencies	12	8	13	7
Indicative Behaviour	12	8	15	5
Indicative Circumstances	11	9	13	7
Mental Health Issues	11	9	14	6
Reflections	11	9	11	9
Total	57	43	66	34

Table 2: Results from expert study where '#good rep' refer to the number of good representative seeds that the expert selected while '#bad rep' refer to the number of samples that the expert deemed not good representatives of the themes

4 Results and Analysis

The aims of our analysis is (1) to identify the most suitable method for fine-tuning GPT-2 model to ensure generating higher quality training data (see Section 4.1), and (2) to understand whether and which seed selection strategies are beneficial for improving DA methods, especially for specialised domains which require domain experts to perform manual annotation (see Section 4.2). The results for the three datasets are displayed in Table 3.

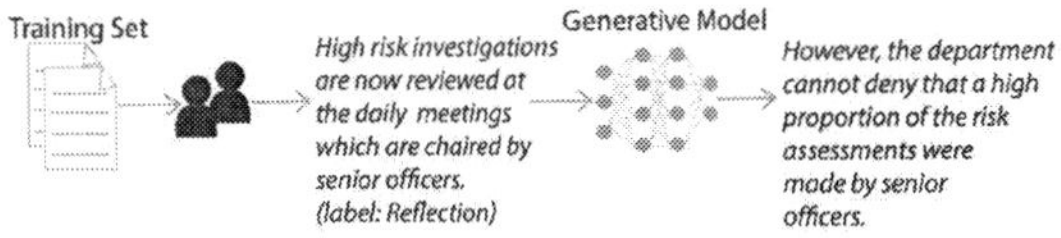

Figure 2: Example of expert-guided seed selection

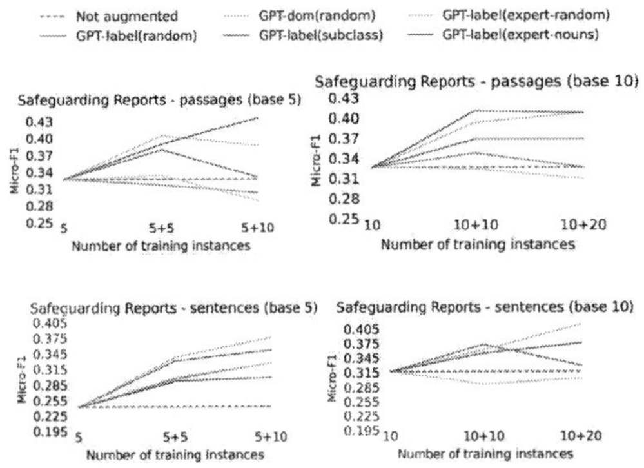

Figure 3: Micro-F1 results with 5 and 10 'base' instances per label for the Safeguarding reports dataset.

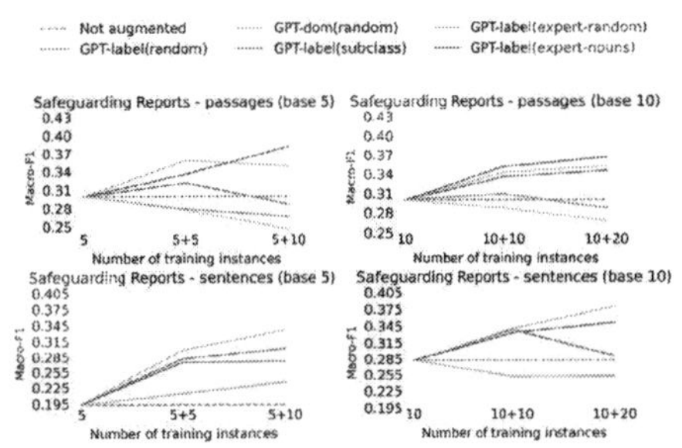

Figure 4: Macro-F1 results with 5 and 10 'base' instances per label for the Safeguarding reports dataset.

4.1 *Can GPT-based Data Augmentation Help Few-Shot Text Classification?*

The results in Table 3 indeed confirm the benefits of GPT-based data augmentation. Comparing different methods for fine-tuning GPT-2 models for DA, the classification results show that GPT-2 fine-tuned per label lead to better results, compared to the pre-trained model or GPT-2 fine-tuned on the entire dataset. These results also show that using a fine-tuned GPT-2 model per label does help label-preservation for the generated instances. Surprisingly, the results for the safeguarding reports at

	DA type	Tuning type	DA method	**Micro-F1**				**Macro-F1**			
				5base		10base		5base		10base	
				+5add	+10add	+10add	+20add	+5add	+10add	+10add	+20add
20 Newsgroups	None	-	-	.509		.578		.481		.567	
		gen	random	.539	.536	.572	.555	.519	.519	.564	.548
	TG (GPT2)	dom	random	.526	.502	.548	.539	.511	.485	.534	.526
			random	**.609***	**.602***	**.627***	**.637***	**.591***	**.587***	.615	.627
blue		label	nouns	.569	.549	.599	.576	.552	.533	.583	.562
			subclass	.563	.585	.624	.632	.549	.571	**.620***	**.628***
		-	BERT	.519	.516	.567	.571	.511	.505	.554	.556
	WR	-	embeddings	.556	.540	.556	.552	.534	.516	.544	.539
		-	synonyms	.517	.508	.554	.549	.502	.493	.542	.537
	SR	-	translation	.529	.525	.559	.563	.515	.509	.549	.552
Original data (upperbound)				.601	.641	.648	.654	.589	.624	.633	.639
	None	-	-	.423		.442		.423		.442	
		gen	random	.447	.424	.405	.423	.447	.424	.405	.423
	TG (GPT2)	dom	random	.401	.417	.369	.343	.401	.417	.369	.343
			random	**.453***	**.452***	.453	.442	**.453***	**.452***	.453	.442
Toxic comments		label	nouns	.417	.399	**.502***	**.461***	.417	.399	**.502***	**.461***
			subclass	.427	.440	.419	.421	.427	.440	.419	.421
		-	BERT	.447	.443	.426	.422	.447	.443	.426	.422
	WR	-	embeddings	.441	.441	.432	.432	.441	.441	.432	.432
		-	synonyms	.423	.411	.433	.429	.423	.411	.433	.429
	SR	-	translation	.446	-	.436	-	.446	-	.436	-
Original data (upperbound)				.442	.435	.448	.463	.442	.435	.448	.463
	None	-	-	.326		.326		.299		.300	
		gen	random	.298	.305	.382	.358	.254	.264	.335	.330
		dom	random	.333	.288	.323	.309	.276	.246	.287	.267
	TG (GPT2)		random	.316	.302	.347	.326	.278	.266	.309	.287
			nouns	.375	.337	.375	.379	.329	.281	.338	.351
Safeguard (pass)		label*	subclass	.379	.330	.368	.368	.321	.286	.335	.345
			expert-random	**.404***	.386	.393	**.407***	**.358***	.349	.342	.352
			expert-nouns	.389	**.435***	**.410***	**.407***	.335	**.382***	**.351***	**.366***
		-	BERT	.287	.294	.326	.336	.282	.278	.294	.297
	WR	-	embeddings	.389	.382	.305	.319	.343	.341	.283	.287
		-	synonyms	.277	.267	.312	.315	.256	.245	.285	.292
	SR	-	translation	.333	.336	.298	.312	.294	.301	.273	.286
Original data (upperbound)				.336	.337	.358	.368	.301	.304	.307	.320
	None	-	-	.242		.316		.193		.282	
		gen	random	.294	.326	.291	.298	.212	.235	.252	.251
		dom	random	.298	.326	.291	.302	.214	.236	.252	.250
			random	.295	.326	.291	.302	.213	.235	.251	.252
			nouns	.358	.368	.361	.389*	.285	.302	.327	.358
Safeguard (sent)	TG (GPT2)	label	subclass	.330	.351	.372	.329	.281	.301	.338	.290
			expert-random	**.337***	**.375***	**.361***	**.414***	**.298***	**.336***	**.340***	**.379***
			expert-nouns	.291	.298	.354	.375	.274	.276	.332	.351
		-	BERT	.249	.284	.319	.315	.245	.274	.278	.274
	WR	-	embeddings	.242	.280	.316	.319	.226	.259	.276	.283
		-	synonyms	.256	.266	.319	.326	.241	.256	.281	.288
	SR	-	translation	.287	.294	.336	.329	.257	.263	.296	.291
Original data (upperbound)				.368	.452	.432	.453	.332	.386	.386	.389

Table 3: FasText classification results based on Micro-F1 and Macro-F1. Text generation is based on GPT-2, where 'gen' refers to the pre-trained general-domain model, 'dom' refers to the same model fine-tuned on domain data, and 'label', fine-tuned per label. Data is split using 5 or 10 'base' instances per label plus additional 5, 10, or 20 'add' instances, 'sent' refers to sentences. The baselines we compare our approaches to are: the word-based replacement (WR) and sentence-based replacement (SR) strategies, 'Original data (upperbound)' refers the training data extracted from the original dataset using the same amount of 'base' and 'additional' instances as for the generative models

.* – Best performing DA methods based on GPT-2 fine-tuned per label lead to statistically significant differences over non-augmented classification (*'None'*) based on t-test results where $p_{value} < 0.05$.

the passage level (see Table 3) show that the pre-trained model outperforms the model fine-tuned on the entire dataset for all settings except for '5+5'. This is not the case, however, at the sentence-level where the model fine-tuned on the entire dataset performs very similarly to the model fine-tuned per label. In general, the results clearly suggest that fine-tuning the GPT-2 model on smaller but labelled data works better for classification than fine-tuning it on a larger unlabelled corpus, especially in settings with longer input sequences. These findings are also supported by the results for the other two datasets,20 Newsgroups and Toxic comments. The main reason for this behaviour can be found in that the fine-tuned model without using label-preservation techniques leads to label-distortions which add noise in the generated dataset. We have given examples of generated instances in the Appendix.

Statistical significance tests. We used t-test (Student, 1908) to measure whether TG-based DA give a significant improvement over the non-augmented classifiers. In particular, we compared the best performing techniques, which are all based on GPT-2 models fine-tuned per label, and the base classifier ('None' in Table 3). We use as a threshold $\alpha = 0.05$. Results showed that $p_{value} < \alpha$ for every setting. This confirms that fine-tuning GPT-2 model with a small number of labelled instances leads to consistent (and statistically significant) improvements for the safeguarding reports [45]

4.2 Seed Selection Strategies Comparison

Results on comparing seed selection strategies for the specialised domain (i.e., safeguarding reports) (see Figures 3 and 4) showed that both seed selection strategies (noun-guided and subclass-guided selection) lead to larger improvements over random selection even for a small number of seed samples. In contrast, experiments on the toxic comments dataset and the 20 newsgroups (see Table 3) showed that random selection is sufficient for improving classification performance over baselines, especially for smaller amount of seeds. This shows that for domains that are similar to the datasets used to train GPT-2 (Newsgroups and Wikipedia) random selection especially for a smaller amount of seeds is sufficient for improving classification performance over baselines. In contrast, applying seed selection techniques to a more specialised domain, such as the safeguarding reports, can be highly beneficial for improving classification.

Finally, the human-in-the-loop approach (see Section 3.5) revealed that seed selection strategy guided by experts outperform all other seed strategies and baselines for both sentences and passages (see Table 3, Figures 3 and 4). This highlights the potential benefits for incorporating expert knowledge into guiding large pre-trained language models in highly specialised domains. This study shows that using active learning techniques in combination with generative models can help increase the efficiency of data augmentation methods and thus be beneficial for few-shot learning.

5 Conclusion

In this paper, we presented and evaluated data augmentation methods using text generation techniques and seed selection strategies for improving the quality of generated artificial sequences and subsequently classifier's performance in few-shot settings. Our results showed that GPT-2 fine-tuned per label, even using only handful of instances, leads to consistent classification improvements, and is shown to outperform competitive baselines and the same GPT-2 model fine-tuned on the entire dataset. This highlights the importance of label preservation techniques in the performance of TG-based DA methods, especially for generating longer sequences (such as passages or full documents). Seed selection strategies proved to be highly beneficial for the specialised domain analysed in this paper, especially when experts are involved in the selection of class-indicative instances. This shows that combining generative models and active learning techniques, i.e., injecting experts knowledge, can lead to significant improvements in data augmentation methods especially for more specialised domains which require domain experts for the annotation of documents. In future, we plan on expanding the experiments for wider range of specialised domains and compare the performance of bigger generative models such as GPT-3 (Brown et al., 2020), Transformer-XL (Dai et al., 2019) and CTRL (Clive et al., 2021). Further, we want to investigate what is the optimum amount of artificial training data which can be generated with the described techniques before effecting the classifier's performance negatively.

[4]These results are also supported by the results for the other two datasets presented in the Appendix

[5]We include full results and t-test details in the Appendix.

Limitations

The main limitation of this research is the lack of further analysis into the performance of text generation models and seed selection strategies when generating higher number of additional training samples. As future work, we plan to investigate the optimal number of generated instances using GPT-based generation as well as experiment with other generative models. Another limitation of the work is that generating artificial training data using GPT-2 requires access to large GPU resources which limits the usability of the approach in real-world scenarios where such resources are unavailable or responses have to be generated in real-time manner. Moreover, the paper presents human-in-the-loop analysis for a single specialised domain (i.e., safeguarding). Safeguarding is a multi-disciplinary domain involving terminology and issues from various other domains such as criminology, medical domain, and legal domain. While the results presented in the paper show clear advantage of leveraging expert knowledge into guiding text generation models, we believe that extending the analysis for a wider range of datasets (such as those datasets where we present extended results in the Appendix) can be beneficial. Additionally, the human-in-the-loop seed selection has been carried by two experts which may cause biases in the process of selecting seeds. However, the participants are practitioners from the safeguarding domain who used standard methodology in thematic analysis for selecting the seeds. These methods do not require inter-annotators agreement, instead experts achieve agreement through discussion. Further, analysis have been performed on sentence- and passage-level where both experiments showed clear advantage of the human-in-the-loop approach. Finally, the paper presents results for a single high-resource language (English). Experiments for other languages (especially low-resource) could show a different tendency in which the expert involved may be even more necessary.

References

Amanuel Alambo, Cori Lohstroh, Erik Madaus, Swati Padhee, Brandy Foster, Tanvi Banerjee, Krishnaprasad Thirunarayan, and Michael Raymer. 2020. Topic-centric unsupervised multi-document summarization of scientific and news articles. *arXiv preprint arXiv:2011.08072*.

Zuhair Ali. 2019. Text classification based on fuzzy radial basis function. *Iraqi Journal for Computers and Informatics*, 45(1):11–14.

Ali Amin-Nejad, Julia Ive, and Sumithra Velupillai. 2020. Exploring transformer text generation for medical dataset augmentation. In *Proceedings of The 12th Language Resources and Evaluation Conference*, pages 4699–4708.

Ateret Anaby-Tavor, Boaz Carmeli, Esther Goldbraich, Amir Kantor, George Kour, Segev Shlomov, Naama Tepper, and Naama Zwerdling. 2020. Do not have enough data? Deep learning to the rescue! In *Proceedings of AAAI*, pages 7383–7390.

Ashutosh Baheti, Alan Ritter, and Kevin Small. 2020. Fluent response generation for conversational question answering. *arXiv preprint arXiv:2005.10464*.

Steven Bird and Edward Loper. 2004. NLTK: The natural language toolkit. In *Proceedings of the ACL Interactive Poster and Demonstration Sessions*, pages 214–217, Barcelona, Spain. Association for Computational Linguistics.

Piotr Bojanowski, Edouard Grave, Armand Joulin, and Tomas Mikolov. 2017. Enriching word vectors with subword information. *Transactions of the Association for Computational Linguistics*, 5:135–146.

Tom Brown, Benjamin Mann, Nick Ryder, Melanie Subbiah, Jared D Kaplan, Prafulla Dhariwal, Arvind Neelakantan, Pranav Shyam, Girish Sastry, Amanda Askell, et al. 2020. Language models are few-shot learners. *Advances in neural information processing systems*, 33:1877–1901.

Jordan Clive, Kris Cao, and Marek Rei. 2021. Control prefixes for text generation. *arXiv preprint arXiv:2110.08329*.

Xiaodong Cui, Vaibhava Goel, and Brian Kingsbury. 2015. Data augmentation for deep neural network acoustic modeling. *IEEE/ACM Transactions on Audio, Speech, and Language Processing*, 23(9):1469–1477.

Zihang Dai, Zhilin Yang, Yiming Yang, Jaime G Carbonell, Quoc Le, and Ruslan Salakhutdinov. 2019. Transformer-xl: Attentive language models beyond a fixed-length context. In *Proceedings of the 57th Annual Meeting of the Association for Computational Linguistics*, pages 2978–2988.

Jacob Devlin, Ming-Wei Chang, Kenton Lee, and Kristina Toutanova. 2019. Bert: Pre-training of deep bidirectional transformers for language understanding. In *Proceedings of the 2019 Conference of the North American Chapter of the Association for Computational Linguistics: Human Language Technologies, Volume 1 (Long and Short Papers)*, pages 4171–4186.

Aleksandra Edwards, Jose Camacho-Collados, Hélène de Ribaupierre, and Alun Preece. 2020. Go simple and pre-train on domain-specific corpora: On the role of training data for text classification. In *Proceedings of COLING*.

Aleksandra Edwards, Alun Preece, and Helene De Ribaupierre. 2019. Knowledge extraction from a small corpus of unstructured safeguarding reports. In *European Semantic Web Conference*, pages 38–42, Portorož, Slovenia. Springer.

Aleksandra Edwards, David Rogers, Jose Camacho-Collados, Hélène de Ribaupierre, and Alun Preece. 2021. Predicting themes within complex unstructured texts: A case study on safeguarding reports. In *Proceedings of the ESWC Workshop Deep Learning meets Ontologies and Natural Language Processing*.

Marzieh Fadaee, Arianna Bisazza, and Christof Monz. 2017. Data augmentation for low-resource neural machine translation. In *Proceedings of the 55th Annual Meeting of the Association for Computational Linguistics (Volume 2: Short Papers)*, pages 567–573, Vancouver, Canada. Association for Computational Linguistics.

Praveen Kumar Badimala Giridhara, Chinmaya Mishra, Reddy Kumar Modam Venkataramana, Syed Saqib Bukhari, and Andreas Dengel. 2019. A study of various text augmentation techniques for relation classification in free text. *ICPRAM*, 3:5.

Ari Holtzman, Jan Buys, Li Du, Maxwell Forbes, and Yejin Choi. 2019. The curious case of neural text degeneration. In *Proceedings of the International Conference on Learning Representations (ICLR)*.

Hossein Hosseini, Sreeram Kannan, Baosen Zhang, and Radha Poovendran. 2017. Deceiving google's perspective api built for detecting toxic comments. *arXiv preprint arXiv:1702.08138*.

Brihi Joshi, Neil Shah, Francesco Barbieri, and Leonardo Neves. 2020. The devil is in the details: Evaluating limitations of transformer-based methods for granular tasks. In *Proceedings of COLING*.

Armand Joulin, Edouard Grave, Piotr Bojanowski, and Tomas Mikolov. 2017. Bag of tricks for efficient text classification. In *Proceedings of the 15th Conference of the European Chapter of the Association for Computational Linguistics: Volume 2, Short Papers*, pages 427–431. Association for Computational Linguistics.

Virapat Kieuvongngam, Bowen Tan, and Yiming Niu. 2020. Automatic text summarization of covid-19 medical research articles using bert and gpt-2. *arXiv preprint arXiv:2006.01997*.

Tassilo Klein and Moin Nabi. 2019. Learning to answer by learning to ask: Getting the best of gpt-2 and bert worlds. *arXiv preprint arXiv:1911.02365*.

Tom Ko, Vijayaditya Peddinti, Daniel Povey, and Sanjeev Khudanpur. 2015. Audio augmentation for speech recognition. In *Sixteenth Annual Conference of the International Speech Communication Association*.

Alex Krizhevsky, Ilya Sutskever, and Geoffrey E. Hinton. 2017. Imagenet classification with deep convolutional neural networks. *Commun. ACM*, 60(6):84–90.

Varun Kumar, Ashutosh Choudhary, and Eunah Cho. 2020. Data augmentation using pre-trained transformer models. *arXiv preprint arXiv:2003.02245*.

Ken Lang. 1995. Newsweeder: Learning to filter netnews. In *Proceedings of the 12th International Conference on Machine Learning*, pages 331–339, Tahoe City, California.

Mike Lewis, Yinhan Liu, Naman Goyal, Marjan Ghazvininejad, Abdelrahman Mohamed, Omer Levy, Ves Stoyanov, and Luke Zettlemoyer. 2019. Bart: Denoising sequence-to-sequence pre-training for natural language generation, translation, and comprehension. *arXiv preprint arXiv:1910.13461*.

Shuai Liu and Xiaojun Huang. 2019. A chinese question answering system based on gpt. In *2019 IEEE 10th International Conference on Software Engineering and Service Science (ICSESS)*, pages 533–537. IEEE.

Jinghui Lu, Maeve Henchion, Ivan Bacher, and Brian Mac Namee. 2021. A sentence-level hierarchical bert model for document classification with limited labelled data. In *International Conference on Discovery Science*, pages 231–241. Springer.

Edward Ma. 2019. Nlp augmentation. https://github.com/makcedward/nlpaug.

George A Miller. 1998. *WordNet: An electronic lexical database*. MIT press.

John X. Morris, Eli Lifland, Jin Yong Yoo, Jake Grigsby, Di Jin, and Yanjun Qi. 2020. Textattack: A framework for adversarial attacks, data augmentation, and adversarial training in nlp.

Yannis Papanikolaou and Andrea Pierleoni. 2019. Data augmented relation extraction (dare) with gpt-2. *Neuropharmacology*.

Alec Radford, Karthik Narasimhan, Tim Salimans, and Ilya Sutskever. 2018. Improving language understanding by generative pre-training.

Alec Radford, Jeffrey Wu, Rewon Child, David Luan, Dario Amodei, and Ilya Sutskever. 2019. Language models are unsupervised multitask learners. *OpenAI blog*, 1(8):9.

Amanda Lea Robinson, Alyson Rees, and Roxanna Dehaghani. 2019. Making connections: A multidisciplinary analysis of domestic homicide, mental health homicide and adult practice reviews. *The Journal of Adult Protection*, 21(1):16–26.

Roy Schwartz, Jesse Dodge, Noah A Smith, and Oren Etzioni. 2019. Green ai. *arXiv preprint arXiv:1907.10597*.

Rico Sennrich, Barry Haddow, and Alexandra Birch. 2016. Improving neural machine translation models with monolingual data. In *Proceedings of the 54th Annual Meeting of the Association for Computational Linguistics (Volume 1: Long Papers)*, pages 86–96, Berlin, Germany. Association for Computational Linguistics.

Rushdi Shams. 2014. Semi-supervised classification for natural language processing. *arXiv preprint arXiv:1409.7612*.

Emma Strubell, Ananya Ganesh, and Andrew McCallum. 2019. Energy and policy considerations for deep learning in NLP. In *Proceedings of the 57th Annual Meeting of the Association for Computational Linguistics*, pages 3645–3650, Florence, Italy. Association for Computational Linguistics.

Student. 1908. The probable error of a mean. *Biometrika*, pages 1–25.

Christian Szegedy, Wei Liu, Yangqing Jia, Pierre Sermanet, Scott Reed, Dragomir Anguelov, Dumitru Erhan, Vincent Vanhoucke, and Andrew Rabinovich. 2015. Going deeper with convolutions. In *Proceedings of the IEEE conference on computer vision and pattern recognition*, pages 1–9.

Rima Türker, Lei Zhang, Maria Koutraki, and Harald Sack. 2019. Knowledge-based short text categorization using entity and category embedding. In *European Semantic Web Conference*, pages 346–362. Springer.

Ashish Vaswani, Noam Shazeer, Niki Parmar, Jakob Uszkoreit, Llion Jones, Aidan N Gomez, Łukasz Kaiser, and Illia Polosukhin. 2017. Attention is all you need. In *Advances in neural information processing systems*, pages 5998–6008.

Congcong Wang and David Lillis. 2019. Classification for crisis-related tweets leveraging word embeddings and data augmentation. In *TREC*.

Jason Wei and Kai Zou. 2019. Eda: Easy data augmentation techniques for boosting performance on text classification tasks. In *Proceedings of the 2019 Conference on Empirical Methods in Natural Language Processing and the 9th International Joint Conference on Natural Language Processing (EMNLP-IJCNLP)*, pages 6383–6389.

Thomas Wolf, Lysandre Debut, Victor Sanh, Julien Chaumond, Clement Delangue, Anthony Moi, Pierric Cistac, Tim Rault, R'emi Louf, Morgan Funtowicz, and Jamie Brew. 2019. Huggingface's transformers: State-of-the-art natural language processing. *ArXiv*, abs/1910.03771.

Xing Wu, Shangwen Lv, Liangjun Zang, Jizhong Han, and Songlin Hu. 2019. Conditional bert contextual augmentation. In *International Conference on Computational Science*, pages 84–95. Springer.

Liqiang Xiao, Lu Wang, Hao He, and Yaohui Jin. 2020. Modeling content importance for summarization with pre-trained language models. In *Proceedings of the 2020 Conference on Empirical Methods in Natural Language Processing (EMNLP)*, pages 3606–3611.

Yiben Yang, Chaitanya Malaviya, Jared Fernandez, Swabha Swayamdipta, Ronan Le Bras, Ji-Ping Wang, Chandra Bhagavatula, Yejin Choi, and Doug Downey. 2020. G-daug: Generative data augmentation for commonsense reasoning. In *Proceedings of the 2020 Conference on Empirical Methods in Natural Language Processing: Findings*, pages 1008–1025.

Yiming Yang. 1999. An evaluation of statistical approaches to text categorization. *Information retrieval*, 1(1-2):69–90.

Danqing Zhang, Tao Li, Haiyang Zhang, and Bing Yin. 2020. On data augmentation for extreme multi-label classification. *arXiv preprint arXiv:2009.10778*.

Xinwei Zhang and Bin Wu. 2015. Short text classification based on feature extension using the n-gram model. In *2015 12th International Conference on Fuzzy Systems and Knowledge Discovery (FSKD)*, pages 710–716. IEEE.

Appendix

In Section A we present related research on data augmentation strategies. In Section B we describe the classification framework for all three datasets. We also present the statistics for the entire datasets and the classification results using the entire training data per dataset, with no augmentation. In Section C, we present examples of generated samples between the GPT models we used in our analysis.

A Data Augmentation: Related Work

The task of data augmentation consists of generating synthetic additional training samples from existing labelled data (Anaby-Tavor et al., 2020). In the following, we describe standard text augmentation methods which we use as baselines. We also explain recent DA methods based on text generation models.

Word replacement-based (WR). Simple but commonly used DA techniques are based on word-replacement strategies using knowledge bases (Wei and Zou, 2019) such as WordNet (Miller, 1998). Such methods often struggle to preserve the class label and lead to grammatical distortions of the data (Kumar et al., 2020; Giridhara et al., 2019; Anaby-Tavor et al., 2020). Recent DA approaches address the above issues by using language models to provide more contextual knowledge such as CBERT (Wu et al., 2019) in the word replacement process. However, methods that make only local changes to given instances produce sentences with a structure similar to the original ones and thus lead to low variability of training instances in the corpus (Anaby-Tavor et al., 2020).

Sentence replacement-based (SR). Common sentence replacement-based methods are based on back-translation strategies where a given sentence is translated to a language and then back to the original language in order to change the syntax but not the meaning of the sentence (Sennrich et al., 2016; Fadaee et al., 2017).

Text Generation (TG). Recent language models such as GPT-2 (Radford et al., 2019) can address the issues associated with the previous strategies by generating completely new instances from given seed samples. GPT-2 was trained with a causal language modeling (CLM) objective which makes it suitable for predicting the next token in a sequence. This model has been used successfully in text generation tasks such as summarising (Xiao et al., 2020; Kieuvongngam et al., 2020; Alambo et al., 2020) and question answering (Liu and Huang, 2019; Baheti et al., 2020; Klein and Nabi, 2019). Previous research on using text generation techniques for DA for text classification focused on the creation of label-preservation techniques for the generated synthetic data samples and comparing different TG techniques (Anaby-Tavor et al., 2020; Wang and Lillis, 2019; Zhang et al., 2020; Kumar et al., 2020). However, these works are limited in scale and solutions for improving quality of generated data.Further, There are two main methods used for label preservation of generated samples. The first approach, using a classifier to re-label artificial sequences, requires either a large training corpus to ensure high performance of the classifier in first place or the generation of large volume of artificial data to ensure that a substantial amount of these will not be filtered because of a low threshold (Anaby-Tavor et al., 2020). The other, more widely accepted approach, is prepending the class labels to text sequences during fine-tuning of the Transformer-based model (Wang and Lillis, 2019; Zhang et al., 2020; Kumar et al., 2020). Such an approach cannot ensure label-preservation for all generated sequences. However, our priority is to allow a fair comparison for seed selection approaches without introducing additional noise. Therefore, we consider a simple technique based on fine-tuning a model per label more suitable for performing our analysis.

B Datasets description

The 20 Newsgroups collection is a popular data set for experiments in machine learning. The data is organized into 20 different newsgroups, each corresponding to a different news topic such as computer systems, religion, politics (Lang, 1995). The collection of the Toxic comments dataset is obtained from Wikipedia and it is the result from the collaboration between Google and Jigsaw for creating a machine learning-based system for automatically detecting online insults, harassment, and abusive speech (Hosseini et al., 2017). Table 4 shows that for the 20 Newsgroups dataset there are 20 subclasses split between 6 overall classes. The Toxic comments consists of two overall classes - 'toxic' and 'non-toxic' where the 'toxic' class is overarching 6 subclasses. The Safeguarding reports consists of 5 overall classes and 34 subclasses.

The full description of the original datasets is given in Table 6. Results from performing classification using unmodified datasets (using the full training data) are given in Table 5.

B.1 Statistical significance test

To further evaluate the effect the additional data generated with GPT-2 have over the classifier's performance, we performed a statistical test, t-test (Student, 1908), used to compare the means of two groups. It is used to determine if there is a significant difference between the means of two groups, which may be related in certain features. It is often used to determine whether a process or treatment actually has an effect on the population of interest, or whether two groups are different from one another.

We use t-test to measure whether the addition of GPT-2 generated training data does actually lead to improvements compared to non-augmented classifier. We specifically perform t-test between best performing seed selection strategy, highlighted in bold and 'None' row in Tables 3 and 4). Our H_0 is: *Generated data does not lead to overall im-*

Dataset	Label	Sub-labels
Toxic comments	non-toxic	non-toxic
	toxic	mild toxic, severe toxic, obscene,threat, insult,identity hate
Newsgroups	computers	comp.graphics, comp.os.ms-windows.misc, comp.sys.ibm.pc.hardware, comp.sys.mac.hardware, comp.windows.x
	recreational activities	rec.autos, rec.motorcycles, rec.sport.baseball, rec.sport.hockey
	science	sci.crypt, sci.electronics, sci.med, sci.space
	forsale	misc.forsale
	politics	talk.politics.misc, talk.politics.guns, talk.politics.mideast
	religion	talk.religion.misc, alt.atheism, soc.religion.christian
Safeguarding Reports	Contact with Agencies	Health Practitioners, Contact with Third sector orgs, Educational Institutions, Contact with Social Care, Police Contact, Contact with councils or LAs
	Indicative Behaviour	Lying, Offending, Serious Threats to Life, Weapons, Emotional Abuse, Domestic Violence, Substance Misuse, Alcohol Misuse, Harassment, Self Inflicted Harm, Stalking, Controlling Behaviour, Aggression
	Indicative Circumstances	Bereavement,NFA, Homelessness or Constantly changing Address, Family Structure, Child Safeguarding, Relationship Breakdown, Debt or Financial Exploitation, Sex Work, Relationship with Children, Quality of Relationship
	Mental Health Issues	Children, Victim, Perpetrator, Suicidal Ideation
	Reflections	Reports Assessments and Conferences, Failures or Missed Opportunities

Table 4: Subclasses for the three datasets

Dataset	Micro-F1	Macro-F1
20 Newsgroups	0.768	0.759
Toxic comments	0.908	0.908
Safeguarding Reports (passages)	0.463	0.404
Safeguarding Reports (sentences)	0.505	0.477

Table 5: FastText classification results for the entire datasets with no augmentation.

provements in classifier performance and H_a: *Generated data does lead to overall improvements in classifier performance*. We use as a threshold $\alpha = 0.05$. Results in Table 7 showed that $p_{value} < \alpha$ for every dataset. This confirms that augmenting approaches using seed selection strategies do lead to improvements in classifier's performance versus non-augmented classifiers.

Dataset	Avg tokens	# Train	# Test
Safeguarding Reports (passages)	45	1,261	284
Safeguarding Reports (sentences)	18	3,591	284
20 Newsgroups	285	11,231	6,728
Toxic comments	46	159,571	63,978

Table 6: Description of unmodified datasets

Dataset	p_{micro}	p_{macro}	α
20 Newsgroups	0.01	0.02	0.05
Toxic comments	0.03	0.03	0.05
Safeguarding Reports (passages)	0.0001	0.0001	0.05
Safeguarding Reports (sentences)	0.006	0.016	0.05

Table 7: T-test results - compare classification performance with no additional data and results with additional data where performance is the highest

C Analysis GPT-2 models: Comparison between generated samples

In Table 8 we provide examples of generated instances per GPT model. Results showed that the fine-tuned model leads to miss-classifications for the 20 Newsgroup dataset and the Toxic comments dataset.

Dataset	Label	Original Text	GPT(gen) generation	GPT(dom) generation	GPT(label) generation
20 Newsgroups	Computers	There are 3 alternatives: You can try to write a small C program something like: int my_int_var;my_int_var = system(command);	4. It's a bit confusing and requires very little programming knowledge.5. It uses only your current CPU and some extra memory.	I am now posting the following FAQs to a group of individuals whose answers are from people who are now either atheists, agnostics, etc.	It appears that I am having a problem in trying to use XRemoteAddInput(xmodmap) in windows.
Toxic Comments	non-toxic	I think the recent editing by all has been brilliant. If I see anything that could be improved I'll speak up here. I would like to see a Christian Theosophy section also.	Thank you for your help, H, for your work on my blog.You are welcome to submit comments in this section, but please note I am not allowed to comment on other forums because they may interfere with my work.	No need to be an encyclopedic asshole. You don't see me deleting things because of something that was on my watchlist. I just wanted you to know that my name is now on my watchlist, and I will try to improve it.	I hope to see the article finished as soon as possible. But I would like to thank you for your contributions.
Safeguarding reports	Indicative Circumstances	Medical records show that she struggled for many years with depression, for which she was treated with antidepressants, also receiving referrals for counselling. She also had issues with her physical health.	Her lawyer, Richard Gage, has asked the court to intervene if Mr. McDevitt was not criminally liable in his decision.	She attended at her GP with a range of depressive symptoms and her medication was improved. It is not known how she gained her weight but it is said that her mental health declined and she started following a diet with vitamin C, which was associated with being better at controlling her mood.	In the early 1970s she moved from Los Angeles to New York. During this time she suffered from depression and other problems, but there was little support in New York.She moved into a small apartment and was living with friends, but had to move into a house next to her apartment to support her mental health.

Table 8: Examples of generated samples using GPT-2 models, where Safeguarding Reports examples are non-verbatim due to data sensitivity.

Partially Humanizing Weak Supervision: Towards a Better Low Resource Pipeline for Spoken Language Understanding

Ayush Kumar[†], **Rishabh Kumar Tripathi**[†*], **Jithendra Vepa**
Observe.AI, India
{ayush,rishabh.tripathi,jithendra}@observe.ai

Abstract

Weak Supervised Learning (WSL) is a popular paradigm to develop machine learning models in absence of labeled training data. WSL involves training over noisy labels which are traditionally obtained from hand-engineered semantic rules and task-specific pre-trained models. Such rules offer limited coverage and generalization over tasks. On the other hand, pre-trained models are available only for limited tasks. Thus, obtaining weak labels is a bottleneck in weak supervised learning. In this work, we propose to utilize the prompting paradigm to generate weak labels for the underlying tasks. We show that task-agnostic prompts are generalizable and can be used to obtain noisy labels for different Spoken Language Understanding (SLU) tasks such as sentiment classification, disfluency detection and emotion classification. These prompts can additionally be updated with '*human-in-the-loop*' to add task-specific contexts. Our proposed WSL pipeline outperforms other competitive low-resource benchmarks on zero and few-shot learning by more than 4% on Macro-F1 and a conventional rule-based WSL baseline by more than 5% across all the benchmark datasets. We demonstrate that prompt-based method helps to generate more reliable labels for the above SLU tasks in less than 72% of time compared to a traditional rule-based method to obtain noisy labels and thus can be used as a universal strategy to obtain weak labels in a weak-supervised framework.

1 Introduction

Weak supervised learning (WSL) (Yu et al., 2021; Ren et al., 2020) has gained interest in the research community because of the success shown by leveraging the high availability of large volumes of unlabeled data (Zhou, 2018). In these weak supervision setups, the unlabeled samples are pseudo-annotated by noisy labels and a noise correction strategy is applied to train the model over such labels. These noisy labels are derived using source(s), commonly known as weak source(s). Most common forms of weak sources observed in the area of weak supervision are: rule-based weak sources (Hutto and Gilbert, 2014; Nielsen, 2011) and task-specific fine-tuned models (Schweter and Akbik, 2020).

Rule-based weak sources require designing the labeling functions using the heuristics, lexicons and external knowledge bases (like *SentiWordNet* (Esuli and Sebastiani, 2006)) to map an input to the class labels expected in the task. It is a challenge to extend such rules to dataset from different domains or to perform a different task. Additionally, designing rules for an individual dataset is a manually time intensive task. While, there are a few rule-based sources available for common tasks like sentiment, it is hard to find such readily available weak sources for tasks like disfluency detection (Godfrey et al., 1992).

The other type of weak-sources utilize a task specific fine-tuned language model. For example, BERT-NER, which is BERT (Devlin et al., 2019) fine-tuned for NER task, can be utilized as a weak source to identify named entities from the data. Such task-specific models cannot be used to predict class labels for a task different than what the model is trained on.

The common challenge imposed by both of these weak sources is the lack of generalizability across a wide variety of tasks. In this paper, we propose a universal weak source which not only generates better quality noisy class labels for wide range of tasks, but can also be tweaked to write '*human-in-the-loop*' task-specific details with minimal efforts. We present *prompt-based weak source*, a hybrid source which utilizes a pre-trained language model (PLM) as a knowledge base and limited human intervention as a prompter to address the labeling problems observed in traditionally used weak sources. A prompt-based weak source requires prompting a

*Work done during internship at Observe.AI, †Equal contribution

Proceedings of the Fourth Workshop on Data Science with Human-in-the-Loop (Language Advances), pages 64 - 73
December 8, 2022 ©2022 Association for Computational Linguistics

PLM (Gao et al., 2021; Schick and Schütze, 2021; Logan IV et al., 2021) to derive weak class labels. A prompt refers to a pattern string that is designed to coax the model into producing an output corresponding to a given class (Scao and Rush, 2021). We study different ways to prompt PLMs in 3.1.1 and 3.1.2. We study 3 key features of prompt-based sources as: *Generalizability* (utilize task-agnostic prompts to cater to various tasks and effectively create prompts for multiple tasks within same generic framework.), *Flexibility* (to modify the prompts to add task and class-label specific contexts in an easy manner to improve over task-agnostic prompts), *Potency* (to derive weak labels with reliable source performance).

Our major contributions in this work are:

- Instead of the classical application of prompting in a few-shot and zero-shot settings, we propose utilization of prompting paradigm to generate noisy labels needed in WSL.
- We demonstrate a generalizable, flexible and time-efficient low-resource '*human-in-the-loop*' setup to train a weak supervised model using task-agnostic and task-specific prompt-based weak sources.
- We perform extensive experiments on three benchmark SLU datasets and demonstrate the effectiveness of the proposed *'human-in-the-loop'* in reducing manual overhead along with improving the performance over the traditional rule-intensive weak sources and other competitive low resource setups.

2 Related Work

Existing works (Wang et al., 2019; Hedderich and Klakow, 2018) in WSL learns on a few gold data, while another group of work (Yu et al., 2021; Ren et al., 2020; Ratner et al., 2020) assumes that no labeled data is available. In the scope of our work, we explore approaches that do not rely on labeled data to train a weak supervised model (WSM). Ren et al. (2020) utilized BERT to learn conditional reliability scores between multiple weak sources using an attention mechanism, while Ratner et al. (2020) proposed a generative model to combine outputs from various weak sources. Yu et al. (2021) proposed a contrastive self-training strategy to learn over weak labels and outperformed prior works (Ren et al., 2020; Ratner et al., 2020). Hence, our work borrows ideas from Yu et al. (2021) to train a weak supervised model (WSM) considering its robustness towards high intensities of label noise.

Prompt-based methods utilize templates structured as *natural language inference (NLI)*-style prompts (section 3.1.1) or *cloze*-style prompts (section 3.1.2) in a zero-shot and/or few-shot setup to predict the labels for the downstream task. Works such as Logan IV et al. (2021) demonstrated few-shot training using *cloze*-style task-agnostic null-prompt, while FLAN (Wei et al., 2021) utilized NLI-style instruction templates and performed instruction tuning to improve the zeroshot performance. However, due to the large size of the model (137B parameters), we find the work unsuitable to be used in creating a low resource pipeline. On the other hand, LMBFF (Gao et al., 2021) and Pattern Exploiting Training (PET) (Schick and Schütze, 2021) utilized a relatively smaller PLM (340M parameters) on *cloze*-style prompts. LMBFF showed that a few demonstrative examples during task fine-tuning provide additional context to better learn the prompts and report improvements over PET (Schick and Schütze, 2021). Considering the benefits of LMBFF (Gao et al., 2021) over other methods in creating a low resource pipeline, we utilize this approach to perform prompt-based fine-tuning.

3 Methodology

The proposed methodology is a two-step process (Figure 1). First, we *prompt the PLMs with 'human-in-the-loop'* as a strategy to produce weak labels for the unlabeled training data. Next, we train a WSM on these weak labels. In the subsequent sections, we describe the two steps in detail.

3.1 Prompting PLMs to obtain weak labels

3.1.1 Prompting: NLI-style

In NLI-style prompts, the input utterance is transformed to a premise-hypothesis pair of an utterance and a prompt respectively. This transformed input is fed to an entailment model. For example, for input utterance *'I am happy.'* and prompt *'The sentiment of the speaker is positive'*, an entailment in this case denotes that class-label is positive. Prompt is designed to reflect the class label of utterance if prompt (hypothesis) entails the utterance (premise). For each premise, the class label associated with the prompt having highest entailment score is treated as the weak label. For prompting, we compare a couple of pre-trained models

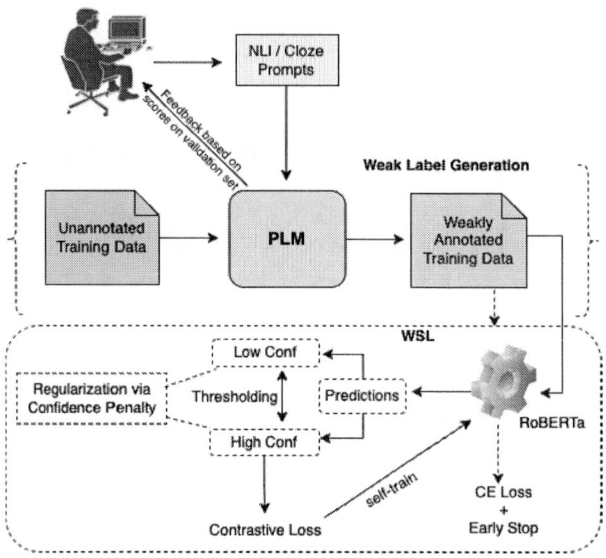

Figure 1: Proposed weak supervised framework.

namely `bart-large-mnli-yahoo-answers` and `roberta-large-mnli` available at Hugging Face library[1] (Wolf et al., 2019). Based on the results over the same set of prompts, we find that bart-based model predicts more accurate class labels, which we select for conducting all the NLI experiments.

3.1.2 Prompting: *Cloze*-style

In *cloze* prompts, a piece of text is inserted in the input examples, so that the original task can be formulated as a masked language modeling (MLM) problem. For example, considering input utterance *'I am happy.'*, the prompt based system is fed a transformed utterance containing a `[mask]` token to form utterance-instruction pair, where instruction is *'The sentiment of the speaker is* `[mask]`*'*. For the masked token, PLM generates a probability distribution over a set of verbalizers representing individual classes (Table 5 in A.1). The class corresponding to the verbalizer with highest probability is taken as the weak label. Inspired by LMBFF (Gao et al., 2021), we leverage pre-trained `roberta-large` (Liu et al., 2019) with an objective to fill the `[mask]` token in the prompt. The resulting sentence is concatenated with one demonstration per class, in the similar fashion as Gao et al. (2021). This scheme leverages additional context around the input sentence to predict appropriate class labels. However, we note *cloze* prompts to be more sensitive than NLI prompts to the changes in the demonstrations chosen. Hence, we take into account an extended version of *cloze* prompts which also requires demonstrations and performs a task fine-tuning using a few-shot setup to solve a specific task. The need of task fine-tuning with *cloze*-style prompts is studied in detail in A.3.

[1] https://huggingface.co/models

3.2 Weak Supervised Learning

The noisy labels obtained in the previous step are utilized to train a WSM following a certain noise-correction mechanism (Ren et al., 2020; Yu et al., 2021). We observe that Yu et al. (2021) with its contrastive self-training label correction strategy outperforms various recent WSL baselines (Ren et al., 2020; Wang et al., 2019). Directly inspired by the technique utilized in Yu et al. (2021), we adopt a noise-handling strategy which uses contrastive loss for self-training to improve over the performance of weak source(s) iteratively. This strategy is robust to the label noise. Further, we assume that there is no gold annotations available for training. The model undergoes two steps:

Initial fine-tuning: Firstly, it trains a `roberta-base` (Liu et al., 2019) encoder over noisy labels with cross-entropy objective only for fewer steps (early epochs). This prevents the model from over-fitting the label noise and simultaneously helps to generalize the learning. During training, the model encourages to utilize soft labels to reduce the aggressive gradient updates. This prevents over-fitting the label noise.

Self-training: Further, the fine-tuned encoder

continues to learn over its own highly confident predictions (identified by keeping a threshold on confidence scores of model predictions obtained from the first step) via optimising a contrastive loss (Huang et al., 2022; Yu et al., 2021). In particular, contrastive loss is applied to regularize the feature space by bringing samples with the same weak labels closer together while separating apart the samples with different weak labels. This makes it easier to discern between the representations for data belonging to various classes and aids the classifier in producing more accurate predictions. As noise can aggressively back-propagate through the model during training on noisy labels, we prevent such events by employing confidence-based sample re-weighting and regularisation schemes. In order to lessen the impact of incorrect predictions, the re-weighting technique promotes the inclusion of samples with high prediction confidence scores solely, anticipating that these samples are likely to be correctly classified. Additionally, we explore a couple of prior works (Yu et al., 2021; Pereyra et al., 2017) on entropy-based confidence penalty (using KL-divergence) for label smoothing and model regularization. As a result, the model smoothens the confident predictions to avoid sampling overconfident samples, hence reducing the impact of inaccurate noisy class labels. This process is continued for several iterations to help the model progressively learn over its own confident predictions and is called self-training (Yu et al., 2021; Wang et al., 2019; Ren et al., 2020). The one which we utilize in our work is a result of the combination of ideas strategized from a few strong prior works (Yu et al., 2021; Pereyra et al., 2017; Huang et al., 2022). The model utilized in our work is applicable to learn effectively and efficiently over weak annotations derived from various noisier sources and is robust to high intensity of label noise.

4 Experiments

4.1 Dataset

We consider three SLU datasets from various domains for conducting our experiments. **CMU-MOSI** is a sentiment dataset consisting of multiple modalities (Zadeh et al., 2016). In this work, we only consider text modality to perform sentiment classification. Similar to previous works (Kumar and Vepa, 2020; Tsai et al., 2019), we use train-test-valid split of 1284, 654 and 229 samples respectively. We use the **Switchboard Disfluency** (Godfrey et al., 1992) (SWBD-D) to classify the utterances into *fluent* and *disfluent* categories. We use the provided splits of train, test and validation set. For emotion task, we utilize **IEMOCAP** (Busso et al., 2008). Since distinguishing between *happy* and *excited* or *angry* and *sad* is a challenging task without audio modality, in the scope of this work, we binarize the emotion in IEMOCAP dataset to *positive* and *negative* emotion. *Positive* emotions comprise of *happy* and *excited* while *negative* emotions comprise of *sad, angry* and *frustrated.* We use the provided split of train, test and validation having 3270, 1207, 867 samples respectively. *It is to be noted that we use training set as unlabeled data and hence do not use ground-truth of the training splits to train the WSM.*

4.2 Weak Sources

Rule-based weak source: For sentiment and emotion classification, we use SentiWordNet (Esuli and Sebastiani, 2006) and AFINN (Nielsen, 2011) lexicons along with a rule based system called VADER (Hutto and Gilbert, 2014). We map the positive scores to positive sentiment/emotion and similarly, for negative sentiment/emotion. Empirically, we find VADER and AFINN to perform better for sentiment, while SentiWordNet and VADER perform best for emotion. For disfluency classification on SWBD-D, the labeling functions are created based on the occurrence of filler words, repetitions and soundex (Odell and Russell, 1918) codes. We create an additional rule by aggregating the weak sources via majority voting. We report the mean performance of rule-based weak sources on Macro-F1 and Coverage metrics in Table 1.

Dataset	Coverage	Macro-F1
MOSI	74.3±4.2	71.0±3.7
SWBD-D	84.4±10.5	73.6±7.4
IEMOCAP	63.9±17.2	46.6±0.3

Table 1: Rule-based weak source performance; Coverage represents %samples labeled by the rules; Macro-F1 is reported only over the samples covered by the rules

Prompt-based weak source: Since rule-based weak sources have varying coverage and require significant manual efforts and time, there is a need of a low-effort method that can generate weak labels over a given dataset with reliable performance. We propose prompting PLMs to obtain the weak labels. Specifically, we compare task-agnostic and task-specific prompts. Task-agnostic prompt represents a general instruction that can be shared across tasks while a task-specific prompt incorporates the task information in its verbiage which helps model with an additional context. To better understand what generalizability in prompts means and how are the generalized (task-agnostic) prompts different from the task-specific ones, we provide representative examples of task-specific and task-agnostic prompts in A.1 in a *cloze*-style template. Such prompts contain a `[mask]` which is expected to be replaced by an appropriate token called *verbalizer*. The *verbalizer* determines the task under the consideration. By choosing different verbalizers, we can utilize same prompt for multiple tasks in a task-agnostic setting. While, in a task-specific setting, contextual prompts (Table 5) are utilized to help predict the verbalizers more accurately. We can translate *cloze*-style prompts used in our experiments to *NLI*-style (i.e. hypotheses) by replacing the `[mask]` tokens with appropriate *verbalizers*. The hypotheses are entailed with the premises and yields entailment scores for each premise-hypothesis pair. The class which is a mapping to the verbalizer with highest entailment score is selected as the weak label for the premise.

Dataset	TSP	TAP
MOSI	83.5±3.3	82.8±1.3
SWBD-D	74.6±5.1	68.9±6.5
IEMOCAP	68.7±3.3	68.0±1.8

Table 2: Mean performance (Macro-F1) of task-specific (TSP) and task-agnostic (TAP) prompts on test set. Mean is computed across both NLI and *cloze* prompts.

Dataset	NLI	Cloze
MOSI	83.2±1.6	82.7±1.0
SWBD-D	42.0±15.6	75.2±3.9
IEMOCAP	70.3±0.4	71.4±0.6

Table 3: Mean performance (Macro-F1) of NLI and Cloze prompts on test set. We utilize both TAP and TSP for the average calculation.

With differences in prompts and verbalizers, the performance of the weak source may vary. Thus, experiments are performed on multiple prompts and/or verbalizers involving '*human-in-the-loop*'. We ask the annotators to sample 16 data points per class and annotate them with ground truth labels which we use as a validation set to evaluate the performance and fairly compare the varieties of prompts. The performance of each prompt acts as a feedback to direct the prompt curators whether or not to continue designing more variations of prompts. The process of designing more prompts terminates when no improvement in performance of prompts is observed for 5 consecutive attempts. Among the wide range of prompts designed as a consequence of the *to-and-fro* process between PLM and humans, we choose to report average across the top-3 performing prompts in Table 2. In the process, by leveraging *flexibility* as a feature of prompt-based source, we modify the prompt structure to create various task-specific prompts. On the other hand, the task-agnostic prompts can be utilized across various tasks performed in our experiments demonstrating *generalizability* of the proposed approach. Additionally, the performance scores of prompt-based weak source reported in Table 2 shows that PLMs when prompted, have potential to generate accurate weak labels (*potency*). We note that for every dataset, task-specific prompts work better than the task-agnostic prompts. This gain is significant for SWBD-D dataset denoting the need for language models to rely on task specific context unlike other tasks. Additionally, we note that NLI-style prompt produces better results for MOSI, while *cloze*-style prompt produces more reliable labels for SWBD-D and IEMOCAP dataset (Table 3). This could mean that complex tasks like disfluency and emotion classification require the model to learn on task-specific contexts which we perform with *cloze*-style prompts.

4.3 Baseline

We compare the performance of the proposed setups with a fully-supervised and other low-resource setups like few-shot learning (FSL) and zero-shot learning (ZSL): ***Oracle*** represents the performance score on test set obtained when a pre-trained RoBERTa (Liu et al., 2019) is trained on gold labels in a fully-supervised fashion. ***Meta-tuning*** is a state-of-the-art work (Zhong et al., 2021) in ZSL where authors propose utilizing question prompts for classification tasks, where zero-shot objective is directly optimized by fine-tuning on a meta-dataset. ***k-Classifier*** is a few-shot setup, a RoBERTa learns on a train-set consisting of only 16 examples per class. ***DNNC*** (Zhang et al., 2020) utilizes discriminative nearest neighbor classifier, is a state-of-the-art model for few-shot and out-of-scope intent prediction task. We use a 16-shot setup.

Further, we compare the performance of various weak sources on the test set: ***Rule*** represents the

	MOSI	SWBD-D	IEMOCAP
Oracle	*86.1±0.4*	*94.5±2.0*	*80.5±0.4*
Meta-tuning	80.3±2.0	49.1±2.7	61.6±1.8
k-Classifier	73.1±7.0	74.3±7.3	61.4±5.9
DNNC	79.9±0.8	63.9±1.7	62.3±7.4
Rule	63.0±3.2	70.9±7.1	33.8±3.1
TAP	81.5±1.6	71.1±7.5	69.0±2.8
TSP	83.5±1.2	73.2±5.2	69.8±1.7
WSL-Rule	74.6±5.4	76.4±1.5	41.0±1.8
WSL-TAP	82.8±1.8	77.5±3.9	71.5±0.3
WSL-TSP	**84.5±0.9**	**81.9±3.7**	**71.9±0.9**
Best WSL	85.26	83.86	72.47

Table 4: Comparative results of the baselines and proposed weak supervised pipeline on Macro-F1 scores.

performance of rule-based weak sources. For the calculation of recall, the samples not covered by the rules are considered to represent false negatives. This represents a heuristic-based classifier. ***Task-Agnostic-Prompt (TAP)*** and ***Task-Specific-Prompt (TSP)*** represent the performance scores obtained by prompting the PLM with a task-agnostic and task-specific prompt directly over the samples in test set, without training a WSM.

Once the weak labels are obtained on the unlabeled training data, a WSM is trained to design: ***WSL-rule*** where a WSM is trained over the weak labels derived from rule-based weak source discussed in Section 4.2. ***WSL-TAP*** and ***WSL-TSP*** are the proposed low-resource pipelines which train a WSM on weak labels obtained from task-agnostic and task-specific prompts respectively.

5 Results and Analysis

We compare our proposed framework (WSL-TAP, WSL-TSP) with other baselines in Table 4. We report the experimental results as mean performance scores with standard deviations. *Rule*, TSP and TAP represent the mean performance score across various rule-based weak sources (refer section 4.2), task-specific and task-agnostic prompts (considering various styles - NLI and *cloze* both) respectively. *WSL-Rule*, *WSL-TSP*, *WSL-TAP* represent the average scores obtained on training the WSM over various rule-based heuristics, task-specific prompts and task-agnostic prompts.

Proposed WSL vs Low-Resource Baselines: The results show that a WSM trained on prompt based weak labels (*WSL-TAP, WSL-TSP*) outperforms other baselines including state-of-the-art zero-shot (meta-tuning) and few-shot (DNNC) approaches. *WSL-TSP* outperforms the few-shot method by more than 4% on MOSI, 7% on SWBD-D and 9% on IEMOCAP dataset. Further results show that training a weak supervision model (*WSL-TAP, WSL-TSP*) over prompt-based weak labels bridges the gap with the Oracle model. Specifically, training a WSM improves the F1 scores by 1% for MOSI, 8.2% for SWBD-D and 2.1% for IEMOCAP. This shows the effectiveness of proposed pipelines for training a low-resource model against few-shot and zero-shot methods.

Proposed WSL vs Rule-based WSL: The proposed weak supervision pipeline on prompt-based weak source also outperforms a traditional rule based weak supervision pipeline (*WSL-Rule*). The distinction between the performance of rule and prompt-based WSL pipeline is more evident for MOSI and IEMOCAP datasets. The proposed method outperforms rule based pipeline by 10% in MOSI, 5% in SWBD-D and 31% in IEMOCAP dataset (*WSL-TSP* vs *WSL-Rule* in Table 4). The higher gap in performances on MOSI and IEMOCAP could be related to the worse performance of rules, where weak labels generated from semantic rules are less accurate and have lower coverage than SWBD-D dataset (Table 1). We see that *Rule* has particularly lower performance on IEMOCAP owing to limited coverage of such rules, while both *TAP* and *TSP* consistently outperform the weak labels obtained from rules. Thus, in addition to reducing the manual effort in writing rules for labeling the data, the prompt-based method generates more accurate labels to annotate the unlabeled data.

Task-agnostic vs Task-specific Prompts: We observe that weak labels obtained from task-specific prompts (*TSP*) are consistently better than task-agnostic prompts (*TAP*). Likewise, *WSL-TSP* outperforms *WSL-TAP* on all tasks. While the best results are obtained from task-specific prompts, even task-agnostic prompts outperform a rule-based pipeline. Hence, the proposed pipeline (WSL-TAP, WSL-TSP) could solve the bottleneck of labeling the data while training a WSM.

Best WSL Scores: Finally, we report the best scores obtained with proposed pipeline: MOSI = 85.26%; SWBD = 83.86%; IEMOCAP = 72.47%. We note that the best score obtained on MOSI dataset is competitive with the Oracle results, which could be explained by a highly reliable weak labels obtained from prompt-based method on MOSI. However, the performance on SWBD-D and IEMOCAP are lower than Oracle (refer to section A.4 for explanation) but are strongly better than state-of-the-art low resource methods on zero-shot and few-shot methods. Thus, we show that low resource pipeline for SLU tasks could be effectively trained via proposed pipeline.

Quantifying the importance of human efforts: We outsource the task of curating prompts to 5 proficient English speakers. We observe that it takes around 17.0±6.0 minutes on an average across the speakers to come-up with the first good prompt for the benchmark SLU tasks. While creating rules for the same under the restriction of given guidelines (section A.5), it takes *roughly around an hour* to come up with pattern-based heuristics for a certain dataset. This observation shows that we can save around 72% of annotation time by avoiding rule-based heuristics and relying only on prompt-based weak source. The reason why designing prompts takes relatively lesser time compared to designing rules is due to the fact that rule-based baselines have to be balanced between coverage and precision, along with the higher complexity of coding the rules against the designing the prompts. We consider rules (or a set of rules unioned together) to be good if it performs better than a baseline of majority class in terms of precision and cover at least 25% of the unlabeled samples. Additionally, these rules have to written in a framework which is a time-consuming step as well against simply writing a prompt which is nothing but a textual sentence. So, iterating with prompts is much faster as compared to iterating on rules. Furthermore, in many cases, a bunch of rules have to be unioned to achieve this criteria on coverage and precision and hence, it takes a longer cycle to identify the set of rules required to generate weakly labeled training data. As it is evident in Table 4 that prompt-based baselines (TAP, TSP) outperform heuristics (Rule), thus, instead of creating rules, we rather encourage human effort in curating more variations of prompts by utilizing a fraction of the expensive time we saved using the proposed weak sources.

6 Conclusion

In this work, we show effectiveness of utilizing prompt-based methods as universal weak sources to develop low-resource models for wide range of benchmark SLU tasks. We show that the proposed method outperforms traditional methods of rule based WSL as well as state-of-the-art methods on other low resource settings like ZSL and FSL. In future, we would like to study the application of automatic and soft prompts to generate the weak labels and the extension of work to multilingual tasks where limited training data is available. We would also like to explore areas around incorporating the human-in-the-loop feedback during the training process instead of only restricting it to improve on the quality of weak labels.

Limitations

The proposed work has dependency on manual prompts. Curating prompts can be subjective across different individual. This can cause variations in the results. Moreover, we also notice that the score on test set for the predictions generated by PLMs is sensitive to the change in prompt tokens. However, our work offers a future opportunity for researchers to use the proposed setup with continuous prompts to address the problem of sensitivity caused by such manually curated prompts. Moreover, the technique of prompt-based fine-tuning (Gao et al., 2021) of PLM which we utilize to infer weak label for a *cloze*-style prompt is constrained to predict class label consisting of a single token only.

References

Carlos Busso et al. 2008. IEMOCAP: interactive emotional dyadic motion capture database. *Lang. Resour. Evaluation*, 42(4):335–359.

Jacob Devlin, Ming-Wei Chang, Kenton Lee, and Kristina Toutanova. 2019. BERT: pre-training of deep bidirectional transformers for language understanding. In *Proceedings of the 2019 Conference of the North American Chapter of the Association for Computational Linguistics: Human Language Technologies, NAACL-HLT 2019, Minneapolis, USA*, pages 4171–4186.

Andrea Esuli and Fabrizio Sebastiani. 2006. SENTIWORDNET: A publicly available lexical resource for opinion mining. In *Proceedings of the Fifth International Conference on Language Resources and Evaluation, LREC, Genoa, Italy*, pages 417–422.

Tianyu Gao, Adam Fisch, and Danqi Chen. 2021. Making pre-trained language models better few-shot learners. In *Proceedings of the 59th Annual Meeting of the Association for Computational Linguistics and the 11th International Joint Conference on Natural Language Processing, ACL/IJCNLP 2021*, pages 3816–3830.

John J. Godfrey, Edward Holliman, and Jane McDaniel. 1992. SWITCHBOARD: telephone speech corpus for research and development. In *1992 IEEE International Conference on Acoustics, Speech, and Signal Processing, ICASSP, California, USA*, pages 517–520.

Michael A. Hedderich and Dietrich Klakow. 2018. Training a neural network in a low-resource setting on automatically annotated noisy data. In *Proceedings of the Workshop on Deep Learning Approaches for Low-Resource NLP, DeepLo@ACL 2018, Melbourne, Australia*, pages 12–18.

Bin Huang, Adi Alhudhaif, Fayadh Alenezi, Sara A. Althubiti, and Chaoyang Xu. 2022. Balance label correction using contrastive loss. *Inf. Sci.*, 607:1061–1073.

Clayton J. Hutto and Eric Gilbert. 2014. VADER: A parsimonious rule-based model for sentiment analysis of social media text. In *Proceedings of the Eighth International Conference on Weblogs and Social Media, ICWSM, Michigan, USA*.

Ayush Kumar and Jithendra Vepa. 2020. Gated mechanism for attention based multi modal sentiment analysis. In *2020 IEEE International Conference on Acoustics, Speech and Signal Processing, ICASSP 2020, Barcelona, Spain*, pages 4477–4481.

Yinhan Liu et al. 2019. Roberta: A robustly optimized BERT pretraining approach. *CoRR*, abs/1907.11692.

Robert L Logan IV, Ivana Balažević, Eric Wallace, Fabio Petroni, Sameer Singh, and Sebastian Riedel. 2021. Cutting down on prompts and parameters: Simple few-shot learning with language models. *arXiv preprint arXiv:2106.13353*.

Ilya Loshchilov and Frank Hutter. 2019. Decoupled weight decay regularization. In *7th International Conference on Learning Representations, ICLR 2019, New Orleans, LA, USA, May 6-9, 2019*. OpenReview.net.

Finn Årup Nielsen. 2011. A new ANEW: evaluation of a word list for sentiment analysis in microblogs. In *Proceedings of the ESWC2011 Workshop on 'Making Sense of Microposts': Big things come in small packages, Crete, Greece*, volume 718 of *CEUR Workshop Proceedings*, pages 93–98.

KM Odell and RC Russell. 1918. Soundex phonetic comparison system. *US Patent*, 1261167.

Gabriel Pereyra, George Tucker, Jan Chorowski, Lukasz Kaiser, and Geoffrey E. Hinton. 2017. Regularizing neural networks by penalizing confident output distributions. In *5th International Conference on Learning Representations, ICLR 2017, Toulon, France, April 24-26, 2017, Workshop Track Proceedings*. OpenReview.net.

Alexander Ratner, Stephen H. Bach, Henry R. Ehrenberg, Jason A. Fries, Sen Wu, and Christopher Ré. 2020. Snorkel: rapid training data creation with weak supervision. *VLDB J.*, 29(2-3):709–730.

Wendi Ren, Yinghao Li, Hanting Su, David Kartchner, Cassie Mitchell, and Chao Zhang. 2020. Denoising multi-source weak supervision for neural text classification. In *Findings of the Association for Computational Linguistics: EMNLP 2020, Online Event*, volume EMNLP 2020 of *Findings of ACL*, pages 3739–3754.

Teven Le Scao and Alexander M. Rush. 2021. How many data points is a prompt worth? In *NAACL-HLT, 2021, Online*, pages 2627–2636.

Timo Schick and Hinrich Schütze. 2021. Exploiting cloze-questions for few-shot text classification and natural language inference. In *Proceedings of the 16th Conference of the European Chapter of the Association for Computational Linguistics: Main Volume, EACL*, pages 255–269.

Stefan Schweter and Alan Akbik. 2020. FLERT: document-level features for named entity recognition. *CoRR*, abs/2011.06993.

Yao-Hung Hubert Tsai, Shaojie Bai, Paul Pu Liang, J. Zico Kolter, Louis-Philippe Morency, and Ruslan Salakhutdinov. 2019. Multimodal transformer for unaligned multimodal language sequences. In *Proceedings of the 57th Conference of the Association for Computational Linguistics, ACL 2019, Florence, Italy*, pages 6558–6569.

Hao Wang, Bing Liu, Chaozhuo Li, Yan Yang, and Tianrui Li. 2019. Learning with noisy labels for sentence-level sentiment classification. In *Proceedings of the 2019 Conference on Empirical Methods in Natural Language Processing and the 9th International Joint Conference on Natural Language Processing, EMNLP-IJCNLP 2019, Hong Kong*, pages 6285–6291.

Jason Wei et al. 2021. Finetuned language models are zero-shot learners. *CoRR*, abs/2109.01652.

Thomas Wolf et al. 2019. Huggingface's transformers: State-of-the-art natural language processing. *CoRR*, abs/1910.03771.

Yue Yu, Simiao Zuo, Haoming Jiang, Wendi Ren, Tuo Zhao, and Chao Zhang. 2021. Fine-tuning pre-trained language model with weak supervision: A contrastive-regularized self-training approach. In *Proceedings of the 2021 Conference of the North American Chapter of the Association for Computational Linguistics: Human Language Technologies, NAACL-HLT 2021*, pages 1063–1077.

Amir Zadeh, Rowan Zellers, Eli Pincus, and Louis-Philippe Morency. 2016. MOSI: multimodal corpus of sentiment intensity and subjectivity analysis in online opinion videos. *CoRR*, abs/1606.06259.

Jianguo Zhang et al. 2020. Discriminative nearest neighbor few-shot intent detection by transferring natural language inference. In *Proceedings of the 2020 Conference on Empirical Methods in Natural Language Processing, EMNLP 2020, Online*, pages 5064–5082.

Ruiqi Zhong, Kristy Lee, Zheng Zhang, and Dan Klein. 2021. Adapting language models for zero-shot learning by meta-tuning on dataset and prompt collections. In *Findings of the Association for Computational Linguistics: EMNLP 2021, Virtual Event / Punta Cana, Dominican Republic*, pages 2856–2878.

Zhi-Hua Zhou. 2018. A brief introduction to weakly supervised learning. *National science review*, 5(1):44–53.

A Appendix

A.1 Representatives: TAP and TSP prompts

We present some of the representative examples of task-agnostic (TAP) and task-specific (TSP) prompts we used in our work. Table 5 demonstrates examples of TSP. Here, we observe that the prompts design vary according to the task and associated class labels. However, design for TAP is independent of any task and its underlying class labels. Here, we demonstrate some examples of TAP:

- *The class best describing the text is* `[mask]`.
- *The text can be classified as* `[mask]`.

A.2 Hyper-parameters

We discuss the hyper-parameters used to run our experiments. We perform a grid search to optimize the performance of the proposed weak source with *cloze*-style prompts (as they require fine-tuning) on development set. Batch size is searched over {2, 4, 8} set. The best learning rate is searched in {1e-5, 2e-5, 3e-5}. We fix the number of demonstrations to 1 for faster training. As we use NLI-style prompts to directly infer the weak labels without performing any task fine-tuning, we do not need any hyper-parameter specifications for prompt-based weak source with this style of prompts. For training the weak supervised model on noisy labels obtained via prompt-based weak source, our experimental setup utilizes the AdamW optimizer (Loshchilov and Hutter, 2019) and the optimal learning rate is searched over {1e-5 , 2e-5, 3e-5}. The weak-supervised learning is carried out for a maximum of 5 epochs. A scheduler (with linear learning rate decay strategy) is utilized with 0.1 warm-up. However, there are some hyper-parameters which are specific to the model and the involved training strategy. Hence, we recommend to look into the works of Yu et al. (2021) and Gao et al. (2021) as our work is inspired by them. Their research work demonstrates the behavioral change in model performance due to change in such hyper-parameters, which we directly use in our work.

A.3 *Cloze*-style prompts with demonstrations

In the scope of our work, we utilize only the extended version of *cloze*-style prompt which require task fine-tuning as discussed in section 3.1.2 but we do not change the nomenclature and refer to it as *cloze*-style prompts everywhere. However, we would now like to differentiate the *cloze-style prompt-based weak source WITH (w/) task fine-tuning* and *cloze-style prompt-based weak source WITHOUT (w/o) task fine-tuning*. We conduct an experiment on the benchmark SLU datasets to investigate if *cloze*-style prompts w/o task fine-tuning can be used to infer class labels and we observe that there is a mandatory need for fine-tuning the PLM with this category of prompts on downstream tasks. We compare the columns in Table 6 to demonstrate the incapability of *cloze-style prompt-based weak source w/o task fine-tuning* in deriving good quality weak labels for training a WSM. We also observe the higher gains in performance post task fine-tuning. These observations encourage us to rely only on the extended version of *cloze*-style prompts to derive weak labels for training a WSM.

A.4 Does a PLM naturally understand some tasks better than the others?

From Table 4, we surprisingly observe that the performance gap between Oracle result and the proposed frameworks (WSL-TSP and WSL-TAP) is low for MOSI but significantly higher for IEMOCAP and SWBD-D. This could be related to the nature and complexity of the tasks performed with each of these datasets. We define the complexity of a task by a measure of how well a PLM performs on that task without any downstream task fine-tuning. As we use NLI-style prompts to directly infer the class labels for unlabeled samples, these prompts can be useful in quantifying the difficulty faced by PLM in solving a certain task. Hence, we compare our results on NLI prompts across the tasks from Table 3.

Apparently, the order of complexity is MOSI (sentiment) < IEMOCAP (emotion) < SWBD-D (disfluency). This shows that a PLM already comprehends the sentiment task to some degree. Hence, without requiring any task fine-tuning, PLM predicts class labels quite accurately. However, dis-

Dataset	Task-specific prompt	verbalizer : class label
MOSI	The sentiment of the speaker is `[mask]`.	positive : positive, negative : negative
SWBD-D	The speaker `[mask]` takes a pause while speaking!	never : fluent, often : disfluent
IEMOCAP	I have `[mask]` emotions.	happy : positive, sad : negative

Table 5: Representative examples of TAP

Dataset	w/o fine-tuning	w/ fine-tuning
MOSI	67.5±2.7	83.3±1.2
SWBD-D	49.3±5.6	73.2±1.6
IEMOCAP	51.6±8.4	69.1±2.7

Table 6: Performance (Macro-F1) of *cloze*-style prompts on the train-set of WSM w/ and w/o task fine-tuning

fluency classification appears to be a task that a PLM is not particularly adept at. The fact that we do not deduce the class labels for the disfluency classification using NLI-style prompts is an evidence for this. We come to a conclusion that PLMs straightaway do not comprehend the pauses in conversation. Hence, we fine-tune the PLM with few-shots to help it understand the conversational pauses (refer to Cloze column in Table 3). However, the performance gap between the Oracle and proposed approaches still remains high which explains that disfluency classification is not a natural property of PLM. For emotion classification, the training is challenging as it is performed at utterance level excluding the surrounding informative context in the dialogue. The struggle in learning intensifies when the PLM is trained on few shots only. This could be a logical justification for the large disparity between Oracle and the suggested technique on IEMOCAP.

However, we encourage further investigations on ways to figure out the reasons for the uneven variations in gaps between Oracle and proposed pipelines.

A.5 Guidelines for Designing Rules

While creating rules for a dataset, it requires efforts to keenly observe the data to identify patterns and map them to the class labels. We ask the experts to manually create the rules for the benchmark datasets, under the assumption that rule-based tools pre-exist only for limited tasks. A rule is considered acceptable if it performs better than a majority baseline in accuracy and can cover at least 25% of the unlabeled samples. As observing the patterns across the complete dataset is tedious, we ask them to consider only 16 annotated samples per class to observe the patterns and use them to evaluate the accuracy of the rules. To design heuristics, we ask annotators to observe the common patterns (lexicons, phrases) to design a strategy that can be utilized to annotate the unseen samples. We also provide liberty to annotators to combine a bunch of rules for a certain dataset or task as necessary.

Improving Human Annotation Effectiveness for Fact Collection by Identifying the Most Relevant Answers

Pranav Kamath[1*], **Yiwen Sun**[2], **Thomas Semere**[2], **Adam Green**[2], **Scott Manley**[2], **Xiaoguang Qi**[2], **Kun Qian**[2], **Yunyao Li**[2], **and Mina Farid**[2]
University of Washington[1], Apple[2]
pranavpk@uw.edu,
{yiwen_sun, tsemere, adam_green2}@apple.com
{scott_manley, xiaoguang_qi, kunqian, yunyaoli, m_farid}@apple.com

Abstract

Identifying and integrating missing facts is a crucial task for knowledge graph completion to ensure robustness towards downstream applications such as question answering. Adding new facts to a knowledge graph in real world system often involves human verification effort, where candidate facts are verified for accuracy by human annotators. This process is labor-intensive, time-consuming, and inefficient since only a small number of missing facts can be identified. This paper proposes a simple but effective human-in-the-loop framework for fact collection that searches for a diverse set of highly relevant candidate facts for human annotation. Empirical results presented in this work demonstrate that the proposed solution leads to both improvements in i) the quality of the candidate facts as well as ii) the ability of discovering more facts to grow the knowledge graph without requiring additional human effort.

1 Introduction

A knowledge graph (KG) is an efficient way of storing information and relations between different types of entities, and is an integral part of many real-world applications such as question answering (Chen et al., 2020). However, incompleteness is a well-known issue that inherently exists in a KG caused by missing facts and entities, and it significantly limits the capability of the downstream applications (Socher et al., 2013). Since richness of the facts in a KG can directly impact its quality, identifying and collecting missing facts is a crucial task. Additionally, it is essential to ensure that the facts being added to KG are verified to be highly accurate.

There is research work published on how to automatically identify missing facts using machine learning models (Ji et al., 2021). Many of them use embedding models over the entities and relations in a KG to train link prediction models to predict missing facts within the KG (Nguyen et al., 2017; Wang et al., 2015), while some use a search-based question-answering approach to get candidate answers from the web and then identify the correct missing fact by aggregating the found answers (West et al., 2014). These approaches can automatically identify a large number of missing facts, but there was usually no human verification (which is also infeasible given the volume of the identified facts) to make sure that the newly discovered facts meet real-world-system-level accuracy.

Collecting high-quality new facts for a live KG is a very complicated process that often requires human effort. For example, the success of finding the birth date of a person from the web heavily depends on the popularity of the person and the uniqueness of their name. On the other hand, open access to the web makes it hard to protect the accuracy of its information; even Wikipedia suffers from vandalism (Šarūnė Bar). This influenced our initial design of a fact collection framework with a human-in-the-loop component. The system starts with an unanswerable query, leverages state-of-the-art technologies to identify the intent and entity of the input query, retrieves a few candidate answers via web search using a natural language based question-answering (QA) system, then instead of using a machine learning model to aggregate the results, e.g., (West et al., 2014), we direct the candidate facts to human annotators for review.

While this pipeline is successfully deployed in a real world system, there is an opportunity for improvements to be made. We observed that the natural language-based QA system sometimes returns no candidate answer for a query, leading to a low coverage problem. On the other hand, even if the QA system returns some candidate answers for certain queries, many of them do not contain the correct answers. In such cases, the human annotations ended up with negative responses, indicating a waste of human labor. To address this problem,

*Work done during an internship at Apple.

Proceedings of the Fourth Workshop on Data Science with Human-in-the-Loop (Language Advances), pages 74 - 80
December 8, 2022 ©2022 Association for Computational Linguistics

one option is to train a better QA system either by using more data or adopting more complicated models, which needs expensive engineering efforts. Another option is to increase the number of candidates returned by the QA system and involve more human annotators for fact verification, but because of the low-correct-ratio nature of the candidate answers, this approach would mean an even more severe waste of human effort.

In this paper a new human-in-the-loop fact collection framework is proposed that addresses the aforementioned problems without training new QA systems nor adding additional human annotators. To solve the low coverage problem of the QA system, the input query is perturbed by generating semantically equivalent variations of it. These variations are then input to the QA system to get diverse answer sets (similar to what has been done in (West et al., 2014)). Then, to address the low-correct-answer-ratio problem, a candidate answer selector is introduced, inspired by the well-known uncertainty-based active sampling strategy Query-by-Committee (QbC) (Seung et al., 1992; Freund et al., 1997; Gurajada et al., 2019), to choose the most relevant answers for human annotation. To summarize, the main contributions of this work are:

- A simple but effective human-in-the-loop fact collection framework that uses a natural language-based QA system as a black-box model to collect diverse candidate answers from the open web.
- By employing a QbC-based selector, the proposed framework can identify more relevant candidate answers and filter out less relevant ones to effectively identify more missing facts with limited human annotation budget.
- Empirically it is observed that this approach can significantly improve both recall and relevancy of the fact collection process in real world settings. Moreover, although only two intent use cases were reported in the experiments, the framework is generic enough to be immediately extended to many more scenarios.

The rest of this paper is organized as follows: Sections 2 describes our human-in-the-loop fact collection framework. Section 3 demonstrates experimental results. Section 4 reviews related work. Finally, concluding remarks and future works are included in Section 5.

2 Methodology

Architecture of the proposed system is illustrated in Figure 1. User query answering is generally carried out by a two-stage model that first extracts the relevant information relating to the intent of the query from a web page, then ranks and selects the most relevant articles that match the entity and the intent of the query. This process can be improved by fine tuning the model used, though it requires quality data and is time-consuming. The proposed framework does not rely on fine tuning but makes changes to the input of the model. The system leverages the sensitivity of language based models to the input and combines it with a selector that works on the principle of Query-by-Committee. The rest of the section shall illustrate each component of the proposed pipeline via a concrete example.

2.1 Query Annotator

The input to Query Annotator is a user query that is unanswerable by the current KG. Assuming the KG does not currently contain the height of Michael Jordan, the following query is an example of an unanswerable query

q_1: `how tall is Michael Jordan?`

Given such a query, the main task for Query Annotator is to identify the intent of the query (e.g., '`height`') as well as the key named entities (e.g., '`Michael Jordan`') in the query. All these rich annotations will be added to the original query and sent to the next component Query Synthesizer to generate query variations. As a concrete example, for the unanswerable query mentioned earlier, the output of Query Annotator would be:

q'_1: `how tall is Michael Jordan?`
`- entity:` $\langle$ `'Michael Jordan',` $kgid$ $\rangle$
`- intent: 'height',`

where $kgid$ is an identifier of the entity in the KG.

2.2 Query Synthesizer

Given a query q' enriched with key named entities and intent, the Query Synthesizer tries to generate semantically equivalent variations and perturbations of q'. A template-based approach is used to create new synthetic queries by replacing the entities in the sentence (e.g., '`how tall is [PERSON ENTITY]`'). Additional information about the detected entities from the KG, such as *occupation* or *aliases* are also used to generate new variations

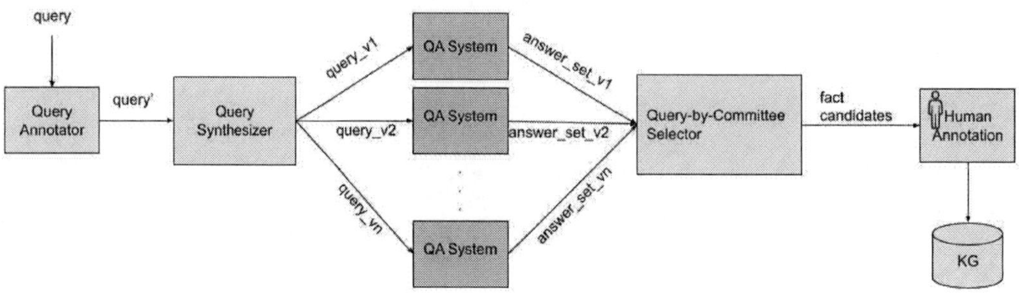

Figure 1: Proposed System Architecture using query by committee. Note that the QA System is kept fixed.

(e.g., '`Michael Jordan`' can be replaced with one of the aliases '`Michael Jeffrey Jordan`').

There are two main requirements for the Query Synthesizer: (1) only semantically equivalent queries should be created; (2) the generated queries should be natural and realistic. It is evident that semantically nonequivalent queries lead to undesirable results, which would hurt precision. Moreover, it is also crucial that the newly generated queries remain natural to humans, so the QA system which was trained to understand natural language questions can return meaningful answers. To meet these requirements, a randomly sampled anonymous query log is analyzed in order to understand user behaviour and how users interact with web search. Based on that, multiple templates to ask single question are determined. The question templates depend heavily on the intent of the query, and therefore different templates for each intent and entity pair were generated. For example, the query '`how tall is Michael Jordan?`' might be translated to

q_1^1: `what's the height of Michael Jordan?`
q_1^2: `tell me Michael Jordan's height.`
q_1^3: `how tall is Michael Jeffrey Jordan?`
...

The main benefit of creating such variations of the input query is to provide the QA system with more diverse signals, leading to more potential answers that might not be found by asking the original query alone.

2.3 QA System

The QA system is responsible for searching and retrieving answers from the internet that are relevant to the input question. In the proposed system, a state-of-the-art QA system is used as a black-box to get candidate answers for a given query. The input to the QA system is a natural question, and the output is a ranked list of answer tuples, where each tuple is of the format `(passage, fact, score)`. `Passage` is the passage from a web page that may contain the fact that can answer the question, `fact` is an extracted and normalized answer to the question, and `score` is a confidence score that the QA system calculated that indicates the quality of the answer found. As a running example, one answer tuple could be `(...a height he himself claimed in 1994 "I'm 6-foot-6"... , '6-foot-6', 0.49)`. Although the QA system may return a lot of answers for a given query, only the top-k tuples by score are kept, where k is a hyperparameter of the system usually set to a small number such as 3 or 5.

One thing to emphasize is that the QA system is very sensitive to the input. Changing the language or ordering of the input query may lead to obtaining different types of answers as the output. This also motivated us to use semantically equivalent variations of the original query to get diverse answer sets to improve the recall. While, one potential pitfall is that the answer sets returned from the QA system can be noisy. For example, for the query `How tall is Michael Jordan?`, some of the passages the QA system returns are extracted from the following webpages:

- `anonymous-url-1` - a webpage that contains multiple different answers
- `anonymous-url-2` - a webpage that contains the word height and Michael Jordan, but not the answer

These issues can come up with any entity and intent. It is very difficult to identify. This is a major motivation for us to adopt multiple variations of the query. Additionally, the noisy results indicate that blindly trusting the results returned by the QA system may hurt precision of the system, therefore, the next component Query-by-Committee selector is adopted to prune the answer sets.

2.4 Query-by-Committee Selector

While the previous Query Synthesizer and QA system components focus on improving the recall by creating semantically equivalent variations, the Query-by-Committee Selector aims to improve precision by selecting the most relevant candidate answers. After receiving the likely noisy answer sets from the QA system in previous step, an immediate question is how to distinguish relevant and irrelevant answer sets. Towards this, a selection approach motivated by the well-known sampling strategy Query-by-Committee is introduced.

QbC is an uncertainty-based modal agnostic active learning algorithm. The core idea of QbC is to form a voting committee consisting of multiple classifiers that were trained in slightly different ways. The degree of agreement among the committee is used as a proxy for uncertainty. If the committee highly disagrees on the label of a data point, then it is an uncertain example, which should have higher priority to be manually verified than those examples where the committee highly agree. Active learning uses this approach to choose the most uncertain and informative examples for human annotation.

Motivated by the idea of using degree of agreement to measure uncertainty, the proposed solution uses QbC in an opposite way, that is, instead of identifying uncertain examples, the goal is to identify highly certain examples. To simulate the QbC-based sampling, a voting committee has to be formed. One option is to perturb the models, i.e., train multiple variations of the QA systems, and another option is to perturb the input query. The proposed solution chooses the second one because it requires much less computational resources, and it is easier to maintain. Therefore, semantically equivalent variations of the input query are generated, which will be sent to the same QA system to get multiple, but likely different answer sets. Next, to identify the most relevant answer among these answer sets, all the answer tuples are ordered based on the number of occurrences in the returned answer sets, finally the top-p answer tuples are chosen as candidates for human annotation.

Note that, the voting mechanism provides a good way to overrule the confidence score returned by the QA system, because an answer tuple with lower confidence score might rank higher than a higher-scoring answer tuple if it gets more votes, which is a way to mitigate the potential bias existed in the QA system. The confidence scores calculated by the QA system is only used as a secondary metric to rank answer tuples.

In this example illustrated here, assuming that it is required of the Selector to select only the top 2 candidate answers that are relevant to `{height, Michael Jordan}`. The first answer set contains `anonymous-url-1` and `anonymous-url-2`. The second answer set contains `anonymous-url-1`, `Wikipedia`, and `anonymous-url-3`. Assuming that the order of score for these answer sets is: `Wikipedia > anonymous-url-1 > anonymous-url-3 > anonymous-url-2`. Since `anonymous-url-1` appeared in both runs of the model, it is ranked the highest. The other three candidates all appear only once. Then, based on the tie-breaker condition, i.e., ordered by confidence scores returned by the QA system, `Wikipedia`, which has the highest score, is selected as the second candidate answer. These selected answers move on to the next step human annotation.

2.5 Human Annotation

The candidate answers received from the QbC Selector will be verified by human annotators before integrated with the KG. Considering the given example, the human annotator would open the url of the website (e.g., `anonymous-url-1`) in a candidate answer tuple, check if the passage indeed comes from the webpage, then make a judgment call on whether or not the extracted fact (e.g., `6-foot-6`) is the correct answer.

3 Experiments

Implementation and Dataset. We implemented the system in python and used PySpark[1] for distributed computation tasks. A randomly sampled anonymous set from query logs is used to evaluate the proposed framework. It contains queries (entity-intent pairs) that did not have answers available in the knowledge graph. The dataset consists of 3648 unique entities for 2 intents.

Experiment setting. The proposed solution is compared against a baseline system, i.e., the system without the Query Synthesizer and QbC Selector. Concretely, the baseline model simply takes an unanswerable query, sends it to the QA system to

[1]https://spark.apache.org/docs/latest/api/python/

	Baseline	Proposed framework (ours)
Failed Answer Ratio	6.69%	**0.10%**
Recall	1102/1441 = 76.5%	1418/1441 = **98%**
Avg. Answer Confidence Score	0.5734	**0.5944**

Table 1: Results for intent 1.

	Baseline	Proposed framework(ours)
Failed Answer Ratio	5.69%	**0.07%**
Recall	1719/2207 = 77.9%	2183/2207 = **98.9%**
Avg. Answer Confidence Score	0.4297	**0.4492**

Table 2: Results for intent 2.

get the top-p answer candidates, then request human annotation. For both the baseline system and the proposed solution, the top-5 (i.e., $p = 5$) answers from the QA system are requested. In this comparison study, the following evaluation metrics are considered:

- ***Recall*** - fraction of input queries that can be answered.
- ***Failed Answer Ratio*** - fraction of input queries that result in an empty candidate answer set from the QA system.
- ***Answer Confidence*** - the average confidence scores of candidate answers provided by the QA system.
- ***Inter-annotator agreement (IAA)*** - given a query q and a candidate answer set A, the IAA of q and A is, the fraction of annotators found the correct answer to the query q from the answer set A, i.e.,

$$\text{IAA}_A^q = \frac{\text{\# annotators found the answer for } q \text{ in} A}{\text{\# of annotators reviewed } q},$$

These metrics evaluate the system in different aspects. Recall evaluates that the proposed method can indeed find more missing facts and increase the number of answerable queries. The failed answer ratio is different from recall in the sense that the former acts as a coverage metric to measure how well the system can find potential answers (not necessarily correct answers) for an input query. Answer confidence serves as a guardrail metric for the QbC Selector. Candidate answers with more votes should have higher confidence scores calculated by the QA system. Finally, IAA is a proxy for evaluating the relevancy of the answer set. Higher IAA values indicate that the candidate answers have higher relevancy and quality, hence easier to reach a consensus among annotators, though not directly related to recall.

Results. Tables 1 and 2 show that our proposed framework performs better across all measurements when compared to the baseline.

For both intents, we observed significant recall boosts indicating that our method is much more effective than the baseline model at finding the correct answers for broader input queries. To make the baseline system reach the parity, an intuitive approach would be to retrieve more candidate answers, so instead of the top-5, top-10 answers from the QA systems could be sent to annotators for review. This would substantially increase the amount of human annotation effort, though a good portion of it will be used to verify incorrect answers, which is actually saved by our system. Another observation is that our approach significantly decreased the Failed Answer Ratio, which can be explained by the fact that introducing Query Synthesizer to generate variations of the input query triggered the QA system to retrieve candidate answers that might have been overlooked by the baseline which runs the QA system only once per query. The average Answer Confidence score returned by the QA system is higher for our framework, which indicates that when using QbC method more relevant candidate answers can be identified. Meanwhile, less relevant answers with lower confidence scores are filtered out by the committee vote. Hence, higher scores indicate higher precision in finding quality answers to questions.

Table 3 shows the IAA comparison between both frameworks for the two intents respectively. As seen in the table, the IAA for our framework is higher than the baseline, which suggests that the candidate answers from our framework are more relevant to the queries, so different annotators come to an agreement more often. Although the IAA number increased only by a small margin, keep

	Baseline	Ours
IAA(intent 1)	64.81%	65%
IAA(intent 2)	68.89%	70.83%

Table 3: Inter-annotator agreement on an average for two intents between baseline and our framework.

in mind that our framework has significantly increased the recall than the baseline. This indicates that our method can find many more answers than the baseline without degrading the quality of the answers.

4 Related Work

In (West et al., 2014), the authors adopted a very similar idea of perturbing the input query, then they used a search-engine with open web access to identify diverse answers, and finally aggregated the answers using scoring model to identify the most likely answers. Although this work is in same spirit, the proposed approach is different from theirs in two ways: first, a much simpler aggregation mechanism without the need to train a scoring model is used, thus the proposed approach is easier to implement and can work with any QA system; second, human-in-the-loop verification is included to ensure the high quality of identified facts.

In addition to improving the human annotation effectiveness, reducing human annotation efforts is another related research topic. A lot of the work try to solve this problem by introducing a deep learning or machine learning model(Varga and Lőrincz, 2020). Certain papers also aim to reduce the annotation work by selecting only samples that are optimal to training the model(Zesch et al., 2015). The proposed solution is different from these works as this solution does not train new machine learning models to reduce annotation efforts rather uses selective sampling.

The use of QbC to identify relevant answers is also related to the ensemble learning paradigm, where the goal is to improve the predictive performance of a single model by training multiple variations and combining their predictions (Sagi and Rokach, 2018; Dietterich et al., 2002). In fact, QbC can be viewed as a way to create the ensemble with the specific purpose of using it to identify uncertain examples for active learning (Melville and Mooney, 2004; Krogh and Vedelsby, 1994). Both QbC and ensemble learning require creating a group of slightly different models so that a diverse predictions or decisions can be later combined or integrated to produce more accurate prediction. The proposed approach was inspired by this idea, and unlike QbC whose primary focus is to identify uncertain examples for human annotation to decrease the uncertainty of the model (Gilad-bachrach et al., 2005), the goal here is to identify certain examples.

Ranking web search results is an important topic in elevating user experience. There are various approaches that try to solve this problem. Aggregated search results and re-ranking based on similarity is one of the solutions(Kumar and Nath, 2013). While this work takes inspiration from the aggregated search results, the proposed solution differs in the re-ranking aspect. Similarity of web pages is not checked for, instead the voting mechanism in the QbC selector to find the best potential answers.

5 Conclusion & Future Work

This paper proposes a new framework that aims to reduce the efforts of human annotators in the fact collection process for enriching a knowledge graph. Empirical observations of the proposed solution when compared against a baseline framework demonstrate that the proposed framework has better recall, and can identify much more relevant facts. This framework is easy to implement, provides an additional automated and scalable layer of enrichment to web answer retrieval, and gives a significant boost to the fact collection process in terms of quality and coverage. Future work shall include testing the proposed framework within other domains such as open domain question answering. Moreover, this framework can significantly boost the recall, which can help in collecting more labeled data to train a model to predict the reliability of a website given a query's intent. In this way, the QA system can be enhanced to provide more relevant candidate answers.

References

Xiaojun Chen, Shengbin Jia, and Yang Xiang. 2020. A review: Knowledge reasoning over knowledge graph. *Expert Systems with Applications*, 141:112948.

Thomas G Dietterich et al. 2002. Ensemble learning. *The handbook of brain theory and neural networks*, 2(1):110–125.

Yoav Freund, H. Sebastian Seung, Eli Shamir, and Naftali Tishby. 1997. Selective sampling using the query by committee algorithm. *Machine Learning*, 28(2):133–168.

Ran Gilad-bachrach, Amir Navot, and Naftali Tishby. 2005. Query by committee made real. In *Advances in Neural Information Processing Systems*, volume 18. MIT Press.

Sairam Gurajada, Lucian Popa, Kun Qian, and Prithviraj Sen. 2019. Learning-based methods with human-in-the-loop for entity resolution. In *Proceedings of the 28th ACM International Conference on Information and Knowledge Management*, pages 2969–2970.

Shaoxiong Ji, Shirui Pan, Erik Cambria, Pekka Marttinen, and S Yu Philip. 2021. A survey on knowledge graphs: Representation, acquisition, and applications. *IEEE Transactions on Neural Networks and Learning Systems*, 33(2):494–514.

Anders Krogh and Jesper Vedelsby. 1994. Neural network ensembles, cross validation, and active learning. *Advances in neural information processing systems*, 7.

Naresh Kumar and Rajender Nath. 2013. A meta search engine approach for organizing web search results using ranking and clustering.

Prem Melville and Raymond J Mooney. 2004. Diverse ensembles for active learning. In *Proceedings of the twenty-first international conference on Machine learning*, page 74.

Dai Quoc Nguyen, Tu Dinh Nguyen, Dat Quoc Nguyen, and Dinh Phung. 2017. A novel embedding model for knowledge base completion based on convolutional neural network. *arXiv preprint arXiv:1712.02121*.

Omer Sagi and Lior Rokach. 2018. Ensemble learning: A survey. *Wiley Interdisciplinary Reviews: Data Mining and Knowledge Discovery*, 8(4):e1249.

H. S. Seung, M. Opper, and H. Sompolinsky. 1992. Query by committee. In *Proceedings of the Fifth Annual Workshop on Computational Learning Theory*, COLT '92, page 287–294, New York, NY, USA. Association for Computing Machinery.

Richard Socher, Danqi Chen, Christopher D Manning, and Andrew Ng. 2013. Reasoning with neural tensor networks for knowledge base completion. *Advances in neural information processing systems*, 26.

Viktor Varga and András Lőrincz. 2020. Reducing human efforts in video segmentation annotation with reinforcement learning. *Neurocomputing*, 405:247–258.

Quan Wang, Bin Wang, and Li Guo. 2015. Knowledge base completion using embeddings and rules. In *Twenty-fourth international joint conference on artificial intelligence*.

Robert West, Evgeniy Gabrilovich, Kevin Murphy, Shaohua Sun, Rahul Gupta, and Dekang Lin. 2014. Knowledge base completion via search-based question answering. In *Proceedings of the 23rd international conference on World wide web*, pages 515–526.

Torsten Zesch, Michael Heilman, and Aoife Cahill. 2015. Reducing annotation efforts in supervised short answer scoring. In *Proceedings of the Tenth Workshop on Innovative Use of NLP for Building Educational Applications*, pages 124–132, Denver, Colorado. Association for Computational Linguistics.

Šarūnė Bar. 64 of the funniest wikipedia edits by internet vandals. `https://www.boredpanda.com/funny-wikipedia-edits/?utm_source=google&utm_medium=organic&utm_campaign=organic`. Accessed: 2022-09-15.

AVA-TMP: A Human-in-the-Loop Multi-layer Dynamic Topic Modeling Pipeline

Viseth Sean, Padideh Danaee, Yang Yang, Hakan Kardes
Alignment Health, Orange, CA
{vsean, pdanaee, yyang, hkardes}@ahcusa.com

Abstract

A phone call is still one of the primary preferred channels for seniors to express their needs, ask questions, and inform potential problems to their health insurance plans. Alignment Health is a next-generation, consumer-centric organization that is providing a variety of Medicare Advantage Products for seniors. We combine our proprietary technology platform, AVA, and our high-touch clinical model to provide seniors with care as it should be: high quality, low cost, and accompanied by a vastly improved consumer experience. Our members have the ability to connect with our member services and concierge teams 24/7 for a wide variety of ever-changing reasons through different channels, such as phone, email, and messages. We strive to provide an excellent member experience and ensure our members are getting the help and information they need at every touch — ideally, even before they reach us. This requires ongoing monitoring of reasons for contacting us, ensuring agents are equipped with the right tools and information to serve members, and coming up with proactive strategies to eliminate the need for the call when possible.

We developed an NLP-based dynamic call reason tagging and reporting pipeline with an optimized human-in-the-loop approach to enable accurate call reason reporting and monitoring with the ability to see high-level trends as well as drill down into more granular sub-reasons. Our system produces 96.4% precision and 30%-50% better recall in tagging calls with proper reasons. We have also consistently achieved a 60+ Net Promoter Score (NPS) score, which illustrates high consumer satisfaction.

1 Introduction

As a consumer-centered healthcare company, we provide our members with experienced member services and concierge teams through our contact center that are available around the clock for a wide variety of inquiries or potential problems. It is crucial for us to monitor the typical causes of why members contact us so that we proactively address the problems or help our members need through their preferred channel even before they reach out to us. To this end, during each call, member service agents take detailed notes on what is discussed during the call, the reason for the call, and any actions taken. They also tag each call with one or more call reason categories from a pre-defined list that was initially built by member experience supervisors to capture call reasons in a more structured manner. There are several drawbacks and limitations to this approach:

- High number of calls that are documented as "General FAQ" or "Other" call reason category due to lack of precise reason category representing the call
- Labor-intensive and not scalable processes to keep pre-defined call reason categories with corresponding subcategories manually up-to-date with high quality while member needs and potential call reasons are continuously changing
- Incomplete and inaccurate call reason reporting

In this paper, we present a novel NLP-based multi-layer dynamic topic modeling pipeline, AVA-TMP, with an effective human-in-the-loop approach that leverages subject matter experts. It enables highly accurate and timely call reason logging, monitoring, and reporting, as well as increased first-time resolution rates. Our pipeline produces a high-quality call reasons list with sub-reason drill-downs and automatically identifies newly emerging high-quality topics eliminating the need for labor-intensive evaluation of high-volume call notes by the customer service supervisors. Our pipeline also increases the efficiency of customer service agents by automatically suggesting a ranked list of relevant topics to tag as

Proceedings of the Fourth Workshop on Data Science with Human-in-the-Loop (Language Advances), pages 81 - 87
December 8, 2022

agents take call notes. The presented pipeline is not limited to inbound calls, and it is applicable to omnichannel communications such as emails, messages, and chats. In the remainder of the paper, we first present the related work in section 2. Next, we describe our approach and evaluate its performance using several real-world datasets in section 3. Then, we evaluate the performance of our algorithm. Finally, we conclude in section 4.

2 Related Work

It has been a great stride in Natural Language Processing (NLP) advancement in recent years for learning, understanding, and producing human language content in more efficient and scalable ways (Hirschberg and Manning, 2015), such as text summarization (Widyassari et al., 2022), name entity recognition (Jiang et al., 2016), sentimental analysis (Bhavitha et al., 2017), text classification (Bhavani and Kumar, 2021), and topic modeling (Sandhiya et al., 2022).

Topic modeling is used to automatically identify the themes, i.e., topics, in unstructured text datasets (Blei et al., 2003b; Boyd-Graber et al., 2017), especially when there is a large volume of document collections and not enough time. These machine-generated topics are then used for reporting and tracking purposes. The traditional topic modeling pipelines (Chaney and Blei, 2012; Gardner et al., 2010; Eisenstein et al., 2012) do not allow the users to refine, clean, or personalize the model-generated topics hence lack an understanding of the end-user needs (Smith et al., 2018). The absence of an interactive and human-centered approach to refine topics and adjust data processing results in bias, noise, and unexpectedly poor real-world model performance. It is crucial to have an efficient and effective level of human contribution with AI to ensure satisfactory model performance.

Previous works have utilized topic modeling techniques with some level of human intervention to address customer needs. For example, a study by Agudelo and Manuel used Latent Dirichlet Allocation (LDA) (Blei et al., 2003b) based topic modeling approach to identify topics of inbound call transcripts for creating a better Interactive Voice Response (IVR) routing option so that customers are routed to the right agents (Agudelo and Manuel, 2019). However, they only provide the most important words to the end users and not the topic. The users then need to manually identify the topic associated with the words presented by the model which can be inconsistent among different users and adds an additional burden to their workflow. This process also results in assigning only one topic to a call which might not be a true representation of customer needs as one call might have multiple reasons and resolutions.

Another study by Chen and Wang utilized the LDA topic modeling technique to extract topics from chat transcripts between librarians and students in order to identify needs, provide help and allocate resources accordingly (Chen and Wang, 2019). However, this work lacks defining a qualitative performance measurement. Also, they assessed the quality of the topics intuitively with visualizations.

Besides topic modeling methods from machine learning, there are also qualitative analytic methods, such as grounded theory methodologies (Charmaz, 2006; Corbin and Strauss, 2008), for identifying topics in text datasets. Previous work by Baumer et al. focused on the comparison between grounded theory and topic modeling (Baumer et al., 2017). The authors found that the results of the two methods exhibited a degree of alignment in which many of the patterns found in the grounded theory were also represented in the topic modeling results. However, grounded theory is time-consuming and resource-intensive. Therefore, it doesn't scale well with large datasets.

Different from these previous works, we implemented a novel NLP-based system with human-in-the-loop stages to accurately tag high-level call reasons (one or multiple) along with sub-category drill-downs in a scalable and timely manner for each call. We also measured the real-world performance of our approach and compared it with the baseline (manual labeling).

3 Methodology

Our comprehensive end-to-end topic modeling pipeline, AVA-TMP, is illustrated in Figure 1. With AVA-TMP, we enhance the traditional NLP topic modeling pipeline with human-in-the-loop stages to significantly improve reporting accuracy, create operational efficiencies and increase member satisfaction.

Standard high-level topic modeling steps include Problem definition, Data collection, Data preparation (tokenization, lemmatization, and stop-word removal), Modeling, Post-processing & model eval-

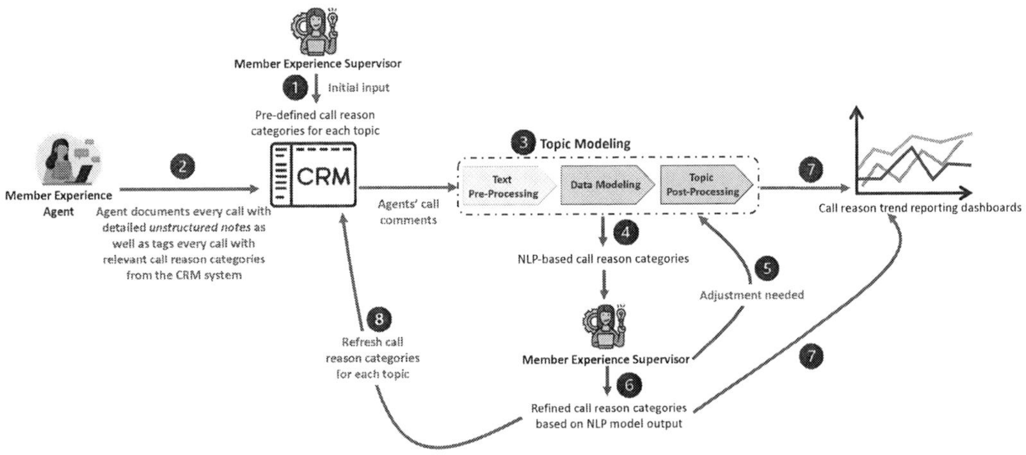

Figure 1: **Overview of AVA-TMP human-in-the-loop pipeline:** 1) Member experience supervisors create an initial list of call reasons for member experience agents to choose from. 2) Member experience agents take notes during calls and also select a reason why member calls from the initial list of reasons in 1). 3) We perform topic modeling on call notes to identify the reason(s) why members call us. 4) The NLP-based reasons are transferred to member experience supervisors for evaluation. 5) Member experience supervisors refine and adjust the newly generated list of reasons by NLP and send it back to step 3) if necessary. 6) Member experience supervisors finalize the new list of call reasons based on the NLP model. 7) We create a call reason trend reporting dashboard based on the new call reason list. 8) We refresh the call reason categories in the CRM system so member experience agents can properly assign reason tags to upcoming calls.

uation, and Model deployment. We altered and improved the standard topic modeling pipeline in three ways:

- First, instead of using call transcripts, which has its own drawbacks and limitations, we use call notes that are already curated by member service agents for documentation purposes. These call notes provide a more contextual and cleaner description of each call (Figure 1 - step 2).

- Second, our pipeline involves subject matter experts (SMEs) to refine call reason categories and sub-reasons to further validate and adjust topics identified by the model (Figure 1 - steps 5 and 6).

- Third, we introduce a multi-layer dynamic hierarchical topic modeling framework to identify hierarchical call reasons and sub-reasons in a flexible manner (Figure 2).

In the following subsections, we describe the major end-to-end steps from initial data collection to the final model deployment, and how they are being used.

3.1 Data Collection

For every member interaction, our member experience agents take notes summarizing what help or information the member needs and what action(s) they take to assist the member. These unstructured call notes provide more contextual information about the call and more standardized and cleaner input to our model compared to using call transcripts. For example, even though actual call conversations might happen in different languages, all call notes are captured in English. Furthermore, there might be incomplete sentences, inaccuracies due to the performance of voice-to-text translation, and other complexities to deal with in call transcripts.

Besides capturing call notes, agents also need to tag each call based on the pre-defined call reason categories. The call reason tagging in this step can help us with immediate reporting within the CRM system so that member experience supervisors can view real-time reports on the pre-defined call reasons as a stopgap measure and respond to the severity of each issue accordingly. However, keeping this list up-to-date is labor-intensive and requires member experience supervisors to manually go through large volume comments, investigate call reasons, and identify frequent emerging patterns. As we describe in section 3.4, our model eliminates the labor-intensive call note reviewing step and helps to keep the call reasons list continuously refreshed. These call reason tagging also help us to measure the real-world performance of our model on an ongoing basis as described in detail in section 3.5.

3.2 Data Preparation

We clean the unstructured text from agents' notes using various standard text pre-processing techniques before feeding it into our model. First, we remove special characters, punctuation, and stop-words from the text, and then convert them to lowercase. Next, the text is lemmatized to return inflected words to their root word. We do not use stemming as it does not provide any performance improvement, which is in line with what other researchers found previously (Schofield and Mimno, 2016). Beyond these common text pre-processing techniques, we clean certain unnecessary and repetitive patterns that do not add value to the call tagging process such as confirmed demographics, or courtesy of callers. The processed dataset is then fed into the model.

3.3 Topic Modeling

After preparing the data, we utilize commonly used topic modeling techniques, LDA (Blei et al., 2003b) and a BERT-based method, BERTopic (Grootendorst, 2022) to achieve the best performance.

To accurately identify the call reason categories and sub-reason drill-downs, we construct a multi-layer topic modeling framework (as illustrated in Figure 2). First, we run the topic modeling with all the call notes to identify the high-level call reasons. Next, we run separate models to extract sub-reasons for each high-level call reason using the subset of call notes associated with the corresponding high-level topic. We repeat this step for another layer to get a further drill-down of each sub-reason. This approach gives us the flexibility to set the different number of topics at each stage and fine-tune the quality of topics. For example, we can start with 50 topics to identify high-level reasons, then in the next layer we can use 10 topics for sub-reasons, and finally 5 topics in the third layer to identify sub-sub-reasons. Each topic generated by the topic model is accompanied by their corresponding top n keywords that explain what the topic is about. We are also able to set different thresholds at each layer to optimize the quality of keyword groups for each topic/sub-topic/sub-sub-topic.

Another benefit of this multi-layer approach is the ability to pick different "n" for "n-gram" construction for the keywords representing each topic. For example, high-level topics have up to tri-grams since they are representing high-level reasons while sub-reasons and sub-sub-reasons are configured to have longer n-grams. We spent significant effort tuning parameters for both LDA and BERTopic within this framework in order to obtain the best possible results.

We choose BERTopic as our final topic modeling technique and 50/10/5 topics for different layers of our multi-layer topic modeling framework as it produced better performance and significantly reduced the review time by SMEs in our use case. Please also note that our multi-layer hierarchical topic modeling framework allows us to have more flexibility and control to adjust various parameters and fine-tune the quality compared to built-in hierarchical topic models like hLDA (Blei et al., 2003a).

3.4 Subject Matter Expert Evaluation

The NLP-based call reason categories from the topic modeling step are then passed to the member experience team for review (Figure 1 - step 4). They start evaluating the list of topics, pinpointing potential issues, identifying bias in the data, and requesting certain refinements such as grouping certain topics into one category, eliminating poor quality and biased topics, and choosing a more user-friendly topic name. These steps help fine-tune the NLP model performance and improve the processes to better understand call trends. This feedback loop might be repeated a few times till desired performance is achieved (Figure 1 - steps 3 to 5).

3.5 Performance Evaluation

In this section, we present the experimental results for our human-in-the-loop topic modeling pipeline, AVA-TMP. There are different ways to measure the performance of the topic models (Hoyle et al., 2021; Chang et al., 2009). We use two different real-world datasets for our experiments to measure both precision and recall of our system. We also compare the performance of the system with the baseline, which is the previous agent tagging using the pre-defined call reasons list during the call prior to developing AVA-TMP.

The first dataset includes randomly selected 500 actual call notes. We run AVA-TMP and generated

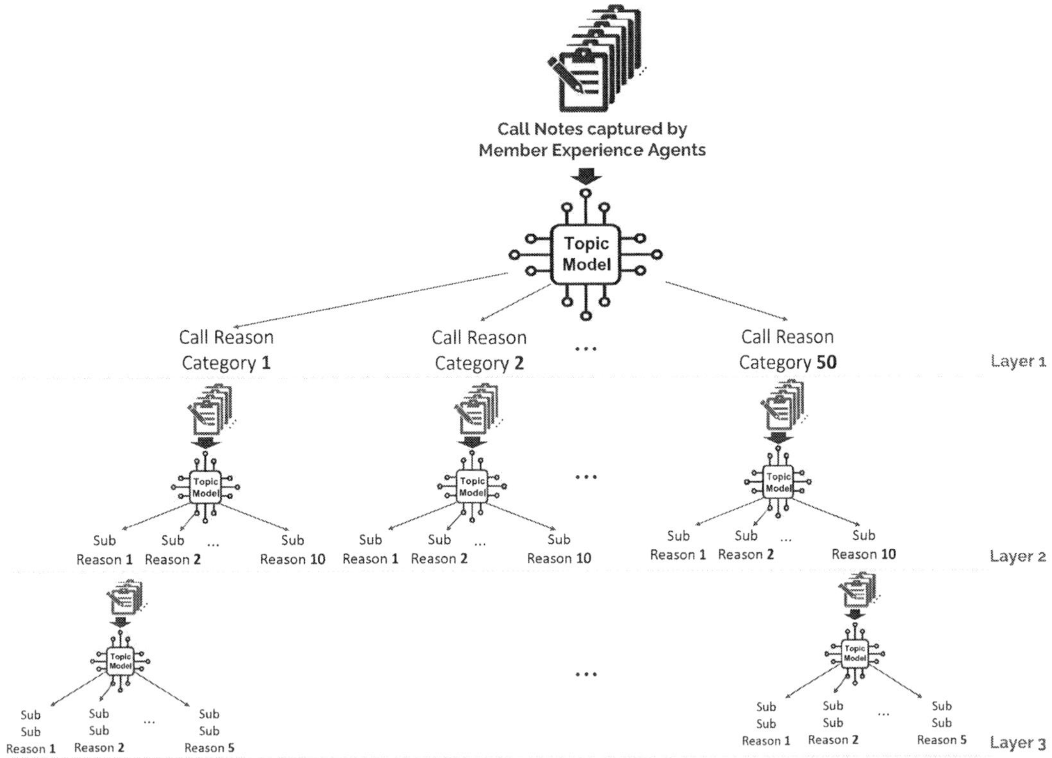

Figure 2: **Multi-layer Dynamic Hierarchical Topic Modeling**

all the call reasons for each call. As mentioned earlier, we already have baseline call reasons for these notes. Three independent SMEs evaluated both AVA-TMP output and baseline tags. SMEs reviewed and labeled each call note and corresponding reasons including all the drill-downs as True Positive (TP) or False Positive (FP). When there are conflicts among SMEs, we use the majority vote. We then computed the precision. AVA-TMP achieved a precision of 96.4% while the baseline precision was 23.4%.

Secondly, we use a much larger dataset to measure the recall improvement with the AVA-TMP system where high-level call reasons overlap with the baseline. We used 3 years of call notes history (1M+ calls) and compared the high-level call reason categories identified by AVA-TMP with the baseline. AVA-TMP achieves 30% to 50% higher recall than baseline depending on the high-level call reason categories. Please note that AVA-TMP identifies new call reason categories that don't exist in the baseline but we didn't include them in the recall analysis since the volume was negligible on a large scale.

3.6 Model Deployment

After generating refined call reason categories and sub-reason drill-downs (Figure 1 - step 6), we deploy our model to production to tag the upcoming calls on an ongoing basis for reporting and tracking purposes (Figure 1 - step 7). The pre-defined call reason categories are also updated in the CRM system accordingly for member experience agents to utilize (Figure 1 - steps 8).

The AVA-TMP is deployed as a real-time service. We run the model on the backend and provide suggested call reasons for tagging in a ranked order. Agents can then select one or multiple labels from the ranked topic list. This process aids the agents to minimize the time going through the entire list and decreases human error in the process.

3.7 Reporting & Tracking Call Trends

It is essential to continuously monitor the call trends to understand members' needs, proactively resolve emerging issues, and measure the member experience improvements. AVA-TMP provides timely and accurate call reasons after every call note is completed. We then feed all these into our reporting and tracking dashboard to monitor newly emerging issues and trends over time (Figure 1 - step 7).

4 Conclusion

In this paper, we demonstrate a novel topic modeling pipeline, AVA-TMP, that consists of multilayer dynamic hierarchical topic modeling with the human-in-the-loop approach for call analytics. Our results illustrate having human-in-the-loop in an advanced NLP pipeline can optimize model performance, reduce manual tasks in the current workflows, and improve overall business outcomes while helping achieve high member satisfaction.

With this framework, we achieved significantly better performance using real-world datasets for evaluation. Alignment Health has also consistently achieved an overall NPS, which is a widely used metric to measure customer experience, of 60+ as a Medicare Advantage plan, compared to the industry average of 30 for healthcare insurance (Ian Luck, 2022; Alignment Healthcare, 2022).

AVA-TMP enables us to have an improved call reporting and tracking system. We can identify seasonal trends for demands, inquiries, or emerging issues and develop proactive and systemic plans for improvement. It also creates operational efficiencies by eliminating the need for various labor-intensive tasks such as i) having an up-to-date call reason list, ii) manual call reason tagging, and iii) manual ad-hoc reports.

Even though we illustrated the AVA-TMP pipeline on call notes, it is applicable to omnichannel communications such as calls, emails, messages, and chats. It can be also used on call transcripts in addition to the call notes for improved outcomes.

References

B. E. Llano Agudelo and Juan Manuel. 2019. Calls' topic recognition.

Alignment Healthcare. 2022. Alignment healthcare esg report. `https://www.alignmenthealth.com/Alignment/media/pdf/Alignment_ESGReport_080422_508.pdf`.

Eric Ps Baumer, David Mimno, Shion Guha, Emily Quan, and Geri Gay. 2017. Comparing grounded theory and topic modeling: Extreme divergence or unlikely convergence? *Journal of the Association for Information Science and Technology*, 68.

A. C. Bhavani and B.J Santhosh Kumar. 2021. A review of state art of text classification algorithms. *2021 5th International Conference on Computing Methodologies and Communication (ICCMC)*, pages 1484–1490.

Budeti Bhavitha, Anisha P. Rodrigues, and Niranjan N. Chiplunkar. 2017. Comparative study of machine learning techniques in sentimental analysis. *2017 International Conference on Inventive Communication and Computational Technologies (ICICCT)*, pages 216–221.

David M. Blei, Thomas L. Griffiths, Michael I. Jordan, and Joshua B. Tenenbaum. 2003a. Hierarchical topic models and the nested chinese restaurant process. In *NIPS*.

David M. Blei, A. Ng, and Michael I. Jordan. 2003b. Latent dirichlet allocation. *J. Mach. Learn. Res.*, 3:993–1022.

Jordan L. Boyd-Graber, Yuening Hu, and David Mimno. 2017. Applications of topic models. *Found. Trends Inf. Retr.*, 11:143–296.

Allison Chaney and David Blei. 2012. Visualizing topic models. In *Proceedings of the International AAAI Conference on Web and Social Media*, volume 6, pages 419–422.

Jonathan Chang, Jordan L. Boyd-Graber, Sean Gerrish, Chong Wang, and David M. Blei. 2009. Reading tea leaves: How humans interpret topic models. In *NIPS*.

Kathy Charmaz. 2006. Constructing grounded theory: A practical guide through qualitative analysis.

Xiaoju Chen and Huajin Wang. 2019. Automated chat transcript analysis using topic modeling for library reference services. *Proceedings of the Association for Information Science and Technology*, 56.

Juliet Corbin and Anselm Strauss. 2008. Basics of qualitative research: Techniques and procedures for developing grounded theory.

Jacob Eisenstein, Duen Horng Chau, Aniket Kittur, and Eric Xing. 2012. Topicviz: Interactive topic exploration in document collections. In *CHI'12 Extended Abstracts on Human Factors in Computing Systems*, pages 2177–2182.

Matthew J Gardner, Joshua Lutes, Jeff Lund, Josh Hansen, Dan Walker, Eric Ringger, and Kevin Seppi. 2010. The topic browser: An interactive tool for browsing topic models. In *Nips workshop on challenges of data visualization*, volume 2, page 2. Whistler Canada.

Maarten R. Grootendorst. 2022. Bertopic: Neural topic modeling with a class-based tf-idf procedure. *ArXiv*, abs/2203.05794.

Julia Hirschberg and Christopher D. Manning. 2015. Advances in natural language processing. *Science*, 349:261 – 266.

Alexander Miserlis Hoyle, Pranav Goel, Denis Peskov, Andrew Hian-Cheong, Jordan L. Boyd-Graber, and Philip Resnik. 2021. Is automated topic model evaluation broken?: The incoherence of coherence. In *NeurIPS*.

Ian Luck. 2022. 25 insurance nps scores for 2022 + nps in insurance guide. https://customergauge.com/benchmarks/blog/nps-insurance-industry-net-promoter-scores.

Ridong Jiang, Rafael E. Banchs, and Haizhou Li. 2016. Evaluating and combining name entity recognition systems. In *NEWS@ACM*.

Ramesh Sandhiya, A. M. Boopika, M. K. Akshatha, S. V. Swetha, and N. M. Hariharan. 2022. A review of topic modeling and its application. *Handbook of Intelligent Computing and Optimization for Sustainable Development*.

Alexandra Schofield and David Mimno. 2016. Comparing apples to apple: The effects of stemmers on topic models. *Transactions of the Association for Computational Linguistics*, 4:287–300.

Alison Smith, Varun Kumar, Jordan Boyd-Graber, Kevin Seppi, and Leah Findlater. 2018. Closing the loop: User-centered design and evaluation of a human-in-the-loop topic modeling system. In *23rd International Conference on Intelligent User Interfaces*, pages 293–304.

Adhika Pramita Widyassari, Supriadi Rustad, Guruh Fajar Shidik, Edi Noersasongko, Abdul Syukur, Affandy Affandy, and De Rosal Ignatius Moses Setiadi. 2022. Review of automatic text summarization techniques & methods. *J. King Saud Univ. Comput. Inf. Sci.*, 34:1029–1046.

Improving Named Entity Recognition in Telephone Conversations via Effective Active Learning with Human in the Loop

Md Tahmid Rahman Laskar, Cheng Chen, Xue-Yong Fu, Shashi Bhushan TN
Dialpad Canada Inc.
Vancouver, BC, Canada
{tahmid.rahman,cchen,xue-yong,sbhushan}@dialpad.com

Abstract

Telephone transcription data can be very noisy due to speech recognition errors, disfluencies, etc. Not only that annotating such data is very challenging for the annotators, but also such data may have lots of annotation errors even after the annotation job is completed, resulting in a very poor model performance. In this paper, we present an active learning framework that leverages human in the loop learning to identify data samples from the annotated dataset for re-annotation that are more likely to contain annotation errors. In this way, we largely reduce the need for data re-annotation for the whole dataset. We conduct extensive experiments with our proposed approach for Named Entity Recognition and observe that by re-annotating only about 6% training instances out of the whole dataset, the F1 score for a certain entity type can be significantly improved by about 25%.

1 Introduction

We describe a Named Entity Recognition (NER) system that needs to provide realtime functionality in a commercial communication-as-a-service (CaaS) platform such as displaying information related to the named entities to a customer support agent during a call with a customer. The primary focus for this NER system is to identify *product* and *organization* type entities that appear in English business telephone conversation transcripts. Since these transcripts are produced by an automatic speech recognition (ASR) system, they are inherently noisy due to the nature of spoken communication as well as limitations of the ASR system, resulting in dysfluencies, filled pauses, and lack of information related to punctuation and case (Fu et al., 2021). These issues make the annotation of such noisy datasets very challenging for the annotators, making the annotation job for such data more difficult than datasets that contain typed text (Meng et al., 2021; Malmasi et al., 2022).

To our best knowledge, the publicly available NER datasets mostly contain typed text. Moreover, there are no existing NER datasets that match the characteristics of the ASR transcripts in the domain of business telephone conversations (Li et al., 2020). Thus, training an NER model in the context of business telephone transcripts requires a large annotated version of such data (Fu et al., 2022b) consisting of *product* or *organization* type entites that usually appear in business conversations (Meng et al., 2021). However, the difficulties to understand noisy data may lead to annotation errors even in the human annotated version of such data.

To address the above issues, in this paper, we present an active learning (Ren et al., 2021) framework for NER that effectively sample instances from the annotated training data that are more likely to contain annotation errors. Moreover, we also address a very challenging task that is not widely studied in most of the existing NER datasets, distinguishing between *organization* and *product* type entities. In addition, since the NER model needs to provide realtime functionality in a commercial CaaS product, we show how data re-annotation through our active learning framework can even help smaller models to obtain impressive performance.

2 Related Work

In recent years, transformer-based pre-trained language models have significantly improved the performance of NER across publicly available academic datasets leading to a new state-of-the-art performance (Devlin et al., 2019; Yamada et al., 2020; Meng et al., 2021). However, there remain several issues in these existing benchmark datasets. For instance, most of these datasets are constructed from articles or the news domain, making these datasets quite well-formed with punctuation and casing information, along with having rich context around

Proceedings of the Fourth Workshop on Data Science with Human-in-the-Loop (Language Advances), pages 88 - 93
December 8, 2022

Sample Utterance
Exactly, yes, absolutely. Health Insurance USA will pay for your physiotherapy and the prescription that you were taking previously um-hum only thing you need to do is to go to our branchand fill out the form required by the insurance company and let me know if you have any questions about the claim process.
You gotta send email to the Netflix team and ask for refund.
The contending discussion of the this guy would setting the TP and other services into the university of Toronto. The one where we just got to the we're just about to serve the meeting vegetables and last week's conference and then, zoom crash.

Table 1: Example Utterances in Noisy Business Conversations.

the entities. Meanwhile, it has been observed recently that the NER models tend to memorize the entities in the training data, resulting in improved entity recognition when those entities also appear in the test data (Lin et al., 2021). Furthermore, it has been found that models trained on such academic datasets tend to perform significantly worse on unseen entities as well as on noisy text (Bodapati et al., 2019; Bernier-Colborne and Langlais, 2020; Malmasi et al., 2022).

To investigate the above issues, Lin et al. (2021) created adversarial examples via replacing target entities with other entities of the same semantic class in Wikidata and observed that existing state-of-the-art models mostly memorized in-domain entity patterns instead of reasoning from the context. Since the dataset that we study in this paper is constructed from real-world business phone conversations, there are many entities that may appear only in our test set as well as in real-world production settings that do not appear in the training set.

Note that due to the presence of speech recognition errors as well as annotation errors, training a model to be more generalized to detect the unseen entities in noisy conversations is fundamentally more challenging than above body of work. In addition, annotating such noisy datasets are also more difficult and expensive (Fu et al., 2021). In such scenarios, techniques such as Active Learning (Ren et al., 2021), that samples only a few instances from the given dataset for annotation could be very effective to train deep learning models. In this paper, we also investigate how active learning can be leveraged to fix the data annotation errors via utilizing an effective human in the loop learning.

3 Dataset Construction

The dataset used in this paper is constructed from transcripts produced by an ASR system (see Table 1 for some sample utterances). Thus, our dataset may miss many punctuation marks while only consisting of partial casing information. This makes the entity recognition on this dataset very challenging since casing information gives a very strong hint of a token being a named entity (Bodapati et al., 2019; Mayhew et al., 2019).

# Examples	Train	Dev	Test
Utterances	55,522	7,947	15,814
Person tags	34,859	4,825	10,270
Product tags	36,553	5,292	10,851
Organization tags	23,942	3,720	6,785
GPE Location tags	22,697	3,309	6,533

Table 2: Labeled in-domain dataset class distribution.

For data annotation, at first, we sampled 78,983 utterances containing human to human business telephone conversation transcripts and sent to Appen[1] for annotation. We asked the annotators in Appen to label four types of entities: *person name*, *product*, *organization*, and *geopolitical location*. The detailed statistic of the dataset labeled by Appen is shown in Table 2.

The initial selection criteria for the annotators is that they were required to be fluent in English. Moreover, the annotators had to pass a screening test where they were given some sample utterances to annotate the named entities. Based on their performance in the screening test, they were selected for the annotation job to ensure better quality for data annotation.

4 Proposed Active Learning Framework

Suppose, there is a sequence $S = s_1, s_2, ..., s_n$ containing n words. For each token s_i, the sequence tagging model will assign the most relevant tag t_j (based on the highest probability score predicted by the model) from a list of m tags $T = t_1, t_2, t_3, ..., t_m$. While constructing a sequence tagging dataset (i.e., NER dataset) from our business conversation data, we ask the annotators to annotate each token with the most relevant tag. Due to the nature of our dataset, there is a high risk of annotation errors. Thus, in this paper,

[1] `https://appen.com/`

Algorithm 1 The Active Learning Framework

```
Folds: {1, 2, 3, 4, 5}
ReAnnotationSet: {}
T: Threshold_Value

for Fold in Folds do
    PredictionSet ← samplePredictionData()
    TrainingSet ← sampleTrainingData()
    Model ← trainModel(TrainingSet)
    for utterance in PredictionSet do
        results ← Model.Predict(utterance)
        for entity, p_tag in results do
            g_tag ← getGoldTag(entity, utterance)
            p_prob_score ← getProbScore(p_tag)
            g_prob_score ← getProbScore(g_tag)
            if p_prob_score − g_prob_score > T then
                ReAnnotationSet.add(utterance)
            end if
        end for
    end for
end for
```

our objective is to reduce the annotation errors that may occur in noisy datasets via utilizing active labeling. Below, we demonstrate our proposed active learning framework.

N-fold Experiments: Given a dataset containing N examples, M fold experiments can be run in the following way to select some samples from the training set that are more likely to contain annotation errors. In each fold, use X% data from the training set as the prediction data (without replacement). Also, the prediction set in each fold should only contain distinct examples (i.e., the examples that do not appear in any other fold's prediction set) such that combining all the prediction sets together covers all the training instances.

In Algorithm 1, we present our framework via demonstrating a 5 fold experiments. The sampled data in each fold will be as follows: 80% data in each fold will contain the training set while 20% data in each fold will contain the prediction set. Moreover, the prediction data in each fold should contain those examples only that do not appear in any other prediction set.

For model training, we fine-tune a BERT-based-cased model on each fold of the training data. In this way, we fine-tune 5 BERT-based-cased models on the training data of 5 different folds. Then each trained model is utilized to predict the NER tags (p_tag refers the predicted tag in Algorithm 1) on the prediction data in their respective folds. Finally, we select some instances from the prediction set for re-annotation based on the following method.

Probability Thresholding: We utilize predicted probabilities to select instances from the prediction set for re-annotation. For an *entity* in an example utterance in the predicted set of the training data, if the predicted tag is p_tag, with the probability score predicted by the NER model for that tag is p_prob_score and the predicted probability score for the gold entity is g_prob_score, then if the probability score difference between p_prob_score and g_prob_score is more than a threshold T (where $p\_prob\_score > g\_prob\_score$), then we add that utterance in our data re-annotation set.

Human in the Loop: Once the data re-annotation set is constructed, it can be sent to the annotators for re-labeling. At first, the annotators can decide whether the given tags for an utterance are correct or not. If they think it is incorrect, then they are asked to re-annotate the utterance. In this way, we speed up the annotation process. Note that for data re-annotation, Labelbox[2] was used.

5 Model Architecture

We use two models in two stages to run our experiments. In stage 1, we fine-tune a BERT-base-cased model (Devlin et al., 2019; Laskar et al., 2019) on each fold of the dataset to identify the instances that are more likely to contain annotation errors. After re-annotating those instances, we run another experiment (i.e., stage 2) in the updated version of the training set containing the instances that are selected for re-annotation along with other instances (i.e., the instances that were not selected for re-annotation). Note that the model trained on stage 2 is the one that is used for production deployment. For this reason, we choose the DistilBERT-base-cased (Sanh et al., 2019) model for stage 2 since it is more efficient than BERT while also being significantly smaller, making it more applicable for industrial scenarios. A general overview of our proposed approach is shown on Figure 1.

5.1 Stage 1: N-fold BERT Fine-Tuning for Re-Annotation

In this section, we describe our N-fold experiments with the BERT-base-cased model to sample the instances for data re-annotation. Though our proposed Active Learning Framework is applicable for all type of entities: *Product*, *Organization*, *GPE Location*, and *Person*; in practice, we observe during

[2] https://labelbox.com/

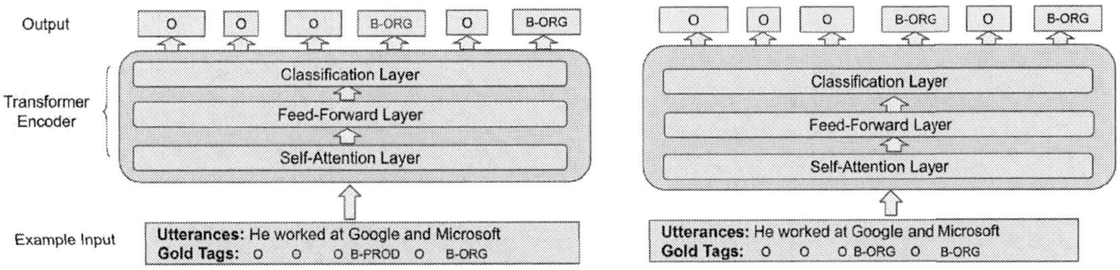

(a) Stage 1: N-Fold Fine-Tuning of BERT on the originally annotated data for Re-Annotation

(b) Stage 2: DistilBERT Fine-Tuning on the updated version of the dataset after re-annotation for Deployment

Figure 1: Our proposed approach: (a) at first, we do fine-tuning using the BERT on the originally annotated dataset to identify utterances where the difference between the predicted probability score for the Organization tag and the gold tag is above a certain threshold T, (b) Next, we fine-tune the DistilBERT model on the updated version of the dataset that is re-annotated in Stage 1. For the given utterance "He worked at Google and Microsoft", suppose the original tag for the token "Google" was B-PROD but during N-fold experiments we get the predicted tag as B-ORG, if the predicted probability score difference between the predicted tag and gold tag is above threshold T, then we select that utterance for re-annotation.

Type	Original Dataset			Re-Annotated Dataset		
	Precision	Recall	F1	Precision	Recall	F1
Person	79.30	**79.68**	**79.73**	**80.82**	78.20	79.49
GPE Location	79.78	79.86	79.82	**82.72**	**79.89**	**81.28**
Product	75.94	74.08	75.01	**77.26**	**74.82**	**76.02**
Organization	48.27	42.45	45.18	**60.47**	**52.50**	**56.21**
Overall (all 4 types)	83.49	81.47	82.41	**85.10**	**82.26**	**83.66**

Table 3: Performance of DistilBERT in the original version and the re-annotated version of the dataset.

our N-fold experiments that most of the times when there is a huge difference between the probability score of the predicted tag and the gold tag is when the predicted tag is *organization* type tag. Thus, when sampling the data for re-annotation, we focus on those utterances that are more likely to contain annotation errors for *organization* type entities and ask the annotators to re-annotate them. Moreover, focusing on annotation errors in *organization* type entities also helps our model to better distinguish between *product* and *organization* type entities.

In this way, we sample 3166 utterances for re-annotation out of 55,222 training samples that are more likely to contain annotation errors for *organization* type entities. To sample these utterances, we define a threshold and measure the difference in probability score between the predicted *'organization' tag* and the *gold tag*. If the probability score difference is above that threshold, we consider this utterance as more likely to contain annotation errors and select it for re-annotation. For this experiment, we set the threshold[3] value $T = 2.0$.

[3]We also tried other values but $T = 2$ performed the best.

5.2 Stage 2: DistilBERT Fine-Tuning for Production Deployment

Since our goal is to deploy an NER model in production for real-time inference while utilizing limited computational resources, we need to choose a model that is fast enough and also requires minimum computational memory. For this reason, we choose DistilBERT (Sanh et al., 2019) as it is much faster and smaller than the original BERT (Devlin et al., 2019) model (though a bit less accurate).

After re-annotation is done for the sampled utterances in Stage 1, we update the labels of those utterances. Then, we fine-tune the DistilBERT-base-cased model in the re-annotated training data.

6 Results and Analyses

We conduct experiments in the original version of the dataset as well as the re-annotated version of the dataset using DistilBERT. During experiments, we run 5 $epochs$ with the $training\_batch\_size$ set to 64. The $learning\_rate$ was set to $1e-4$ with the $max\_sequence\_length$ being set to 200.

We show our experimental results in Table 3 to find that for all entity types, the Precision score is increased when the model is trained on the re-

Type	DistilBERT			DistilBERT$_{\text{dtft}}$		
	Precision	Recall	F1	Precision	Recall	F1
Person	80.82	78.20	79.49	**82.06**	**82.46**	**82.26**
GPE Location	82.72	79.89	81.28	**82.90**	**83.29**	**83.09**
Product	77.26	74.82	76.02	77.23	**75.44**	**76.33**
Organization	60.47	52.50	56.21	**61.97**	**55.55**	**58.59**
Overall (all 4 types)	85.10	82.26	83.66	**85.41**	**84.04**	**84.73**

Table 4: Performance of DistilBERT and DistilBERT$_{\text{dtft}}$ in the re-annotated version of the dataset.

annotated version of the dataset. Moreover, except the Person type entity, Recall and F1 scores are also improved. Out of all 4 types of entities, we observe the highest performance improvement in terms of the *organization* type entity. This is expected since we sample data for re-annotation targeting the annotation errors in *organization* type entities. Meanwhile, we observe improvement in most other entities in addition to *organization* since the annotators were also asked to re-annotate the utterance even if there are annotation errors on any other entity types. By only re-annotating about 6% of the training data using our proposed active learning framework, we observe improvement: i) for *Organization*: 25.27%, 23.67, 24.41%, and (ii) *Overall (for all 4 types)*: 0.73%, 0.97%, and 1.52%, in terms of Precision, Recall, and F1 respectively.

The performance gain using our proposed active learning framework also makes this technique applicable for production deployment. To further improve the performance, we utilize the *distill-then-fine-tune (dtft)* architecture from Fu et al. (2022b) that achieves impressive performance on noisy data. Similar to their knowledge distillation (Hinton et al., 2015; Fu et al., 2022b) technique, we first fine-tune the teacher LUKE (Yamada et al., 2020) model on our re-annotated training set and generate pseudo labels for 483,766 unlabeled utterances collected from telephone conversation transcripts. Then, we fine-tune the student DistilBERT model in this large dataset of pseudo labels as well as the re-annotated training set via leveraging the two-stage fine-tuning mechanism (Fu et al., 2022b; Laskar et al., 2022c). We show the result in Table 4 to find that the DistilBERT$_{\text{dtft}}$ model further improves the performance and so we deploy this model in production.

7 Conclusion

In this paper, we propose an active learning framework that is very effective to fix the annotation errors in a noisy business conversation data. By sampling only about 6% of the training data for re-annotation, we observe a huge performance gain in terms of Precision, Recall, and F1. Moreover, re-annoating the data using the proposed technique also helps the NER model to better distinguish between *product* and *organization* type entities in noisy business conversational data. These findings further validate that our proposed approach is very effective in limited budget scenarios to alleviate the need of human re-labeling of a large amount of noisy data. We also show that a smaller-sized DistilBERT model can be effectively trained on such data and deployed in a minimum computational resource environment. In the future, we will investigate the performance of our proposed technique on other entity types, as well as on other tasks (Fu et al., 2022a; Laskar et al., 2022a,b) similar to NER (Fu et al., 2022b) containing noisy data.

Ethics Statement

The data used in this research is comprised of machine generated utterances. To protect user privacy, sensitive data such as personally identifiable information (e.g., credit card number, phone number) were removed while collecting the data. We also ensure that all the annotators are paid with adequate compensation. There is a data retention policy available for all users so that data will not be collected if the user is not consent to data collection. Since our model is doing classification to predict the named entities in telephone transcripts, incorrect predictions will not cause any harm to the user besides an unsatisfactory experience. While annotator demographics are unknown and therefore may introduce potential bias in the labelled dataset, the annotators are required to pass a screening test before completing any labels used for experiments, thereby mitigating this unknown to some extent.

ACKNOWLEDGEMENTS

We would like to thank Anne Paling and Kevin Sanders for their help with the data annotation job. We also thank the anonymous reviewers for their excellent review comments.

References

Gabriel Bernier-Colborne and Philippe Langlais. 2020. Hardeval: Focusing on challenging tokens to assess robustness of ner. In *Proceedings of the 12th Language Resources and Evaluation Conference*, pages 1704–1711.

Sravan Bodapati, Hyokun Yun, and Yaser Al-Onaizan. 2019. Robustness to capitalization errors in named entity recognition. In *Proceedings of the 5th Workshop on Noisy User-generated Text (W-NUT 2019)*, pages 237–242.

Jacob Devlin, Ming-Wei Chang, Kenton Lee, and Kristina Toutanova. 2019. Bert: Pre-training of deep bidirectional transformers for language understanding. In *Proceedings of the 2019 Conference of the North American Chapter of the Association for Computational Linguistics: Human Language Technologies, Volume 1 (Long and Short Papers)*, pages 4171–4186.

Xue-Yong Fu, Cheng Chen, Md Tahmid Rahman Laskar, Shashi Bhushan, and Simon Corston-Oliver. 2021. Improving punctuation restoration for speech transcripts via external data. In *Proceedings of the Seventh Workshop on Noisy User-generated Text (W-NUT 2021)*, pages 168–174.

Xue-Yong Fu, Cheng Chen, Md Tahmid Rahman Laskar, Shayna Gardiner, Pooja Hiranandani, and Shashi Bhushan TN. 2022a. Entity-level sentiment analysis in contact center telephone conversations. *arXiv preprint arXiv:2210.13401*.

Xue-Yong Fu, Cheng Chen, Md Tahmid Rahman Laskar, Shashi Bhushan Tn, and Simon Corston-Oliver. 2022b. An effective, performant named entity recognition system for noisy business telephone conversation transcripts. In *Proceedings of the Eighth Workshop on Noisy User-generated Text (W-NUT 2022)*, pages 96–100.

Geoffrey Hinton, Oriol Vinyals, Jeff Dean, et al. 2015. Distilling the knowledge in a neural network. *arXiv preprint arXiv:1503.02531*, 2(7).

Md Tahmid Rahman Laskar, Cheng Chen, Jonathan Johnston, Xue-Yong Fu, Shashi Bhushan TN, and Simon Corston-Oliver. 2022a. An auto encoder-based dimensionality reduction technique for efficient entity linking in business phone conversations. In *Proceedings of the 45th International ACM SIGIR Conference on Research and Development in Information Retrieval*, pages 3363–3367.

Md Tahmid Rahman Laskar, Cheng Chen, Aliaksandr Martsinovich, Jonathan Johnston, Xue-Yong Fu, Shashi Bhushan Tn, and Simon Corston-Oliver. 2022b. BLINK with Elasticsearch for efficient entity linking in business conversations. In *Proceedings of the 2022 Conference of the North American Chapter of the Association for Computational Linguistics: Human Language Technologies: Industry Track*, pages 344–352. Association for Computational Linguistics.

Md Tahmid Rahman Laskar, Enamul Hoque, and Jimmy Xiangji Huang. 2022c. Domain adaptation with pre-trained transformers for query-focused abstractive text summarization. *Computational Linguistics*, 48(2):279–320.

Md Tahmid Rahman Laskar, Enamul Hoque, and Jimmy Xiangji Huang. 2019. Utilizing bidirectional encoder representations from transformers for answer selection. In *International Conference on Applied Mathematics, Modeling and Computational Science*, pages 693–703. Springer.

Jing Li, Aixin Sun, Jianglei Han, and Chenliang Li. 2020. A survey on deep learning for named entity recognition. *IEEE Transactions on Knowledge and Data Engineering*, 34(1):50–70.

Bill Yuchen Lin, Wenyang Gao, Jun Yan, Ryan Moreno, and Xiang Ren. 2021. Rockner: A simple method to create adversarial examples for evaluating the robustness of named entity recognition models. In *Proceedings of the 2021 Conference on Empirical Methods in Natural Language Processing*, pages 3728–3737.

Shervin Malmasi, Anjie Fang, Besnik Fetahu, Sudipta Kar, and Oleg Rokhlenko. 2022. Multiconer: a large-scale multilingual dataset for complex named entity recognition. *arXiv preprint arXiv:2208.14536*.

Stephen Mayhew, Tatiana Tsygankova, and Dan Roth. 2019. ner and pos when nothing is capitalized. In *Proceedings of the 2019 Conference on Empirical Methods in Natural Language Processing and the 9th International Joint Conference on Natural Language Processing, EMNLP-IJCNLP 2019, Hong Kong, China, November 3-7, 2019*, pages 6255–6260. Association for Computational Linguistics.

Tao Meng, Anjie Fang, Oleg Rokhlenko, and Shervin Malmasi. 2021. Gemnet: Effective gated gazetteer representations for recognizing complex entities in low-context input. In *Proceedings of the 2021 Conference of the North American Chapter of the Association for Computational Linguistics: Human Language Technologies*, pages 1499–1512.

Pengzhen Ren, Yun Xiao, Xiaojun Chang, Po-Yao Huang, Zhihui Li, Brij B Gupta, Xiaojiang Chen, and Xin Wang. 2021. A survey of deep active learning. *ACM computing surveys (CSUR)*, 54(9):1–40.

Victor Sanh, Lysandre Debut, Julien Chaumond, and Thomas Wolf. 2019. Distilbert, a distilled version of BERT: smaller, faster, cheaper and lighter. *CoRR*, abs/1910.01108.

Ikuya Yamada, Akari Asai, Hiroyuki Shindo, Hideaki Takeda, and Yuji Matsumoto. 2020. LUKE: deep contextualized entity representations with entity-aware self-attention. In *Proceedings of the 2020 Conference on Empirical Methods in Natural Language Processing, EMNLP 2020, Online, November 16-20, 2020*, pages 6442–6454. Association for Computational Linguistics.

Interactively Uncovering Latent Arguments in Social Media Platforms: A Case Study on the Covid-19 Vaccine Debate

Maria Leonor Pacheco[1,2] **Tunazzina Islam**[3] **Lyle Ungar**[4] **Ming Yin**[3] **Dan Goldwasser**[3]
[1]Microsoft Research [2]University of Colorado Boulder
[3]Purdue University [4]University of Pennsylvania
maria.pacheco@colorado.edu ungar@cis.upenn.edu
{islam32,mingyin,dgoldwas}@purdue.edu

Abstract

Automated methods for analyzing public opinion have grown in popularity with the proliferation of social media. While supervised methods can be very good at classifying text, the dynamic nature of social media discourse results in a moving target for supervised learning. Meanwhile, traditional unsupervised techniques for extracting themes from textual repositories, such as topic models, can result in incorrect outputs that are unusable to domain experts. For this reason, a non-trivial amount of research on social media discourse still relies on manual coding techniques. In this paper, we present an interactive, humans-in-the-loop framework that strikes a balance between unsupervised techniques and manual coding for extracting latent arguments from social media discussions. We use the COVID-19 vaccination debate as a case study, and show that our methodology can be used to obtain a more accurate, interpretable set of arguments when compared to traditional topic models. We do this at a relatively low manual cost, as 3 experts take approximately 2 hours to code close to 100k tweets.

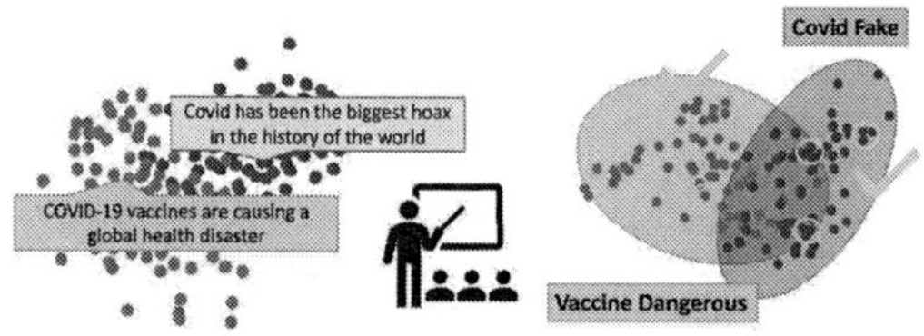

(a) Identifying and Naming Arguments

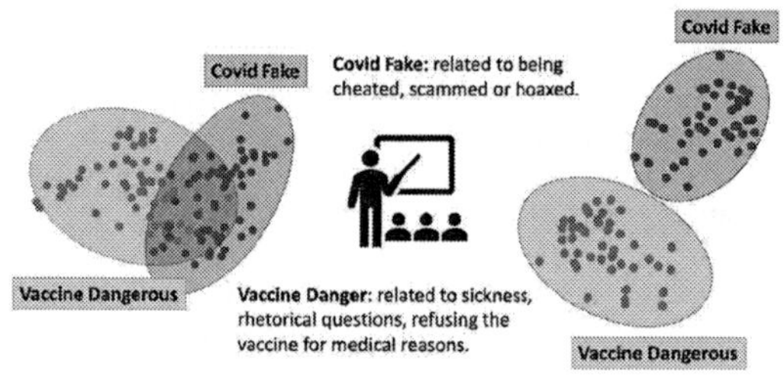

(b) Refining Arguments

Figure 1: Interactive Framework

1 Introduction

Public opinion plays an important role in the making of policy in pluralistic and democratic societies, as it allows the will of citizens to be heard and accounted for (Smith, 1942; Verba, 1995). As social media has become one of the main outlets for political and civic engagement (Rainie et al., 2012), there is a growing body of work focused on automatically analyzing public opinion on social media. The applications studied include identifying the sentiment towards specific governmental measures (Cortis and Davis, 2019; Wang et al., 2020), detecting and analyzing morally charged statements about current events (Hoover et al., 2020; Pacheco et al., 2022), exploring how ordinary citizens frame political issues (Mendelsohn et al., 2021), and contrasting the stances expressed in social media with public opinion surveys (Joseph et al., 2021). In all of these cases, the variables of interest are well defined, and substantial efforts are dedicated to creating manually annotated resources. In other words, we know which issues, governmental measures, or frames are of interest, and the problems can be framed as supervised learning tasks.

In this paper, we take a step back and tackle the problem of defining the space of relevant variables to analyze public opinion online. Given a widely debated topic, we put the focus on uncovering repeating arguments surrounding discussions on Twitter. Uncovering general themes from collections of unstructured textual resources is a common goal for researchers and practitioners across various disciplines. Unsupervised techniques, like topic models and clustering methods, have been the de-facto NLP solution to this problem (Blei et al., 2003; Boyd-Graber et al., 2017; Sia et al., 2020). While widely used, these methods often produce topics that are clearly incorrect to domain experts

Proceedings of the Fourth Workshop on Data Science with Human-in-the-Loop (Language Advances), pages 94 - 111
December 8, 2022

(Mimno et al., 2011). For this reason, and despite the popularity of contemporary NLP techniques, a non-trivial number of recent studies on social media discourse rely on manual, qualitative coding methods instead (Valle et al., 2020; Nguyen et al., 2021; Hagen et al., 2022).

In this work, we strike a balance between unsupervised NLP techniques and manual coding by adopting a humans-in-the-loop approach. We use the Twitter debate surrounding the COVID-19 vaccine as a case study, and present an interactive framework to discover and define the space of arguments frequently cited as reasons to refuse or accept the vaccine. Our framework is designed to address two main challenges: 1) Given a large collection of tweets, how can experts effectively explore the data and identify a set of repeating arguments, and 2) Given a known space of high-level arguments, how can experts create and refine a representation that improves the mapping from tweets to arguments. For example, in Fig. 1a we can observe an initial clustering of arguments provided by the system. Our initial goal is to obtain a resulting set of named arguments with high-quality examples as identified by the experts. Similarly, In Fig. 1b we can observe two overlapping arguments. Our next goal is to source explanations from the experts that result in a better mapping from tweets to arguments. This can be achieved by expanding and refining the theme representation according to the explanations provided. The expected result is a comprehensive set of high-level arguments that explain the discussion about the COVID-19 vaccine, and a partial mapping from tweets to their most likely argument.

To tackle our goals, we design and implement a simple protocol that allows groups of experts to work together towards this goal, and introduce an interactive tool equipped with operations to facilitate the discovery and refinement of arguments in large language resources. Our work is related to interactive systems that leverage clustering techniques to help users discover relevant topics (Bernstein et al., 2010), systems that exploit visualization techniques to label data interactively (Bernard et al., 2017, 2018; Vajiac et al., 2022), and human-in-the-loop topic modeling approaches that let users refine discovered topics (Hu et al., 2011; Lund et al., 2017; Smith et al., 2018). The main differences between these systems and our work are that: 1) we do not assume a known space of relevant labels, 2) we let experts drive and influence the topic discovery procedure in addition to supporting the exploration, and 3) we support open-ended feedback from experts in natural language.

Our experiments show that our framework can be used to uncover a set of arguments that cover a large portion of the discussion about the COVID-19 vaccine on Twitter, and that the resulting mapping from tweets to argument is fairly accurate with respect to human judgements. Additionally, we use the dataset of tweets about the COVID-19 vaccine released by Pacheco et al. (2022), which is annotated for vaccination stance and morality frames, and show that the high-level arguments obtained using our methodology have higher correlations with vaccination stance and moral sentiments than topics obtained using traditional topic models.

2 Interactive Framework

We propose a simple protocol that combines NLP techniques, interactive interfaces and qualitative methods to assist experts in characterizing large tweet repositories about the COVID-19 vaccine. Our protocol takes a large repository of tweets and automatically proposes an initial partition of the data, such that tweets that are thematically similar are clustered together. We provide experts with an interactive interface equipped with a set of exploratory operations that allows them to evaluate the quality of the discovered clusters, as well as to further explore and partition the space by inspecting individual examples, finding similar tweets, and using open text queries. As they interact with the data through interface, a group of experts work together following an inductive thematic analysis approach to identify and code the patterns that emerge within the partitions (Braun and Clarke, 2012). Next, they group the identified patterns into general arguments, and instantiate them using the interface. Although intuitively we could expect a single cluster to result in a single argument, note that this is not enforced. Experts maintain full freedom as to how many arguments they instantiate, if any. Once an argument is created, experts are provided with a set of operations to explain the argument using natural language, select good example tweets, or write down additional examples. At any point during the process, experts can toggle a procedure that assigns tweets to arguments.

Operations	Description
Finding Clusters	Experts can find clusters in the space of unassigned tweets. To do this, we run a clustering algorithm using the tweet representations described in Sec. ??. We support the K-means (Jin and Han, 2010) and Hierarchical Density-Based Clustering (McInnes et al., 2017) algorithms. For all results presented in this paper, we use the K-means algorithm.
Text-based Queries	Experts can type any query in natural language and find tweets that are close to the query in the embedding space.
Finding Similar Tweets	Experts have the ability to select each tweet and find other examples that are close in the embedding space.

Table 1: Discovery Operations

2.1 Interactive Tool

To support our interactive framework, we developed a tool for experts to interact with a large number of tweets. The tool is a simple GUI equipped with a finite set of exploratory and intervention operations. *Exploratory operations* allow experts to discover clusters of tweets and further explore and partition the space, and to evaluate the quality of the discovered clusters and the grounded statements. *Intervention operations* allow experts to name the discovered patterns, as well as to provide examples and judgements to improve the quality of the initial partitions.

Representing Tweets and Arguments: We represent tweets using their Sentence BERT embedding (Reimers and Gurevych, 2019). We represent arguments using a handful of explanatory phrases and a small set of examples, and calculate their SBERT embeddings. Note that our tool is agnostic of the representation used, as the underlying embedding objective can be easily replaced.

Exploratory Operations: These operations allow experts to inspect the current state of the system, both to evaluate the quality of the tweet-argument mappings, as well as to explore the data and discover new emerging arguments. We divide exploratory operations in two types: discovery operations and quality assurance operations. *Discovery operations* allow users to explore the space of tweets and get a sense of what arguments emerge in the data. We enumerate them in Tab. 1. *Quality assurance operations* allow users to evaluate the quality of the discovered clusters and the grounded tweets. We enumerate them in Tab. 2.

Intervention Operations: These operations allow experts to introduce knowledge into the system to improve the discovery and grounding of emerging arguments. We enumerate them in Tab. 3.

Cropped screenshots demonstrating all of these operations can be observed in Appendices, A.1, A.2 and A.3. Additionally, we include screenshots of the full view of all pages in our GUI in Appendix A.4.

Operations	Description
Listing Arguments and Examples	Experts can browse the current list of arguments and their grounded examples. Examples are ranked in order of "goodness", corresponding to the similarity in the embedding space to the argument representation. Examples are listed from closest to most distant, or from most distant to closest.
Visualizing Local Explanations	Experts can visualize aggregated statistics and explanations for each of the grounded arguments. To obtain these explanations, we aggregate all instances that have been identified as being associated with a theme. Explanations include wordclouds, frequent entities and their sentiments, and graphs of feature distributions.
Visualizing Global Explanations	Experts can visualize aggregated statistics and explanations for the global state of the system. To do this, we aggregate all instances in the database. Explanations include argument distribution, coverage statistics, and 2-Dimensional t-sne plots (van der Maaten and Hinton, 2008).

Table 2: Quality Assurance Operations

Operations	Description
Adding and Removing Arguments	Experts can create and remove arguments. The only requirement for creating a new argument is to give it a unique name. Similarly, arguments can be removed at any point. If any instances are assigned to an argument being removed, they will be assigned to the *"Unknown"* argument.
Adding and Removing Examples	Experts can assign "good" and "bad" examples to existing arguments. Good examples are instances that characterize the named argument. Bad examples are instances that could have similar wording to a good example, but that have different meaning. Experts can add examples in two ways: they can mark grounded tweets as "good" or "bad", or they can directly contribute example phrases.

Table 3: Intervention Operations

Argument Grounding: At any point during interaction, experts can toggle a procedure that assigns tweets to arguments. We use a simple distance-based approach for this purpose. To measure the closeness between a tweet and an argument, we compute the cosine distance between the tweet and *all* of the explanatory phrases and examples for the argument, and take the minimum distance score among them. Before this operation is called for the first time, all tweets belong to *unnamed clusters*. In other words, they remain unassigned. Once this operation is called, we assign tweets to their closest argument *if and only if* the newly computed distance is less than or equal to the distance to its previous assignment. Previous assignments can correspond either to different arguments, or to the unnamed space. Note that this way, some tweets can remain unassigned.

3 Case Study

As a case study, we look at tweets written about the COVID-19 vaccine on Twitter. We collected a corpus of 85,000 tweets that mentioned the vaccine. To avoid repetitions, we filter out all retweets ahead of time. The collected tweets are uniformly distributed between January and October, 2021. All tweets in our corpus are written in English, and were posted by users located in the United States. Our main goal is to use the framework introduced in Sec. 2 to identify repeating themes in this corpus, and construct a set of high-level arguments that are frequently used to justify stances on the vaccine.

For our study, we recruited six experts in Natural Language Processing and Computational Social Science, four male and two female, within the ages of 25 and 45. The experts included graduate students, postdoctoral researchers and faculty. To evaluate the different components of our framework, we performed a two-stage analysis. In the first stage, we simplify the problem and assume that we have an initial, known set of high-level arguments, and let three of the experts focus on the challenge of interactively refining the arguments and grounding them in the large Twitter corpus. In the second stage, we remove this assumption and have the remaining three experts discover the space of relevant arguments from scratch. Below, we present each of these scenarios in detail and perform both qualitative and quantitative evaluations to assess the outcome of the interaction.

3.1 Stage 1: Mapping Tweets to Arguments

In this stage, we assume that we know what is the set of relevant arguments, and our main goal is to improve the mapping between tweets and arguments. We build on previous work on health informatics studying the arguments made by Twitter users in Poland when discussing the COVID-19 vaccine (Wawrzuta et al., 2021). This work introduces a code-book of 13 main arguments defined using short phrases in natural language (Tab. 4).

We start by mapping the collection of 85k tweets to the Wawrzuta et al. (2021) arguments using the distance between their SBERT embeddings. Then, we let the experts interact with the system following the protocol outlined in Sec. 2. Below, we outline the interactive sessions performed by the three experts in detail.

Interactive Sessions: The three experts started by looking at the global visualizations. Then, they inspected the arguments one by one, looking at the local explanations and the 10 closest and 10 furthest tweets from each argument. Next, they were involved in a discussion phase to identify arguments that were present in the data, but not covered by the Wawrzuta et al. (2021) set, as well as the argumentation patterns that the system failed to identify for each of the arguments. This process was done in two one-hour sessions.

1	Lack of trust in the government
2	The vaccine will be dangerous to health
3	The COVID-19 vaccine disease does not exist
4	I do not want to be vaccinated because I have freedom of choice
5	The vaccine was created for the profit of pharmaceutical companies
6	Natural methods of protection are better than the vaccine
7	The vaccine does not work
8	The vaccine is not properly tested, it was developed too quickly
9	No one is responsible for the potential side effects of the vaccine
10	Mentioning past development of the swine-flu vaccine
11	The vaccine existed before the epidemic, there is too much resistance
12	Conspiracy theories, hidden vaccine effects (e.g. chips)
13	Positive attitude towards the vaccine

Table 4: 13 Arguments Proposed by Wawrzuta et al. (2021)

PRO VAX	government distrust, vaccine dangerous, covid fake, vaccine oppression, pharma bad, natural immunity effective, vaccine against religion, vaccine does not work, vaccine not tested, bill gates' micro chip, vaccine tested on dogs, vaccine has fetal tissue, vaccine makes you sterile
ANTI VAX	government trust, vaccine safe, covid real, vaccine not oppression, pharma good, natural immunity ineffective, vaccine not against religion, vaccine works, vaccine tested

Table 5: Resulting Arguments

Initially, the experts focused on adding missing arguments and removing arguments that were not frequently referenced in the data. For example, they noticed that the Wawrzuta et al. (2021) set contained mostly anti-vaccine arguments, and added the positive counterpart for each argument (e.g. *"The vaccine is dangerous"* $\Rightarrow$ *"The vaccine is safe"*). In addition to this, they observed and added new arguments such as *"The vaccine is against my religion"*, and separated *"Conspiracy theories and hidden effects"* into sub-arguments related to particular conspiracy theories, such as *"The vaccine contains fetal tissue"*, and *"The vaccine makes you sterile"*. They also removed infrequent arguments, such as *The swine-flu vaccine*, and came up with shorter names/identifiers for each one of the arguments. The resulting set of arguments can be observed in Tab. 5.

Next, the experts turned their attention to identifying the argumentative patterns that were not being captured by the given argument descriptions. They did this by looking at assignments to other arguments that appeared to be a mismatch, as well as inspecting low confidence assignments. Here, the coders followed a qualitative thematic analysis approach to code relevant patterns. For example, in the case of *"vaccine oppression"*, the experts noted that tweets that included legal terms were not being captured, as well as sarcastic expressions, and tweets that had explicit mentions to discrimination and oppression. They followed this process for every argument, and coded the missing argumentative patterns. Then, each expert contributed a set of 2-5 examples for each argument. In Appendix A.5 we include tables enumerating the full list of coded patterns and contributed phrases.

Evaluation: To evaluate the performance of our tweet to argument mapping in the dataset of 85k unlabeled tweets, we sorted the tweets according to their semantic distance to their assigned arguments, computed the three quartiles, and sampled a set of 12 tweets per argument such that 3 tweets are randomly sampled from each interval. Then, we manually annotated whether the mapping was correct or not. We did this both for the initial mapping, before any interaction, and for the resulting mapping, after interaction. This resulted in 156 tweets and 264 tweets, respectively.

To evaluate the performance at different degrees of semantic distance to the argument embedding, we perform the evaluation at each quartile. Results for the first quartile (Q_1) correspond to the 25% closest examples. For the second quartile (Q_2), they correspond to the 50% closest examples, and for the third quartile (Q_3), to the 75% closest examples. Intuitively, we expect better average performance the lower the distance is between the tweets and the argument. Results are outlined in Tab. 6. While both before and after interaction we have comparable performance for the semantically closest tweets, performance degrades faster using the initial set of arguments. This result makes sense, given that for the Wawrzuta et al. (2021) set we are only relying on one short phrase to represent arguments. The positive impact of refining arguments interactively by enriching the argument representation is clear.

Given that we can characterize arguments as the reasons cited by people to accept or refuse the COVID-19 vaccine, we consider assignments to be better if they are more cohesive (e.g. if they are more strongly correlated with vaccination stance). To evaluate this, we perform a correlation test between the identified arguments and the stance expressed in the tweet (i.e. pro or anti-vaccine). To do this, we use the set of 750 tweets annotated for stance and moral foundations released by Pacheco et al. (2022). We calculate the Pearson correlation matrices and present them in Fig. 2. We compare the arguments obtained interactively with the seed set of manual arguments (Wawrzuta et al., 2021), and with a set of topics extracted using Latent Dirichlet Allocation (LDA) (Blei et al., 2003), a generative, unsupervised topic modeling technique that allows a set of textual instances to be explained by unobserved groups of words that explain their similarity. We can observe that our refined arguments (Fig. 2d) have higher, more accurate correlations with vaccination stances and than both the original set of arguments (Fig. 2b) and the derived LDA topics (Fig. 2a, 2c). For example, we find that in the initial arguments baseline, both *"Vaccine Doesn't Work"* and *"Covid Fake"* have a high correlation with the *"pro-vax"* stance, which is opposite from what would be expected. This behavior is corrected after interaction.

Iter.	# Args	Q_1	Q_2	Q_3	All
Before Interaction	13	89.36	73.81	60.87	52.05
After Interaction	22	88.52	84.87	81.98	80.27

Table 6: Argument F1 w.r.t Human Judgements

3.2 Stage 2: Uncovering Latent Arguments

In this stage, we address the challenge of discovering the space of arguments that emerge from our corpus of 85k tweets about the COVID-19 vaccine. Unlike the scenario presented before, we do not assume any prior knowledge, and we make no assumptions about the number of relevant arguments or what they ought to be. Our main goal is to let the three experts leverage our interactive framework to find a set of relevant arguments, as well as a final mapping from tweets to arguments.

The main challenge in this stage is to obtain a set of arguments that accounts for as many tweets as possible, while maintaining the cohesiveness of the partitions and the accuracy of tweet to argument assignments. Below, we explain the interactive process in detail and present an evaluation of the results obtained.

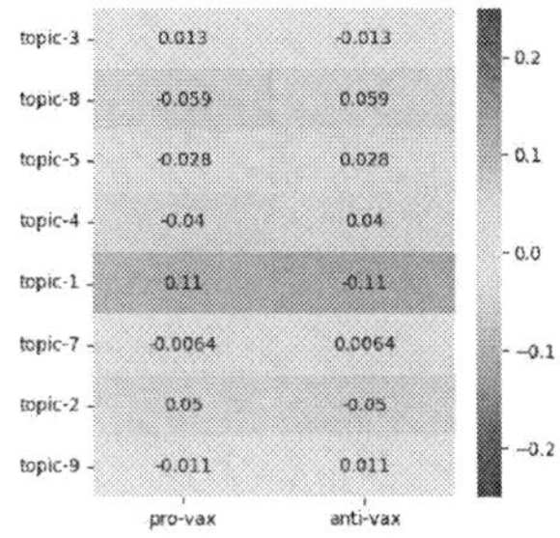

(a) **Baseline**: 10 LDA Topics

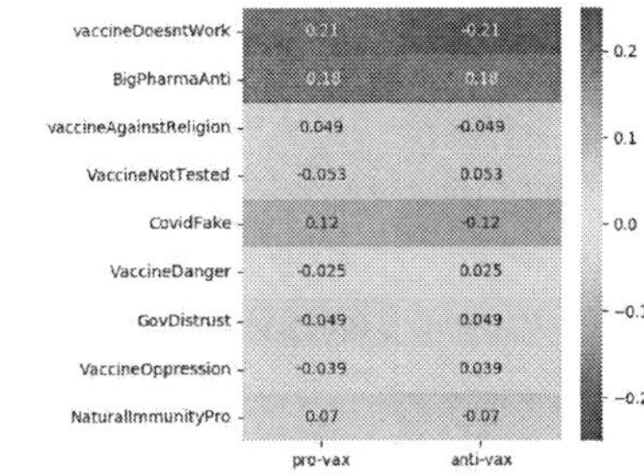

(b) **Baseline**: Manual (Wawrzuta et al., 2021)

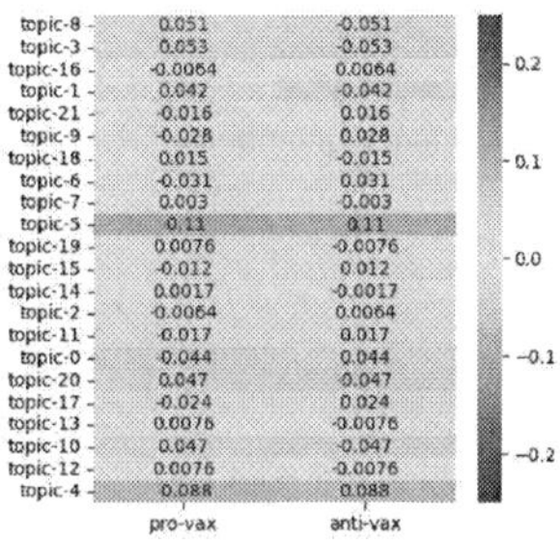

(c) **Baseline**: 20 LDA Topics

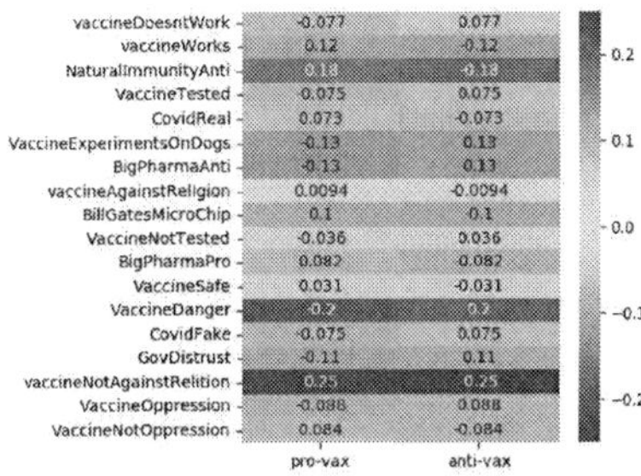

(d) **Ours**: After Interaction

Figure 2: Correlations between arguments and stance

Interactive Sessions: To initialize the system, the experts started by using the clustering operation to find 10 initial clusters of roughly the same size. First, they examined the clusters one by one, looking at the examples closest to the centroid. This was followed by a discussion phase, in which the experts coded the argumentative patterns observed. If one or more cohesive patterns were identified, the experts created a new argument, named it, and marked a set of good example tweets that helped to characterize the named argument. In Appendix A.6 we include a table showing each initial cluster, the argumentative patterns identified, and the named arguments chosen by the experts during the discussion phase. When a pattern was not obvious, the experts explored similar instances to the different tweets found. Whenever the similarity search resulted in a new pattern, the experts coded it and created a new argument.

Next, the experts looked at the local argument explanations and repeated a process similar to the first stage, by enhancing each argument with additional example phrases. Note that each argument already contained a small set of representative tweets, which were marked as "good" in the previous step. Finally, the experts toggled the nearest neighbors operation to map tweets to arguments.

We performed two iterations of this process. In the second iteration, the experts used the clustering operation again over the set of tweets that remained unassigned to existing arguments. Then, they repeated the full process a second time to uncover new arguments. The full table outlining the clusters, coded patterns and resulting arguments for the second iteration are also provided in Appendix A.6.

Evaluation: As in the previous stage, we evaluate the performance of our tweet to argument mapping by sampling a random set of 12 tweets per argument after each iteration of interaction, 3 from each interval. This resulted in a set of 108 tweets for iteration 1 and 192 tweets for iteration 2. Then, we manually annotated whether the mapping was correct or not. To evaluate the performance at different degrees of semantic distance to the argument embedding, we perform the evaluation at each quartile. Results are outlined in Tab. 7.

As expected, we obtained higher F1 scores for tweets that are the closest to the arguments in the embedding space. In addition to the F1 scores, we also look at the percentage of tweets that are covered by the set of arguments uncovered by the

Iter.	# Args	Coverage	Q_1	Q_2	Q_3	All
1	9	9.3%	89.80	87.50	87.50	85.71
2	16	22.9%	90.91	87.06	84.34	77.32

Table 7: Argument F1 w.r.t Human Judgements

experts after each iteration. We remind the reader that we do not enforce that all tweets need to be mapped to arguments, and therefore some tweets remain unassigned. There is a degradation in performance after subsequent iterations, as we increase both the number of arguments and the amount of tweets mapped. However, we find that the gain in coverage is proportionally greater than the drop in performance (x2.5 vs. x1.1). The intuition behind performing subsequent iterations is that we force the system to look at new, previously ignored partitions of the data to find new arguments. In future work, we would like to study how to estimate the optimal number of iterations, as well as when to decide to stop exploring the unassigned space.

4 Conclusions

We presented an initial step towards an interactive, humans-in-the-loop framework for uncovering latent arguments in social media discourse. We implemented a simple protocol that allows groups of experts to work together efficiently to create a comprehensive code-book of high-level arguments, and developed a GUI with a set of computational operations to streamline their coding process. We used the COVID-19 vaccine debate as a case study, and showed that by applying subsequent runs of our methodology, experts can obtain a comprehensive set of arguments that account for a reasonable slice of the data without sacrificing performance. Additionally, we showed that our resulting set of arguments is cleaner and more explainable than themes obtained with topic modeling approaches.

References

Jurgen Bernard, Marco Hutter, Matthias Zeppelzauer, Dieter Fellner, and Michael Sedlmair. 2018. Comparing visual-interactive labeling with active learning: An experimental study. *IEEE transactions on visualization and computer graphics*.

Jürgen Bernard, Matthias Zeppelzauer, Michael Sedlmair, and Wolfgang Aigner. 2017. A Unified Process for Visual-Interactive Labeling. In *EuroVis Workshop on Visual Analytics (EuroVA)*. The Eurographics Association.

Michael S. Bernstein, Bongwon Suh, Lichan Hong, Jilin Chen, Sanjay Kairam, and Ed H. Chi. 2010. Eddi: interactive topic-based browsing of social status streams. In *Proceedings of the 23nd annual ACM symposium on User interface software and technology*, UIST '10, pages 303–312, New York, NY, USA. ACM.

David M. Blei, Andrew Y. Ng, and Michael I. Jordan. 2003. Latent dirichlet allocation. *J. Mach. Learn. Res.*, 3(null):993–1022.

Jordan Boyd-Graber, Yuening Hu, and David Minmo. 2017. *Applications of Topic Models*.

Virginia Braun and Victoria Clarke. 2012. *Thematic analysis.*, pages 57–71.

Keith Cortis and Brian Davis. 2019. A social opinion gold standard for the Malta government budget 2018. In *Proceedings of the 5th Workshop on Noisy User-generated Text (W-NUT 2019)*, pages 364–369, Hong Kong, China. Association for Computational Linguistics.

Loni Hagen, Ashley Fox, Heather O'Leary, DeAndre Dyson, Kimberly Walker, Cecile A Lengacher, and Raquel Hernandez. 2022. The role of influential actors in fostering the polarized covid-19 vaccine discourse on twitter: Mixed methods of machine learning and inductive coding. *JMIR Infodemiology*, 2(1):e34231.

Joe Hoover, Gwenyth Portillo-Wightman, Leigh Yeh, Shreya Havaldar, Aida Mostafazadeh Davani, Ying Lin, Brendan Kennedy, Mohammad Atari, Zahra Kamel, Madelyn Mendlen, Gabriela Moreno, Christina Park, Tingyee E. Chang, Jenna Chin, Christian Leong, Jun Yen Leung, Arineh Mirinjian, and Morteza Dehghani. 2020. Moral foundations twitter corpus: A collection of 35k tweets annotated for moral sentiment. *Social Psychological and Personality Science*, 11(8):1057–1071.

Yuening Hu, Jordan Boyd-Graber, and Brianna Satinoff. 2011. Interactive topic modeling. In *Proceedings of the 49th Annual Meeting of the Association for Computational Linguistics: Human Language Technologies*, pages 248–257, Portland, Oregon, USA. Association for Computational Linguistics.

Xin Jin and Jiawei Han. 2010. *K-Means Clustering*, pages 563–564. Springer US, Boston, MA.

Kenneth Joseph, Sarah Shugars, Ryan Gallagher, Jon Green, Alexi Quintana Mathé, Zijian An, and David Lazer. 2021. (mis)alignment between stance expressed in social media data and public opinion surveys. In *Proceedings of the 2021 Conference on Empirical Methods in Natural Language Processing*, pages 312–324, Online and Punta Cana, Dominican Republic. Association for Computational Linguistics.

Jeffrey Lund, Connor Cook, Kevin Seppi, and Jordan Boyd-Graber. 2017. Tandem anchoring: a multiword anchor approach for interactive topic modeling. In

Proceedings of the 55th Annual Meeting of the Association for Computational Linguistics (Volume 1: Long Papers)*, pages 896–905, Vancouver, Canada. Association for Computational Linguistics.

Leland McInnes, John Healy, and Steve Astels. 2017. hdbscan: Hierarchical density based clustering. *The Journal of Open Source Software*, 2(11):205.

Julia Mendelsohn, Ceren Budak, and David Jurgens. 2021. Modeling framing in immigration discourse on social media. In *Proceedings of the 2021 Conference of the North American Chapter of the Association for Computational Linguistics: Human Language Technologies*, pages 2219–2263, Online. Association for Computational Linguistics.

David Mimno, Hanna Wallach, Edmund Talley, Miriam Leenders, and Andrew McCallum. 2011. Optimizing semantic coherence in topic models. In *Proceedings of the 2011 Conference on Empirical Methods in Natural Language Processing*, pages 262–272, Edinburgh, Scotland, UK. Association for Computational Linguistics.

Thu T. Nguyen, Shaniece Criss, Eli K. Michaels, Rebekah I. Cross, Jackson S. Michaels, Pallavi Dwivedi, Dina Huang, Erica Hsu, Krishay Mukhija, Leah H. Nguyen, Isha Yardi, Amani M. Allen, Quynh C. Nguyen, and Gilbert C. Gee. 2021. Progress and push-back: How the killings of ahmaud arbery, breonna taylor, and george floyd impacted public discourse on race and racism on twitter. *SSM - Population Health*, 15:100922.

Maria Leonor Pacheco, Tunazzina Islam, Monal Mahajan, Andrey Shor, Ming Yin, Lyle Ungar, and Dan Goldwasser. 2022. A holistic framework for analyzing the COVID-19 vaccine debate. In *Proceedings of the 2022 Conference of the North American Chapter of the Association for Computational Linguistics: Human Language Technologies*, pages 5821–5839, Seattle, United States. Association for Computational Linguistics.

Lee Rainie, Aaron Smith, Kay Lehman Schlozman, Henry E. Brady, and Sidney Verba. 2012. Social media and political engagement. *Pew Research Center Reports*.

Nils Reimers and Iryna Gurevych. 2019. Sentence-BERT: Sentence embeddings using Siamese BERT-networks. In *Proceedings of the 2019 Conference on Empirical Methods in Natural Language Processing and the 9th International Joint Conference on Natural Language Processing (EMNLP-IJCNLP)*, pages 3982–3992, Hong Kong, China. Association for Computational Linguistics.

Suzanna Sia, Ayush Dalmia, and Sabrina J. Mielke. 2020. Tired of topic models? clusters of pretrained word embeddings make for fast and good topics too! In *Proceedings of the 2020 Conference on Empirical Methods in Natural Language Processing (EMNLP)*, pages 1728–1736, Online. Association for Computational Linguistics.

Alison Smith, Varun Kumar, Jordan Boyd-Graber, Kevin Seppi, and Leah Findlater. 2018. Closing the loop: User-centered design and evaluation of a human-in-the-loop topic modeling system. In *23rd International Conference on Intelligent User Interfaces*, IUI '18, page 293–304, New York, NY, USA. Association for Computing Machinery.

Charles W. Smith. 1942. Democracy through public opinion. by harold d. lasswell. (menasha, wisconsin: George banta publishing company. 1941. pp. 176. 1.50.). *American Political Science Review*, 36(2):348–349.

Catalina Vajiac, Duen Horng Chau, Andreas Olligschlaeger, Rebecca Mackenzie, Pratheeksha Nair, Meng-Chieh Lee, Yifei Li, Namyong Park, Reihaneh Rabbany, and Christos Faloutsos. 2022. Trafficvis: Visualizing organized activity and spatio-temporal patterns for detecting and labeling human trafficking. *IEEE transactions on visualization and computer graphics*.

Marc Esteve Del Valle, Rimmert Sijtsma, Hanne Stegeman, and Rosa Borge. 2020. Online deliberation and the public sphere: Developing a coding manual to assess deliberation in twitter political networks. *Javnost - The Public*, 27(3):211–229.

Laurens van der Maaten and Geoffrey Hinton. 2008. Visualizing data using t-SNE. *Journal of Machine Learning Research*, 9:2579–2605.

Sidney Verba. 1995. The citizen as respondent: Survey research and american democracy. *American Political Science Review*, March.

Shihan Wang, Marijn Schraagen, Erik Tjong Kim Sang, and Mehdi Dastani. 2020. Public sentiment on governmental COVID-19 measures in Dutch social media. In *Proceedings of the 1st Workshop on NLP for COVID-19 (Part 2) at EMNLP 2020*, Online. Association for Computational Linguistics.

Dominik Wawrzuta, Mariusz Jaworski, Joanna Gotlib, and Mariusz Panczyk. 2021. What arguments against covid-19 vaccines run on facebook in poland: Content analysis of comments. *Vaccines*, 9(5):481.

A Appendix

In this section, we include cropped screenshots of the different operations outlined in Section 2.1, as well as full screenshots of all the views of the GUI. Additionally, we include tables with the full results of the qualitative thematic analysis procedures.

A.1 Discovery Operations

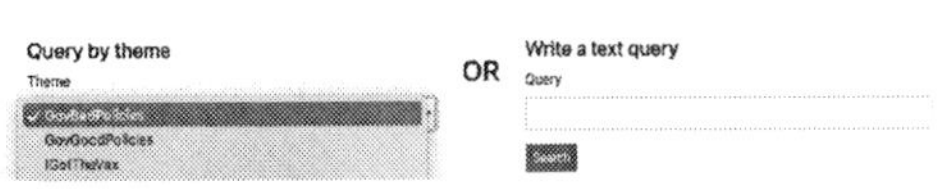

Figure 3: Text-based Queries

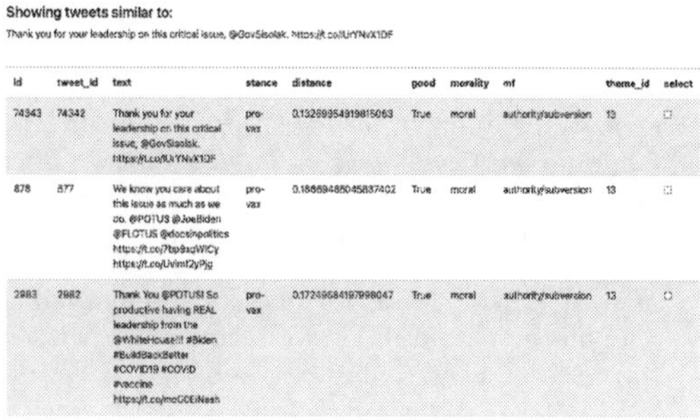

Figure 4: Finding Similar Tweets

A.2 Quality Assurance Operations

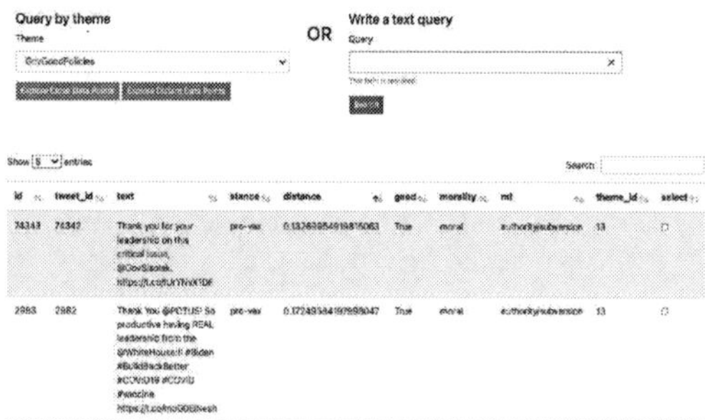

Figure 5: Listing Arguments and Examples

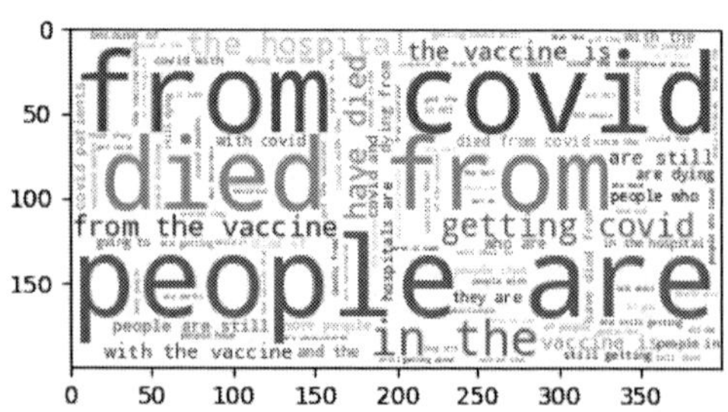

Figure 6: Visualizing Local Explanations: Word Cloud Example for *The Vaccine Doesn't Work*

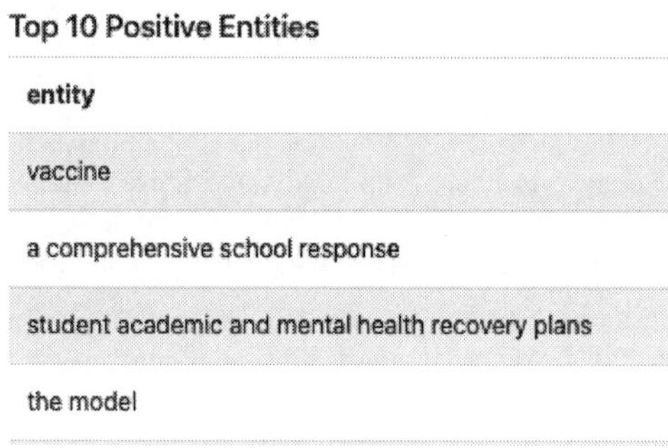

(a) Top Positive Entities

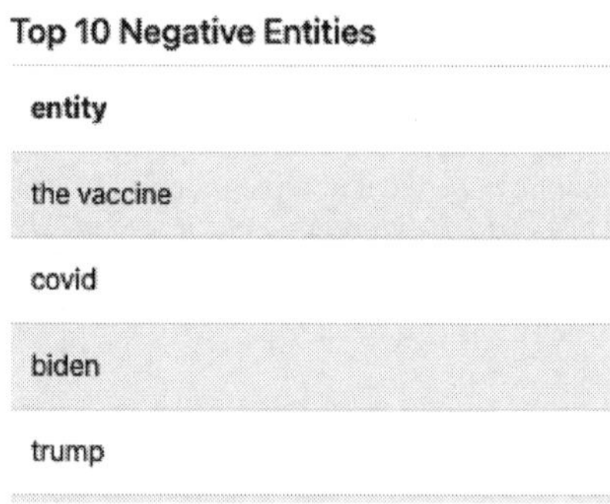

(b) Top Negative Entities

Figure 7: Visualizing Local Explanations: Most Frequent Positive and Negative Entities for *Bad Governmental Policies*

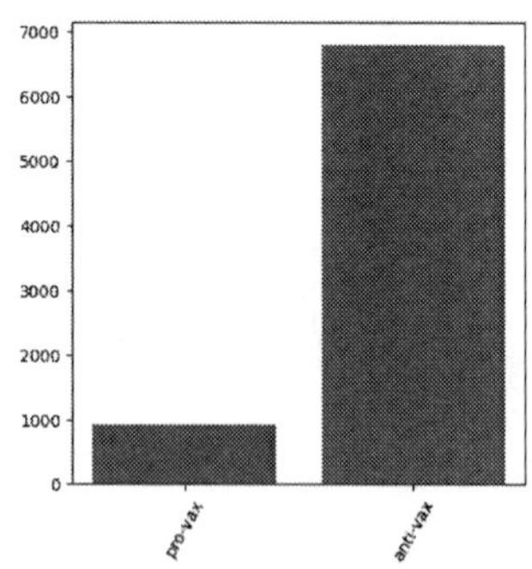

(a) Stance

Figure 8: Visualizing Local Explanations: Attribute Distribution for *The Vaccine Doesn't Work*. Note that attributes can be predicted using external resources. In this case, we predicted stance using a classifier trained on hashtags, as described in (Pacheco et al., 2022).

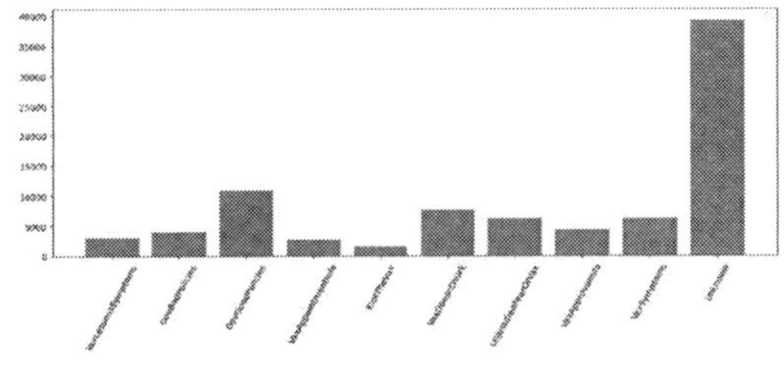

Figure 9: Visualizing Global Explanations: Argument Distribution

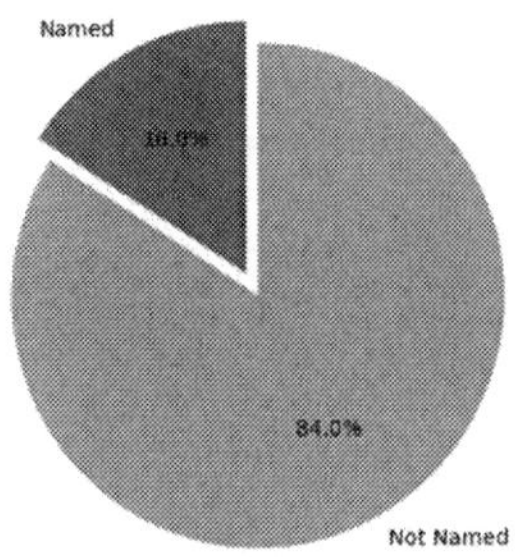

Figure 10: Visualizing Global Explanations: Coverage

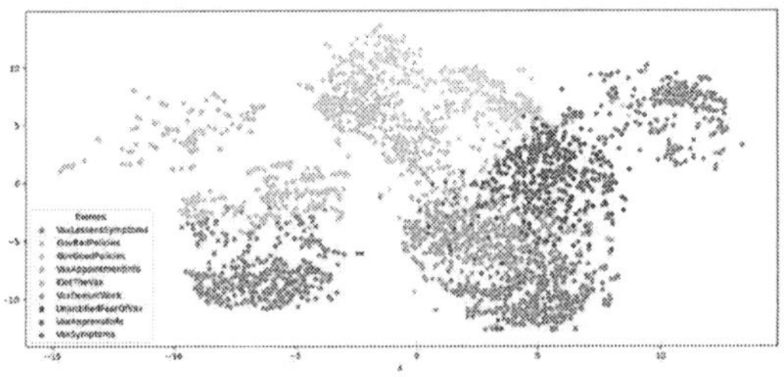

Figure 11: Visualizing Global Explanations: 2D t-SNE

A.3 Intervention Operations

Figure 12: Adding New Themes

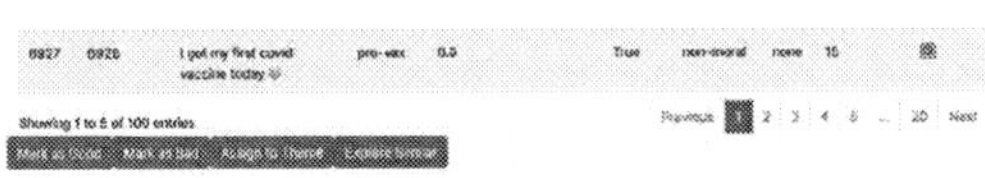

Figure 13: Marking Instances as *Good*

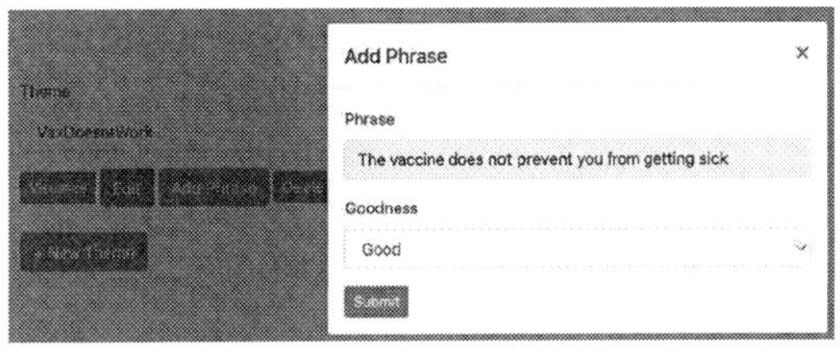

Figure 14: Adding *Good* Examples

A.4 Full Screenshots

Full screenshots of the page views of our GUI can be seen in Figures 15, 16, 17, 18, 19, 20, 21 and 22

A.5 Stage 1: Coded Patterns and Contributed Phrases

Coded patterns for each argument can be observed in Tab. 8. The resulting list of added and removed arguments, as well as their contributed phrases can be observed in Tabs. 9 and 10.

A.6 Stage 2: Argumentative Codes and Resulting Arguments

The clusters for the first iteration of interaction, the coded argumentative patterns and the resulting arguments can be observed in Tab. 11. The same content for the second iteration of interaction can be observed in Tab. 12.

Argument	Argumentative Patterns
GovDistrust	Add phrases with strong word for distrust
	"Good at being bad"
	Explicit negations
GovTrust	Hedging phrases (sort-of trust)
VaxDanger	Closer connection between vaccine words and danger words (related to sickness, bad effects)
	Explit negations
	Rhetorical questions
	Refusing the vaccine for medical reasons
VaxSafe	Explicit mentions of safety
	Explicit negations
CovidFake	Stronger relevant negative words (fake, scam, hoax)
	Explicit negations
CovidReal	Trust the science
	References to Covid hospitalization on the rise, explicit mentions of hospitals
	Explicit negations
VaxOppression	Legal language
	Explicit mentions of discrimination and oppression
	Sarcasm
VaxNotOppression	Justifying mandates
	Freedom to be protected
	Criticizing others using "you/people" language, focus freedom on me/my/I
BigPharmaAnti	Stronger words against pharmaceutical companies (corrupt, evil)
	Not accountable / irresponsible past behavior
	Mentions of negative side-effect of other products (cancer)
BigPharmaPro	Trust science/research and vaccine development process
	Language about intent, the vaccine was created to do something good, explicit names of companies
NaturalImmunityPro	The vaccine is not enough
	Explicit mentions to population immunity, herd immunity and antibodies
NaturalImmunityAnti	Emphasis on global look, collective entities, society
	Natural immunity characterized as dangerous or not effective
	Mentions of experts and trusting science
VaxAgainstReligion	I put it in god hands (god is deciding)
	Treating pro-vax as another religion
VaxNotAgainstReligion	"Religious" in quotes
	Bugus exemptions
	"Where is your faith"
	Call to action: get tested/get vaccinated/put a mask on (mentions of compassion)
	No religion ask members to refuse vaccine
VaxDoesntWork	Reference to "magic vaccine"
	"Never developed", "doesn't work"
	Questions: why are deaths high? Why is corona not going away? Why are vaccinated people dying?
VaxWorks	"ask a doctor", consult with an expert
	Research on the vaccine is good/has been going on for a long time
	Capture differences, e.g. "good trials" vs. rushed ones.
VaxNotTested	Language suggesting "rushed through trials" and "experimental vaccine"
VaxTested	trust the research and development process
	Testing can be confused with covid-test, use other language.

Table 8: Coded Argumentative Patterns for Stage 1

Arguments	Contributed Phrases
GovDistrust	**"lack of trust in the government"**, "Fuck the government", "The government is a total failure", "Never trust the government", "Biden is a failure", "Biden lied people die", "The government and Fauci have been dishonest", "The government always lies", "The government has a strong record of screwing things up", "The government is good at screwing things up", "The government is screwing things up", "The government is lying", "The government only cares about money", "The government doesn't work logically", "Do not trust the government", "The government doesn't care about people's health", "The government won't tell you the truth about the vaccine"
VaxDanger	**"the vaccine will be dangerous to health"**, "Covid vaccines can cause blood clots", "The vaccine is a greater danger to our children's health than COVID itself", "The vaccine will kill you", "The experimental covid vaccine is a death jab", "The covid vaccine causes cancer", "The covid vaccine is harmful for pregnant women and kids", "The vaccine increases health risk", "The vaccine isn't safe", "What are vaccines good for? Nothing, rather it increases risk", "I and many others have medical exemptions", "The vaccine is dangerous for people with medical conditions", "I won't take the vaccine due to medical reasons", "The vaccine has dangerous side effects"
CovidFake	**"Covid-19 disease does not exist"**, "Covid is fake", "covid is a hoax", "covid is a scam", "covid is propaganda", "the pandemic is a lie", "covid isn't real", "I don't think that covid is real", "I don't buy that covid is real", "I don't think there is a pandemic", "I don't think the pandemic is real", "I don't buy that there is a pandemic"
VaxOppression	**"I do not want to be vaccinated because I have freedom of choice"** "Forcing people to take experimental vaccines is oppression", "The vaccine has nothing to do with Covid-19, it's about the vaccine passport and tyranny", "The vaccine mandate is unconstitutional", "I choose not to take the vaccine", "My body my choice", "I'm not against the vaccine but I am against the mandate", "I have freedom to choose not to take the vaccine", "I am free to refuse the vaccine", "It is not about covid, it is about control", "Medical segregation based on vaccine mandates is discrimination", "The vaccine mandate violates my rights", "Falsely labeling the injection as a vaccine is illegal", "Firing over vaccine mandates is oppression", "Vaccine passports are medical tyranny", "I won't let the government tell me what I should do with my body", "I won't have the government tell me what to do"
BigPharmaAnti	**"the vaccine was created only for the profit of pharmaceutical companies"**, "We are the subjects of massive experiments for the Moderna and Pfizer vaccines", "Pharmaceutical companies are corrupt", "The pharmaceutical industry is rotten", "Big Pharma is evil", "How would you trust big pharma with the COVID vaccine? They haven't been liable for vaccine harm in the past", "Covid vaccines are not doing what the pharmaceutical companies promised", "Pharmaceutical companies have a history of irresponsible behavior", "I don't trust Johnson & Johnson after knowing their baby powder caused cancer for decades"
NatImmunityPro	**"natural methods of protection against the disease are better than vaccines"**, "Herd immunity is broad, protective, and durable", "Natural immunity has higher level of protection than the vaccine", "Embrace population immunity", "I trust my immune system", "I have antibodies I do not need the vaccine", "Natural immunity is effective"
VaxAgainstReligion	"The vaccine is against my religion", "The vaccines are the mark of the beast", "The vaccine is a tool of Satan", "The vaccine is haram", "The vaccine is not halal", "I will protect my body from a man made vaccine", "I put it all in God's hands", "God will decide our fate", "The vaccine contains bovine, which conflicts with my religion", "The vaccine contains aborted fetal tissue which is against my religion", "The vaccine contains pork, muslims can't take the vaccine", "Jesus will protect me", "The vaccine doesn't protect you from getting or spreading Covid, God does", "The covid vaccine is another religion"
VaxDoesntWork	**"the vaccine does not work"**, "covid vaccines do not stop the spread", "If the vaccine works, why are deaths so high?", "Why are vaccinated people dying?", "If the vaccine works, why is covid not going away?"
VaxNotTested	**"the vaccine is not properly tested, it has been developed too quickly"**, "Covid-19 vaccines have not been through the same rigorous testing as other vaccines", "The Covid vaccine is experimental", "The covid vaccine was rushed through trials", "The approval of the experimental vaccine was rushed", "How was the vaccine developed so quickly?"
VaxExperimentDogs	"Animal shelters are empty because Dr Fauci allowed experimenting of various Covid vaccines/drugs on dogs and other domestic pets", "Fauci tortures dogs and puppies"
BillGatesMicroChip	"The covid vaccine is a ploy to microchip people", "Bill Gates wants to use vaccines to implant microchips in people", "Globalists support a covert mass chip implantation through the covid vaccine"
VaxFetalTissue	"There is aborted fetal tissue in the Covid Vaccines", "the Covid vaccines contain aborted fetal cells"
VaxMakeYouSterile	"The covid vaccine will make you sterile", "Covid vaccine will affect your fertility"
NoResponsibility	**no one is responsible for the potential side effects of the vaccine**
SwineFluVax	**mentioning the past development of the swine flu vaccine**
VaxResistance	**the vaccine has existed before the Covid-19 epidemic, now there is too much resistance**
ConspiracyTheories	**conspiracy theories, hidden vaccine effects (e.g., chips)**

Table 9: AntiVax arguments and contributed phrases. Arguments that were added during interaction are shown in blue. Arguments that were removed are shown in red. The original definitions/examples are presented in bold.

Arguments	Contributed Phrases
GovTrust	"We trust the government", "The government cares for people", "We are thankful to the government for the vaccine availability", "Hats off to the government for tackling the pandemic", "It is a good thing to be skeptical of the government, but they are right about the covid vaccine", "It is a good thing to be skeptical of the government, but they haven't lied about the covid vaccine", "The government can be corrupt, but they are telling the truth about the covid vaccine", "The government can be corrupt, but they are not lying about the covid vaccine"
VaxSafe	"The vaccine is safe", "Millions have been vaccinated with only mild side effects", "Millions have been safely vaccinated against covid", "The benefits of the vaccine outweigh its risks", "The vaccine has benefits", "The vaccine is safe for women and kids", "The vaccine won't make you sick", "The vaccine isn't dangerous", "The vaccine won't kill you", "The covid vaccine isn't a death jab", "The covid vaccine doesn't harm women and kids"
CovidReal	"Covid is real", "I trust science", "Covid death is real", "The science doesn't lie about covid", "Scientist know what they are doing", "Scientist know what they are saying", "Covid hospitalizations are on the rise", "Covid hospitalizations are climbing as fourth stage surge continues", "Covid's death toll has grown faster", "Covid is not a hoax", "The pandemic is not a lie", "The pandemic is not a lie, hospitalizations are on the rise"
VaxNotOppression	"The vaccine mandate is not oppression because vaccines lower hospitalizations and death rates", "The vaccine mandate is not oppression because it will help to end this pandemic", "The vaccine mandate will help us end the pandemic", "We need a vaccine mandate to end this pandemic", "I support vaccine mandates", "If you don't get the vaccine based on your freedom of choice, don't come crawling to the emergency room when you get COVID", "If you refuse a free FDA-approved vaccine for non-medical reasons, then the government shouldn't continue to give you free COVID tests", "You are free not to take the vaccine, businesses are also free to deny you entry", "You are free not to take the vaccine, businesses are free to protect their customers and employees", "If you choose not to take the vaccine, you have to deal with the consequences", "If it is your body your choice, then insurance companies should stop paying for your hospitalization costs for COVID"
BigPharmaPro	"I trust the science and pharmaceutical research", "Pharmaceutical companies are not hiding anything", "The research behind covid vaccines is public", "The Pfizer vaccine is saving lives", "The Moderna vaccines are helping stop the spread of covid", "The Johnson and Johnson vaccine was created to stop covid", "Pharmaceutical companies are seeking FDA approval", "Pharmaceutical companies are following standard protocols"
NatImmunityAnti	"Only the vaccine will end the pandemic", "Vaccines will allow us to defeat covid without death and sickness", "The vaccine has better long term protection than to natural immunity", "Natural immunity is not effective", "Natural immunity would require a lot of people getting sick", "Experts recommend the vaccine over natural immunity"
VaxReligionOk	"The vaccine is not against religion, get the vaccine", "No religion ask members to refuse the vaccine", "Religious exemptions are bogus", "When turning in your religious exemption forms for the vaccine, remember ignorance is not a religion", "Disregard for others' lives isn't part of your religion", "Jesus is trying to protect us from covid by divinely inspiring scientists to create vaccines"
VaxWorks	"The vaccine works", "Vaccines do work, ask a doctor or consult with an expert", "The covid vaccine helps to stop the spread", "Unvaccinated people are dying at a rapid rate from Covid-19", "There is a lot of research supporting that vaccines work", "The research on the covid vaccine has been going on for a long time"
VaxTested	"Covid vaccine research has been going on for a while", "Plenty of research has been done on the covid vaccine", "The technologies used to develop the Covid-19 vaccines have been in development for years to prepare for outbreaks of infectious viruses", "The testing processes for the vaccines were thorough didn't skip any steps", "The vaccine received FDA approval"
ProVax	**positive attitude**

Table 10: ProVax arguments and contributed phrases. Arguments that were added during interaction are shown in blue. Arguments that were removed are shown in red. The original definition/examples are presented in bold.

Cluster	Experts Rationale	New Named Arguments
K-Means 0	Discusses what the vaccine can and cannot do. Emphasis in reducing COVID-19 symptoms in case of infection ("like a bad cold"). Contains tweets with both stances.	VaxLessensSymptoms
K-Means 1	A lot of mentions to political entities. Politicians get in the way of public safety	GovBadPolicies
K-Means 2	A lot of tweets with mentions and links. Not a lot of textual context. Some examples thanking and praising governmental policies. **Theme added upon inspecting similar tweets**	GovGoodPolicies
K-Means 3	Overarching theme related to vaccine rollout. Mentions to pharmacies that can distribute, distribution in certain states, places with unfulfilled vax appointments. **Too broad to create a theme**	-
K-Means 4	Broadcast of vaccine appointments. Which places you can get vaccine appointments at.	VaxAppointments
K-Means 5	"I got my vaccine" type tweets	GotTheVax
K-Means 6	Mixed cluster, not a clear theme in centroid. Two prominent flavors: the vaccine not working and people complaining about those who are scared of vaccine.	VaxDoesntWork UnjustifiedFearOfVax
K-Means 7	Tweets look the same as K-Means 5	-
K-Means 8	Tweets about development and approval of vaccines	VaxApproval
K-Means 9	Tweets related to common vaccine side-effects	VaxSideEffects

Table 11: **First Iteration**: Patterns Identified in Initial Clusters and Resulting Arguments

Cluster	Experts Rationale	New Named Arguments
K-Means 0	Tweets weighting health benefits/risks, but different arguments. (e.g. it works, doesn't work, makes things worse...) **Too broad to create a theme.**	-
K-Means 1	Messy cluster, relies on link for information.	-
K-Means 2	Relies on link for information.	-
K-Means 3	A lot of mentions to government lying and misinformation. "misinformation" is used when blaming antivax people. "experts and government are lying" is used on the other side. References to alt-treatments on both sides. **Text lookup "give us the real meds", "covid meds"**	AntiVaxSpreadMisinfo ProVaxLie AltTreatmentsGood AltTreatmentsBad
K-Means 4	Some examples are a good fit for old theme, VaxDoesntWork. **Other than that no coherent theme.**	-
K-Means 5	Tweets about free will and choice. **Text lookup "big gov", "free choice", "my body my choice"** Case "my body my choice" - a lot of mentions to abortion People using covid as a metaphor for other issues.	FreeChoiceVax FreeChoiceOther
K-Means 6	Almost exclusively mentions to stories and news.	-
K-Means 7	Availability of the vaccine, policy. Not judgement of good or bad, but of how well it progresses.	VaxEffortsProgression
K-Means 8	Assign to previous theme GotTheVax	-
K-Means 9	Vaccine side effects. Assign to previous theme, VaxSymptoms	-

Table 12: **Second Iteration**: Patterns Identified in Subsequent Clusters and Resulting Arguments

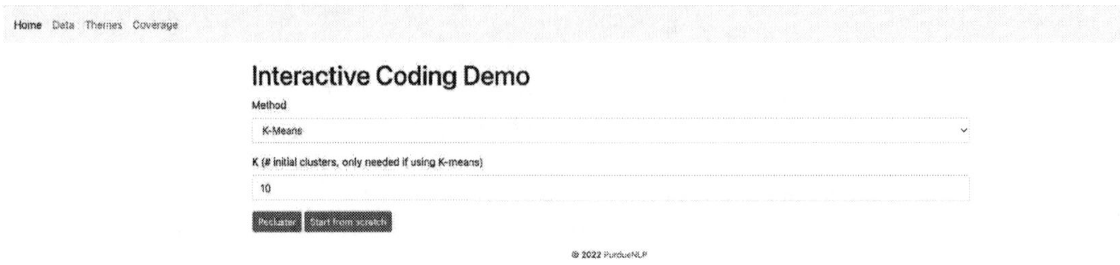

Figure 15: Cluster/Recluster Page

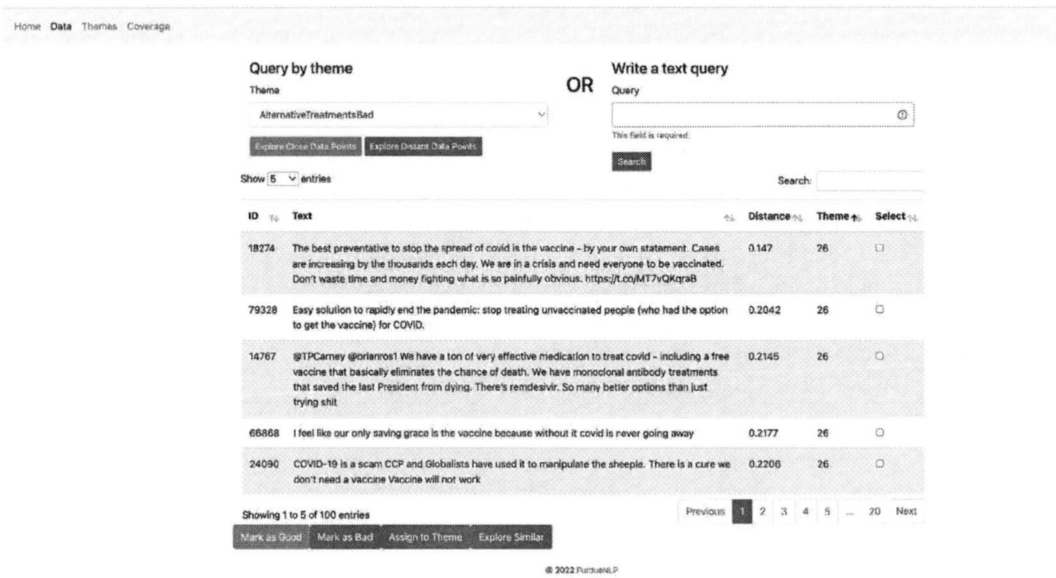

Figure 16: Listing Arguments Page: Named Argument View

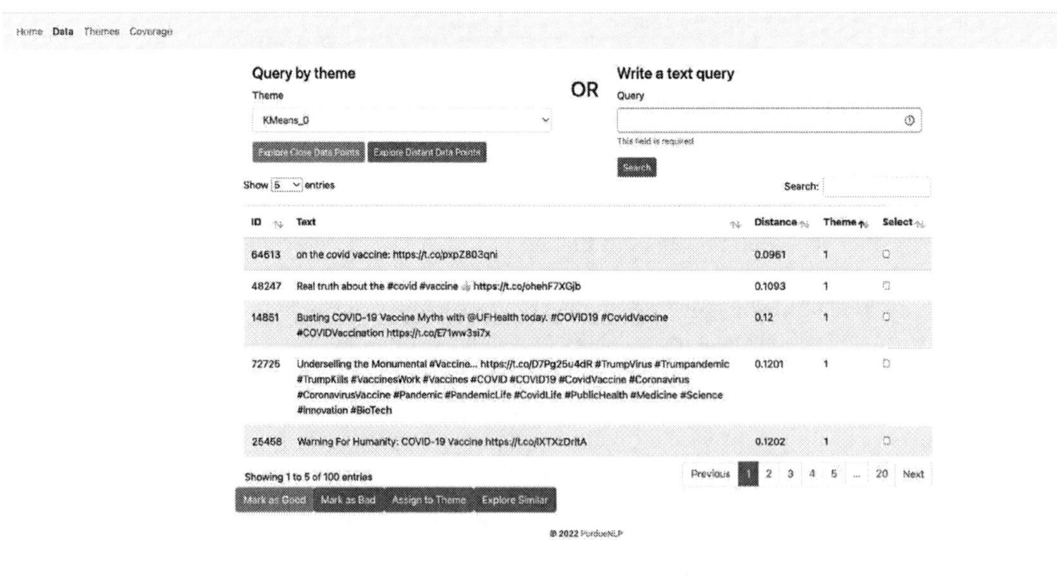

Figure 17: Listing Arguments Page: Unnamed Cluster View

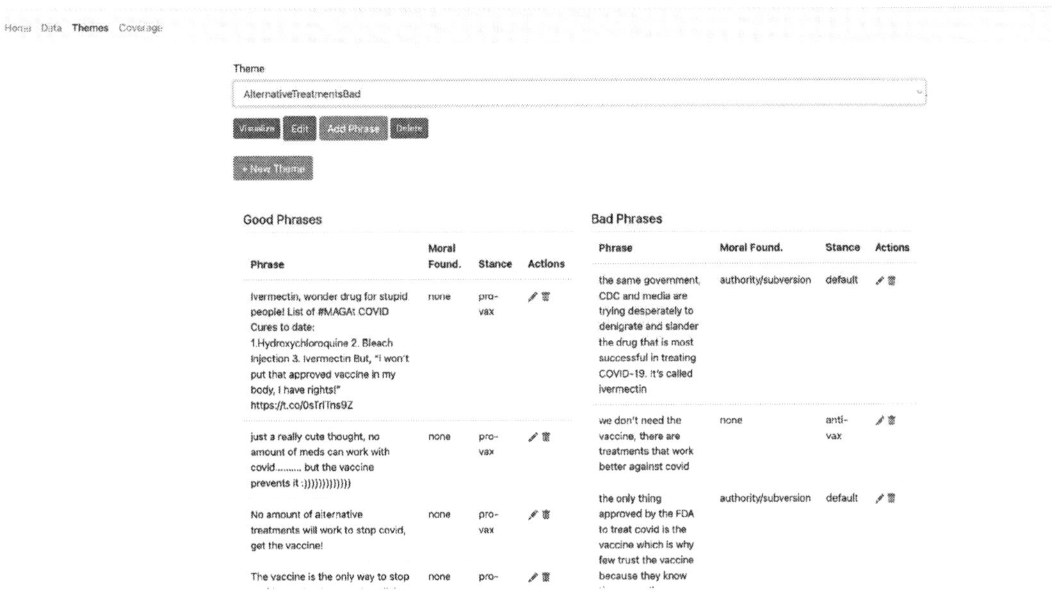

Figure 18: Visualizing Arguments Page

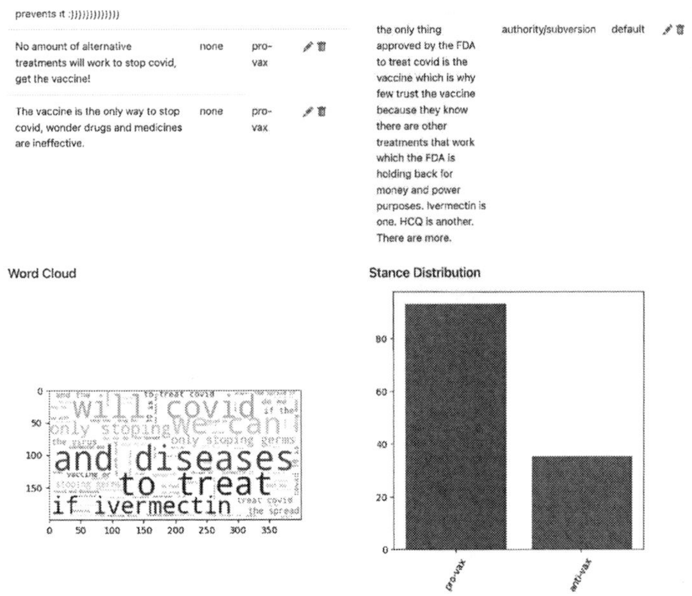

Figure 19: Visualizing Arguments Page: Scroll Down for Local Explanations

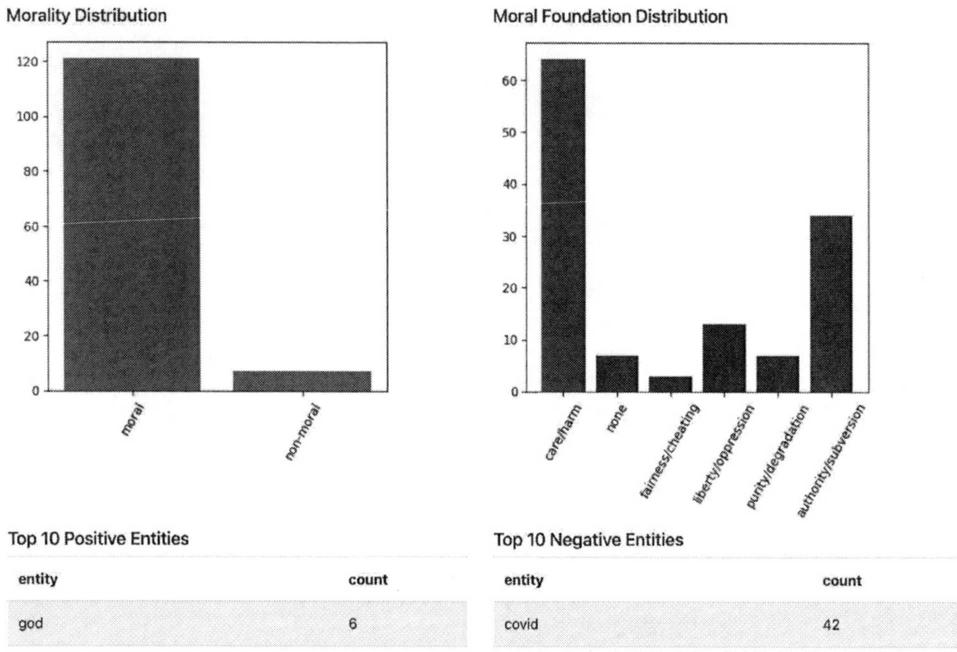

Figure 20: Visualizing Arguments Page: Scroll Down for Local Explanations 2

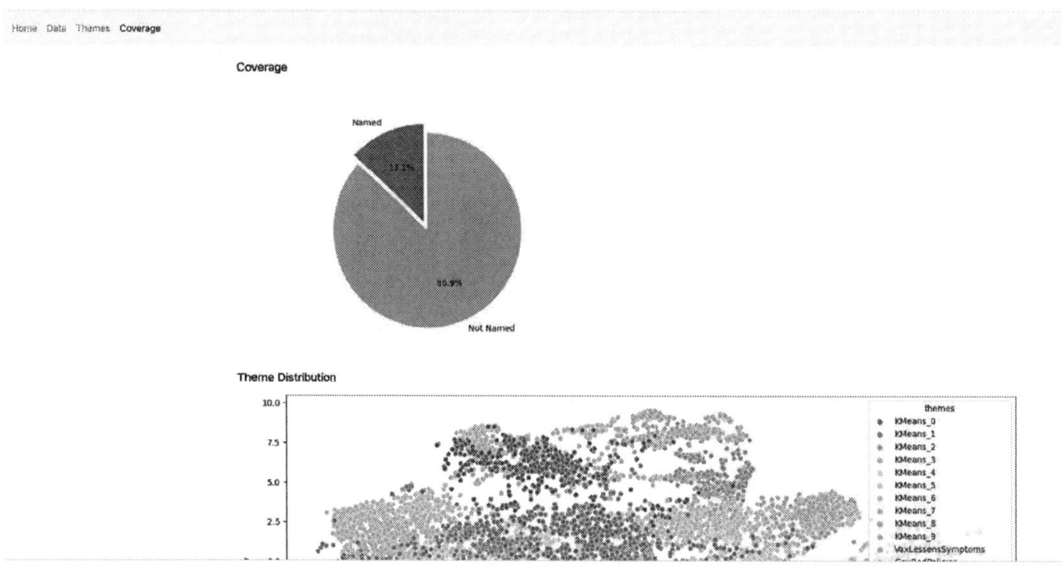

Figure 21: Visualizing Global Explanations Page

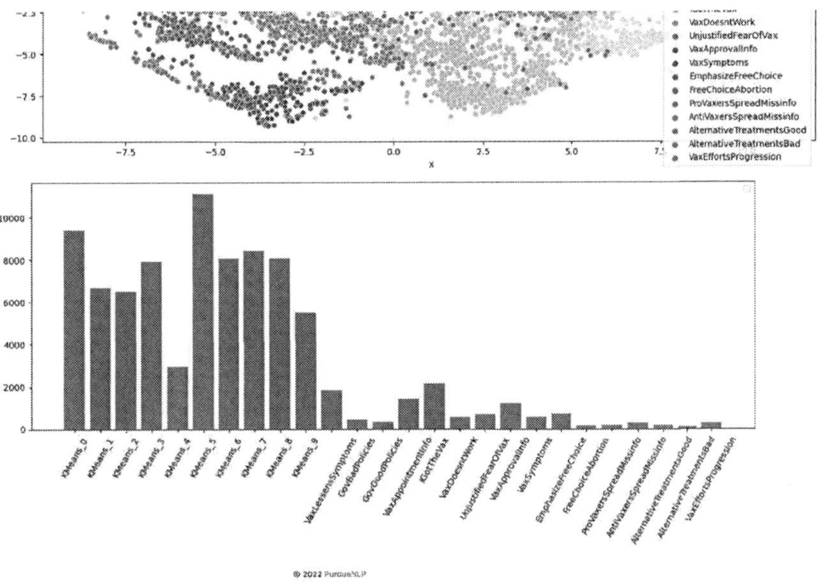

Figure 22: Visualizing Global Explanations Page: Scroll Down for Distributions

User or Labor: An Interaction Framework for Human-Machine Relationships in NLP

Ruyuan Wan
University of Notre Dame
rwan@nd.edu

Naome Etori
University of Minnesota
etori001@umn.edu

Karla Badillo-Urquiola
University of Notre Dame
kbadill3@nd.edu

Dongyeop Kang
University of Minnesota
dongyeop@umn.edu

Abstract

The bridging research between Human-Computer Interaction and Natural Language Processing is developing quickly these years. However, there is still a lack of formative guidelines to understand the human-machine interaction in the NLP loop. When researchers crossing the two fields talk about humans, they may imply a user or labor. Regarding a human as a user, the human is in control, and the machine is used as a tool to achieve the human's goals. Considering a human as a laborer, the machine is in control, and the human is used as a resource to achieve the machine's goals. Through a systematic literature review and thematic analysis, we present an interaction framework for understanding human-machine relationships in NLP. In the framework, we propose four types of human-machine interactions: Human-Teacher and Machine-Learner, Machine-Leading, Human-Leading, and Human-Machine Collaborators. Our analysis shows that the type of interaction is not fixed but can change across tasks as the relationship between the human and the machine develops. We also discuss the implications of this framework for the future of NLP and human-machine relationships.

1 Introduction

Research at the intersection of Natural Language Processing (NLP) and Human-Computer Interaction (HCI) is developing rapidly. Humans and machines are now both engaged in each step of the end-to-end NLP pipeline (Wang et al., 2021; Wu et al., 2022). NLP systems are trained on data created and annotated by humans, such as news articles (Da San Martino et al., 2019), Wikipedia pages (Faruqui et al., 2018), product reviews (Badlani et al., 2019), and social media posts (Joseph et al., 2021). Yet, humans are also empowered by NLP systems, such as writing assistants (Chen et al., 2012), collaborative text revision (Du et al., 2022), and translators (Gu et al., 2016). Nonetheless, humans and machines play distinct roles in these scenarios. From the HCI perspective, researchers usually consider humans as the users of certain technology within the interaction, while many NLP researchers emphasize the labor responsibility of humans to improve the performance of NLP models in tasks.

Humans and machines naturally have different strengths, such as trustworthiness, automation, and assessment ability (Shneiderman, 2020; Maes, 1995). Humans stand out for trustworthiness, while machines are known for automation. Both humans and machines have the competence to evaluate each other, given their own specialties.

While more and more interdisciplinary research and systems are being built to bridge the HCI and NLP fields, we still lack a normative understanding of how human and machine interaction works within the NLP context. More importantly, does the interaction work well? To fill this gap, we address two main research questions:

RQ1: *How does human-machine interaction happen in NLP?*

RQ2: *How do humans and machines interact with each other in NLP?*

We address our research questions by conducting a systematic literature review on the interactive NLP research from leading HCI and NLP venues. Our goal was to define a generalizable human-machine interaction framework in NLP to explain current implementation, guide the design of human-machine interaction, and inspire future research in interactive NLP systems. Based on our synthesis, we defined three properties of interaction: *continuity*, *variety* of interaction options, and *medium* (RQ1). We also conceptualized four re-

Proceedings of the Fourth Workshop on Data Science with Human-in-the-Loop (Language Advances), pages 112 - 121
December 8, 2022 ©2022 Association for Computational Linguistics

lationships summarizing the roles of human and machine interaction patterns in different scenarios: *Human-Teacher and Machine-Learner*, *Machine-Leading*, *Human-Leading*, and *Human-Machine Collaborators* (RQ2). We used these properties and conceptualizations to contribute a theoretical interaction framework for human-machine relationships in NLP. Future research from HCI and NLP can use this framework to design and evaluate human-machine interaction for human and machine needs within their role and responsibility.

2 Related Work

Traditionally, NLP models are trained, fine-tuned, and tested on existing datasets before being deployed to solve real-world problems. While HCI research usually involves users designing, developing, implementing, and evaluating systems. To encourage collaboration between HCI and NLP, combining both approaches is required for successful 'HCI+NLP' applications (Heuer and Buschek, 2021). Further, Heuer and Buschek (2021) proposed five methods for designing and evaluating HCI+NLP Systems: user-centered NLP, co-creating NLP, crowdsourcing, and user models.

The human-machine interaction in NLP focuses on how people interact with machines and how NLP systems can be designed to support humans. In recent years, many researchers and practitioners have made significant advances in interactive NLP systems, such as text classification (Godbole et al., 2004), text summarization (Passali et al., 2021), semantic parsing and entity linking (Liang et al., 2020; He et al., 2016; Klie et al., 2020; Zhong and Chen, 2020), dialogue systems (Sanguinetti et al., 2020; Liu et al., 2018), topic modeling (Smith et al., 2018).

Wang et al. (2021) summarized recent human-in-the-loop NLP work based on their tasks, goals, human interactions, and feedback learning methods. According to Wang et al. (2021), a good human-in-the-loop NLP system must clearly communicate to humans what the model requires, provide user-friendly interfaces for collecting feedback, and effectively learn from it. For example, humans can provide various types of feedback, such as training data providers, annotations, and evaluators of the system's output to improve the model's performance, interpretability, or usability.

Also, it is vital to understand the constraints of collecting and interpreting human inputs correctly. Many design considerations influence the efficiency and effectiveness of interactive learning from human feedback (Cui et al., 2021). For example, noise caused by human error (such as when a human teacher fails to provide the conventional ground truth) could be challenging in designing human-machine interaction systems. In addition, data collected from humans may be poor quality Hsueh et al. (2009). Social bias Fiske (2019) can also be introduced automatically during data collection Garrido-Muñoz et al. (2021) and language model training, which emerging the need of developing fair and responsible models Hutchinson et al. (2020); Mehrabi et al. (2021). Therefore, it is critical to appropriately interpret collected human data and analyze the effects of various interaction types on learning outcomes (Cui et al., 2021).

3 Survey and Analysis Methods

We conducted a systematic literature review to understand the types of interactions humans and machines have within the NLP and HCI context. To select the targeted papers, we searched from ACL anthology (NLP database) and ACM Digital Library (HCI database) for articles that have been published over the last two years and included papers with keywords such as 'human-in-the-loop,' 'interactive,' 'collaborative,' 'active learning,' 'HCI + NLP,' 'human-machine,' and 'human-AI.' We also searched for workshops held in ACL or ACM conferences, such as HCI+NLP in EACL 2021(Blodgett et al., 2021). Further, we conducted a backward reference search on the articles we found to identify any additional missing articles. This resulted in a total of 73 papers at the intersection of NLP and HCI. We narrowed down our search to only include articles that made algorithmic contributions, system contributions, or empirical contributions. We excluded papers that only contributed opinions, theories, surveys, or datasets. This resulted in a total of 54 papers.

Next, we included only papers that had simultaneous interactions between humans and machines. We discarded 21 articles that had no interaction, or the interaction between the human and machine was asynchronous. This resulted in a final set of 33 articles included in our analysis.

Further, We conducted a thematic analysis (Braun and Clarke, 2012) of our dataset. We began by reading through each article and taking notes on observations and insights regarding the inter-

Relationships	Papers
Human-Teacher, Machine-Learner	**OUG** Wiechmann et al. (2021), **IUG** Stiennon et al. (2020), **IVN** Jandot et al. (2016), **IVM** Wallace et al. (2019), **IVM** Liu et al. (2018), **IVM** Settles (2011), **IVM** Godbole et al. (2004)
Machine-Leading	**OUG** Khashabi et al. (2020), **OUG** Lawrence and Riezler (2018), **IUG** Lertvittayakumjorn et al. (2020), **IUG** He et al. (2016), **IUN** Liang et al. (2020), **IVG** Simard et al. (2014), **IVM** Lo and Lim (2020), **IVM** Smith et al. (2018), **IVM** Ross et al. (2021)
Human-Leading	**SUN** Bhat et al. (2021), **SUN** Rao and Daumé III (2018), **SVG** Kim et al. (2021), **SVM** Coenen et al. (2021), **IVM** Chung et al. (2022), **IVM** Passali et al. (2021)
Human-Machine Collaborators	**OUG** Kreutzer et al. (2018), **OUN** Khashabi et al. (2021), **OVG** Head et al. (2021), **SUN** Ashktorab et al. (2021), **IVG** Karmakharm et al. (2019), **IVN** Hancock et al. (2019), **IVN** Van Heerden and Bas (2021), **IVN** Klie et al. (2020), **IVM** Clark and Smith (2021), **IVM** Trivedi et al. (2019), **IVM** Kim et al. (2019),

Table 1: Human-Machine Relationships Mapping Interaction Properties: The properties of the interaction in each paper are coded by the first letter of their three interaction properties: **O/S/I** represents **One-time/Sequential/Iterative**. **U/V** represents **Unitary/Various**. **G/N/M** represents **GUI/NUI/MUI**.

actions between humans and machines. We used these notes to develop a set of guiding questions that helped us generate our initial codes:

- *What is the frequency of the interaction?*
- *What are the different ways humans can interact with machines?*
- *In what form does the interaction take place?*
- *Who starts the interaction?*
- *Who ends the interaction?*
- *Who benefits from the interaction?*

4 Findings

After iterating on our codes informed by the guiding questions, we conceptualized the codes into two major dimensions: 1) the properties of human-machine interaction based on the first three questions, and 2) the types of human-machine relationships based on the last three questions. Table 1 summarizes the mapping between our dimensions, codes, and dataset.

4.1 Properties of Interaction

Within our first dimension, we identified three major properties of how interactions happen, which address the first three guiding questions respectively: 1) continuity, 2) variety of interaction options, and 3) medium of interactions.

4.1.1 Continuity

Continuity measures the frequency of interaction which can be one-time, sequential, or iterative, to perform a single task.

One-time interaction is when the human-machine interaction is designed to happen just once, usually in active learning. For example, ActiveAnno (Wiechmann et al., 2021) offers annotation generator functionality: human annotators will manually label documents at the beginning; if it reaches a threshold of the annotation generator, it will trigger the machine annotation generator to label the remaining documents in the project.

Sequential interaction means that one agent acts first, and the other responds. Furthermore, the latter interactions are based on the previous exchanges. Over multiple rounds to complete the project, the interaction and the model will not update. For example, in the word guessing game to study the effects of communication directionality (Ashktorab et al., 2021), the machine and human play as giver and guesser by giving word hints and word guessing together to let the guess win the game in 10 rounds. The human player is playing with the same machine player in each game, but previous rounds influence the words given in later rounds.

Iterative interaction: the model performance improves through iterating over several interactions. For example, the Interactive Classification and Extraction (ICE) system enables humans to define the appropriate features through interactive features while humans can monitor their classifier's progress(Simard et al., 2014). Researchers usually set up a limitation of the rounds of the interaction for experiments, but they show that theoretically, the continuous interaction (either sequential or iterative interactions) can continue with no end.

4.1.2 Variety of Interaction Actions

Variety represents the number of ways humans can interact with machines. Some interactions are limited to a specific task (unitary), while some are flexible to multiple options (various).

Unitary interaction is a single option of the interaction action, like labeling data (Wiechmann et al., 2021), having humans perform one action to evaluate submissions (Khashabi et al., 2021), ranking candidate questions (Rao and Daumé III, 2018), giving natural language responses to query (Liang et al., 2020), or selecting an answer from the multi-choice questions (Lertvittayakumjorn et al., 2020; He et al., 2016).

Various interaction is that there are multiple options for an interaction action. Humans can select what to do from multiple options, such as choosing continuation writing, rewriting, or filling in an interactive editor (Coenen et al., 2021). In CYOA (Clark and Smith, 2021), human has many options, such as deleting suggestions, submitting suggestions as-is, or writing a new suggestion.

4.1.3 Medium of Interactions

Medium in interactive NLP systems can be Graphical User Interfaces (GUI), Natural Language User Interfaces (NUI), or Mixed User Interfaces (MUI):

Graphical User Interfaces (GUI) allow humans to select given options or highlight text. Such as, in FIND (Lertvittayakumjorn et al., 2020), humans answer multiple-choice questions about whether a given word cloud is relevant to a class to disable irrelevant hidden features. Journalist-in-the-loop (Karmakharm et al., 2019) uses a web-based interface rumour analysis that takes user feedback. (Kreutzer et al., 2018) collects reinforcement signals from humans using a 5-star rating interface.

Natural Language User Interfaces (NUI) let the agent respond with natural language. For instance, GENIE (Khashabi et al., 2021) uses text generation tasks. Liang et al. (2020) 's ALICE utilizes contrastive natural language explanations to improve data efficiency in learning.

Mixed User Interfaces (MUI) contain both graphical and natural language interfaces. For example, in the Interactive NLP in Clinical Care (Trivedi et al., 2019), physicians can add or remove highlighted predicted sentences in a report and write natural language feedback in a separate box. Also, Wordcraft allows humans to start writing with a prompt and change text and selection options for machine editing in the side GUI (Coenen et al., 2021). In CYOA (Clark and Smith, 2021), a human can write a storyline alone and delete suggestions, while models provide suggestions of the story, and then the human can submit the suggestion. Participants are asked to score on a Likert-scale and open-ended questions about the systems and suggestions they received after submitting their stories. In DUALIST (Settles, 2011) humans can label documents by clicking the appropriate class from the drop-down menus below each text, In addition, each column has a text box where users can "inject" domain knowledge by typing in random words. Users must click a large submit button at the top of the screen to retrain the classifier and get a new set of queries. Smoothed dictionary features (Jandot et al., 2016) use a methodology to solicit features from humans or teachers. In Passali et al. (2021) human has the option to view visualization and choose different decoding strategies.

4.2 Relationships of Human and Machine

For our second dimension, we conceptualized four relationships (each based on the last three guiding questions): 1) *Human-Teacher and Machine-Learner*, 2) *Machine-Leading*, 3) *Human-Leading*, and 4) *Human-Machine Collaborators*.

Human-Teacher and Machine-Learner When humans initiate the interaction, then machines learn from humans to mimic the task, after that, humans evaluate and give feedback on the machines' learning results in the end. Through this interaction, humans benefit from machines' automation in finishing tasks, and machines also benefit from learning to improve their performance.

For instance, humans annotate and label data at the beginning in ActiveAnno (Wiechmann et al. (2021)), ICE (Simard et al. (2014)), DUALIST (Settles, 2011) and HIClass (Godbole et al., 2004). Once the machine has learned enough from the human annotation, it can predict labels for the remaining documents. In Trick-Me-If-You-Can (Wallace et al., 2019), human authors are guided to break the model by writing adversarial questions, and the machine exposes the predictions and interpretations of the answers to hu-

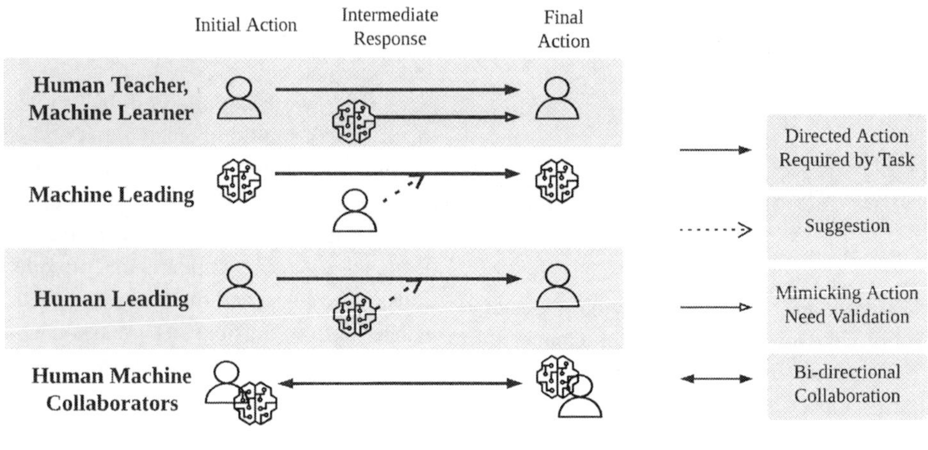

Figure 1: Interaction Framework for Human-Machine relationships in NLP

mans. In smoothed dictionary features (Jandot et al., 2016), the machine elicits dictionary features from a teacher or human.

Machine-Leading Machines initiate interactions with their optimal competence, then humans respond with suggestions, and later, machines iterate on the task based on the intermediate suggestions. From the interaction, machines benefit from humans' knowledge in improving their own capacity, while humans don't earn anything from the process.

For instance, ALICE (Coenen et al., 2021), FIND (Lertvittayakumjorn et al., 2020), Interactive NLP in clinical care (Trivedi et al., 2019), and Human-in-The-Loop Parsing (He et al., 2016), have a baseline model to perform the corresponding NLP tasks. Then human steps into interactively selecting useful features, promoting machine learning efficiency. In Interactive Entity Linking (Lo and Lim, 2020), an instance chooses mentions for human annotation using an active learning approach. The goal is to improve entity linking accuracy while updating the embedding model. The machine triggers the interaction, the human assists the machine in the annotation process, and human annotation feedback is used to update the model. Finally, high machine accuracy determines the end of the interaction process.

Human-Leading Humans initiate the task, then machines give suggestions based on their pre-trained expertise, later, humans select the way they want to interact with machines. Via the interaction, humans gain help from machines, but machines don't take any benefit from these interactions.

Like Wordcraft (Coenen et al. (2021)), human plays the lead role because human triggers the interaction by writing a prompt, selecting collaborative writing options, and eventually deciding what to write and when to end. In Towards Human-Centered Summarization (Passali et al., 2021), human actively participates and takes a leading role in the summarization process, such as deciding on the decoding strategies during the inference stage, choosing visualization color and viewing visualization of the attention weights, combining sentences from the various summaries to create a new one that can be used in fine-tuning the model.

Human-Machine Collaborators Either a human or machine initiates the task, then the other one gives the response. There is no explicit benefit for humans or machines during the interaction.

For example, in Ashktorab et al. (2021), humans and machines can play as giver and guesser and cooperate for a common goal: to help the guesser answer the right word. In GENIE (Khashabi et al., 2021), human annotators work with a machine to assess leaderboard submissions on various axes such as correctness, conciseness, and fluency and compare their responses to a variety of automated metrics. Journalist-in-the-loop (Karmakharm et al., 2019) is a rumor annotation service that continuously allows journalists to provide feedback on social media posts. The feedback is then used to improve the neural network-based rumor classification mode. Also, human-machine collaboration improves the journals' productivity. In AfriKI (Van Heerden and Bas, 2021), human authors collaborate with machines to gener-

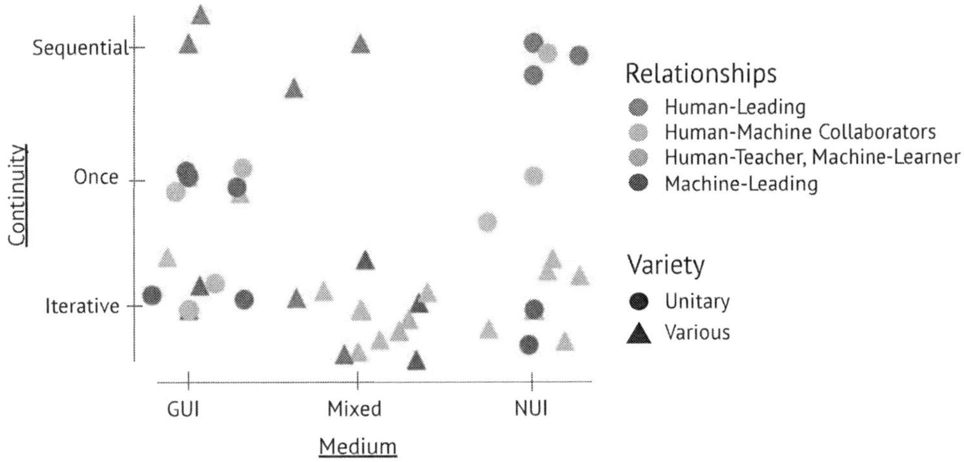

Figure 2: Human-Machine Relationships Mapping Interaction Properties

ate Afrikaans poetry through phrase selection and vertically arranging poetry lines. The collaboration promotes human creativity and also improves the robustness of the model. From Zero to Hero (Klie et al., 2020), an interactive machine learning annotation supports that guides the user in locating text entities and deciding on the correct knowledge base entries. As a result, the annotation speed and quality improve tremendously and reduce human cognitive load. In CYOA (Clark and Smith, 2021), humans and machines take turns writing a story, and two models generate suggestions for the following line after the human writes the story's first line. The human suggestions provide interpretability of the model performance and improve human creativity.

5 Discussion

Based on our findings, we developed an interaction framework for the four types of human-machine relationships in one interaction cycle (see Figure 1). The "human-in-the-loop" concept has become popular in NLP. But it is too broad to describe the nuance in similar but different human-machine interactions. Our interaction framework depicts human and machine actions under different roles.

It is important for NLP and HCI practitioners to define human-machine interactions when designing interactive NLP systems because it builds up a clearer understanding of the human and machine's strengths and weaknesses. We can use the identified strengths to complement the weaknesses. For example, in *Human-Teacher and Machine-Learner interactions*, the strengths of automation in annotation tasks can be leveraged to complete a task more quickly, while the human's strength in assessment can validate the machine's output. For *Human-Leading* or *Machine-Leading*, the leader may have limited knowledge and capacity that could be complemented with external expertise.

Next, we share how NLP and HCI practitioners can use our conceptual framework in practice. While *Human-Leading* is similar to *Human-Teacher, Machine Learner* (since both are driven by humans who take initial and final action with machines' intermediate response), the framework captures the different statuses of machines and the corresponding actions of humans and machines. As a learner, the machine is a novice at the beginning and is launched by mimicking humans finishing their remaining tasks. However, the machines in the *Human-Leading* relationship have their own expertise to offer suggestions. Accordingly, this also leads to different humans' final actions, i.e., humans as teachers will validate machines' learning results, while humans would choose machines' suggestions based on personal interests during human-leading interaction.

Additionally, the framework can be used as a guideline to check whether the interaction design is appropriate. For instance, the machine directly overwrites a human's control will be problematic when *Human-Leading* is required. For instance, someone is writing in colloquial English, using 'ain't' as a general preverbal negator (Rickford, 1999). A machine trained in standard English will detect this as an error and would like to correct it, but it violates the writer's intention.

Figure 2 shows some trends of interactions: *Human-Leading* relationship usually happens with sequential interactions; *Machine-Leading* relationship uses more GUI and has iterative interaction; *Human-Machine Collaborators* mainly use NUI; *Human-Teacher, Machine-Learner* relationship usually happens iteratively as well.

6 Limitations

From the papers we reviewed, we didn't find any interaction that machines validate humans' actions. This might be because humans overall are more trustworthy than machines and may be influenced by the range of literature we reviewed. Additionally, 'collaboration' can sometimes be interchangeable with 'interaction' based on their semantic meanings. But we strive to name our precise definitions of each relationship with clear and straightforward enough abstract names.

In addition, we initially coded *'what are the outcomes of the research paper'* to understand how interaction can influence the research outcome, such as efficiency, creativity, etc. But it didn't synthesize sufficiently with other codes. More importantly, the research outcome is usually the goal of those research papers so we couldn't derive the causal relationship from interaction design to the research outcome. However, this guides us in the future to study how we can manipulate desired research improvement by designing human-machine interaction.

7 Conclusion

Humans and machines interact with each other in a variety of ways. For example, humans may be involved in providing input to a machine learning algorithm, labeling data for training purposes, or evaluating the output of a machine learning system. Additionally, humans may interact with machine learning systems through natural language interfaces, such as chatbots or virtual assistants. We contribute an interaction framework for human-machine interactions through a systematic literature review and thematic analysis, which conceptualizes four human-machine relationships based on three different interaction properties, to help researchers and practitioners better understand and manage human-machine interactions in NLP.

References

Zahra Ashktorab, Casey Dugan, James Johnson, Qian Pan, Wei Zhang, Sadhana Kumaravel, and Murray Campbell. 2021. Effects of communication directionality and ai agent differences in human-ai interaction. In *Proceedings of the 2021 CHI Conference on Human Factors in Computing Systems*, pages 1–15.

Rohan Badlani, Nishit Asnani, and Manan Rai. 2019. Disambiguating sentiment: An ensemble of humour, sarcasm, and hate speech features for sentiment classification. *W-NUT*, 2019:337–345.

Advait Bhat, Saaket Agashe, and Anirudha Joshi. 2021. How do people interact with biased text prediction models while writing? In *Proceedings of the First Workshop on Bridging Human–Computer Interaction and Natural Language Processing*, pages 116–121.

Su Lin Blodgett, Michael Madaio, Brendan O'Connor, Hanna Wallach, and Qian Yang. 2021. Proceedings of the first workshop on bridging human–computer interaction and natural language processing. In *Proceedings of the First Workshop on Bridging Human–Computer Interaction and Natural Language Processing*.

Virginia Braun and Victoria Clarke. 2012. *Thematic analysis*. American Psychological Association.

Mei-Hua Chen, Shih-Ting Huang, Hung-Ting Hsieh, Ting-Hui Kao, and Jason S Chang. 2012. Flow: a first-language-oriented writing assistant system. In *Proceedings of the ACL 2012 System Demonstrations*, pages 157–162.

John Joon Young Chung, Wooseok Kim, Kang Min Yoo, Hwaran Lee, Eytan Adar, and Minsuk Chang. 2022. *TaleBrush: Sketching Stories with Generative Pretrained Language Models*. Association for Computing Machinery, New York, NY, USA.

Elizabeth Clark and Noah A Smith. 2021. Choose your own adventure: Paired suggestions in collaborative writing for evaluating story generation models. In *Proceedings of the 2021 Conference of the North American Chapter of the Association for Computational Linguistics: Human Language Technologies*, pages 3566–3575.

Andy Coenen, Luke Davis, Daphne Ippolito, Emily Reif, and Ann Yuan. 2021. Wordcraft: a human-ai collaborative editor for story writing. *arXiv preprint arXiv:2107.07430*.

Yuchen Cui, Pallavi Koppol, Henny Admoni, Scott Niekum, Reid G Simmons, Aaron Steinfeld, and Tesca Fitzgerald. 2021. Understanding the relationship between interactions and outcomes in human-in-the-loop machine learning. In *IJCAI*, pages 4382–4391.

Giovanni Da San Martino, Seunghak Yu, Alberto Barrón-Cedeno, Rostislav Petrov, and Preslav Nakov. 2019. Fine-grained analysis of propaganda in news article. In *Proceedings of the 2019 conference on empirical methods in natural language processing and the 9th international joint conference on natural language processing (EMNLP-IJCNLP)*, pages 5636–5646.

Wanyu Du, Zae Myung Kim, Vipul Raheja, Dhruv Kumar, and Dongyeop Kang. 2022. Read, revise, repeat: A system demonstration for human-in-the-loop iterative text revision. *arXiv preprint arXiv:2204.03685*.

Manaal Faruqui, Ellie Pavlick, Ian Tenney, and Dipanjan Das. 2018. Wikiatomicedits: A multilingual corpus of wikipedia edits for modeling language and discourse. *arXiv preprint arXiv:1808.09422*.

Susan T Fiske. 2019. 13.4 prejudice, discrimination, and stereotyping. *Introduction to Psychology*.

Ismael Garrido-Muñoz, Arturo Montejo-Ráez, Fernando Martínez-Santiago, and L Alfonso Ureña-López. 2021. A survey on bias in deep nlp. *Applied Sciences*, 11(7):3184.

Shantanu Godbole, Abhay Harpale, Sunita Sarawagi, and Soumen Chakrabarti. 2004. Document classification through interactive supervision of document and term labels. In *European Conference on Principles of Data Mining and Knowledge Discovery*, pages 185–196. Springer.

Jiatao Gu, Graham Neubig, Kyunghyun Cho, and Victor OK Li. 2016. Learning to translate in real-time with neural machine translation. *arXiv preprint arXiv:1610.00388*.

Braden Hancock, Antoine Bordes, Pierre-Emmanuel Mazare, and Jason Weston. 2019. Learning from dialogue after deployment: Feed yourself, chatbot! In *Proceedings of the 57th Annual Meeting of the Association for Computational Linguistics*, pages 3667–3684.

Luheng He, Julian Michael, Mike Lewis, and Luke Zettlemoyer. 2016. Human-in-the-loop parsing. In *Proceedings of the 2016 Conference on Empirical Methods in Natural Language Processing*, pages 2337–2342.

Andrew Head, Kyle Lo, Dongyeop Kang, Raymond Fok, Sam Skjonsberg, Daniel S. Weld, and Marti A. Hearst. 2021. Augmenting scientific papers with just-in-time, position-sensitive definitions of terms and symbols.

Hendrik Heuer and Daniel Buschek. 2021. Methods for the design and evaluation of hci+ nlp systems. In *Proceedings of the First Workshop on Bridging Human–Computer Interaction and Natural Language Processing*, pages 28–33.

Pei-Yun Hsueh, Prem Melville, and Vikas Sindhwani. 2009. Data quality from crowdsourcing: a study of annotation selection criteria. In *Proceedings of the NAACL HLT 2009 workshop on active learning for natural language processing*, pages 27–35.

Ben Hutchinson, Vinodkumar Prabhakaran, Emily Denton, Kellie Webster, Yu Zhong, and Stephen Denuyl. 2020. Social biases in nlp models as barriers for persons with disabilities. *arXiv preprint arXiv:2005.00813*.

Camille Jandot, Patrice Simard, Max Chickering, David Grangier, and Jina Suh. 2016. Interactive semantic featuring for text classification. *arXiv preprint arXiv:1606.07545*.

Kenneth Joseph, Sarah Shugars, Ryan Gallagher, Jon Green, Alexi Quintana Mathé, Zijian An, and David Lazer. 2021. (mis) alignment between stance expressed in social media data and public opinion surveys. *arXiv preprint arXiv:2109.01762*.

Twin Karmakharm, Nikolaos Aletras, and Kalina Bontcheva. 2019. Journalist-in-the-loop: Continuous learning as a service for rumour analysis. In *Proceedings of the 2019 Conference on Empirical Methods in Natural Language Processing and the 9th International Joint Conference on Natural Language Processing (EMNLP-IJCNLP): System Demonstrations*, pages 115–120.

Daniel Khashabi, Tushar Khot, and Ashish Sabharwal. 2020. More bang for your buck: Natural perturbation for robust question answering. In *Proceedings of the 2020 Conference on Empirical Methods in Natural Language Processing (EMNLP)*, pages 163–170.

Daniel Khashabi, Gabriel Stanovsky, Jonathan Bragg, Nicholas Lourie, Jungo Kasai, Yejin Choi, Noah A Smith, and Daniel S Weld. 2021. Genie: A leaderboard for human-in-the-loop evaluation of text generation. *arXiv preprint arXiv:2101.06561*.

Hannah Kim, Dongjin Choi, Barry Drake, Alex Endert, and Haesun Park. 2019. Topicsifter: Interactive search space reduction through targeted topic modeling. In *2019 IEEE Conference on Visual Analytics Science and Technology (VAST)*, pages 35–45. IEEE.

Jeonghwan Kim, Junmo Kang, Suwon Shin, and Sung-Hyon Myaeng. 2021. Can you distinguish truthful from fake reviews? user analysis and assistance tool for fake review detection. In *Proceedings of the First Workshop on Bridging Human–Computer Interaction and Natural Language Processing*, pages 53–59.

Jan-Christoph Klie, Richard Eckart de Castilho, and Iryna Gurevych. 2020. From zero to hero: Human-in-the-loop entity linking in low resource domains. In *Proceedings of the 58th Annual Meeting of the Association for Computational Linguistics*, pages 6982–6993.

Julia Kreutzer, Shahram Khadivi, Evgeny Matusov, and Stefan Riezler. 2018. Can neural machine translation be improved with user feedback? *NAACL HLT 2018*, pages 92–105.

Carolin Lawrence and Stefan Riezler. 2018. Counterfactual learning from human proofreading feedback for semantic parsing. *arXiv preprint arXiv:1811.12239*.

Piyawat Lertvittayakumjorn, Lucia Specia, and Francesca Toni. 2020. Find: human-in-the-loop debugging deep text classifiers. *arXiv preprint arXiv:2010.04987*.

Weixin Liang, James Zou, and Zhou Yu. 2020. Alice: Active learning with contrastive natural language explanations. In *Proceedings of the 2020 Conference on Empirical Methods in Natural Language Processing (EMNLP)*, pages 4380–4391.

Bing Liu, Gokhan Tur, Dilek Hakkani-Tur, Pararth Shah, and Larry Heck. 2018. Dialogue learning with human teaching and feedback in end-to-end trainable task-oriented dialogue systems. *arXiv preprint arXiv:1804.06512*.

Pei-Chi Lo and Ee-Peng Lim. 2020. Interactive entity linking using entity-word representations. In *Proceedings of the 43rd International ACM SIGIR Conference on Research and Development in Information Retrieval*, pages 1801–1804.

Pattie Maes. 1995. Agents that reduce work and information overload. In *Readings in human–computer interaction*, pages 811–821. Elsevier.

Ninareh Mehrabi, Fred Morstatter, Nripsuta Saxena, Kristina Lerman, and Aram Galstyan. 2021. A survey on bias and fairness in machine learning. *ACM Computing Surveys (CSUR)*, 54(6):1–35.

Tatiana Passali, Alexios Gidiotis, Efstathios Chatzikyriakidis, and Grigorios Tsoumakas. 2021. Towards human-centered summarization: A case study on financial news. In *Proceedings of the First Workshop on Bridging Human–Computer Interaction and Natural Language Processing*, pages 21–27.

Sudha Rao and Hal Daumé III. 2018. Learning to ask good questions: Ranking clarification questions using neural expected value of perfect information. *arXiv preprint arXiv:1805.04655*.

John Russell Rickford. 1999. *African American vernacular English: Features, evolution, educational implications*. Wiley-Blackwell.

Andrew Ross, Nina Chen, Elisa Zhao Hang, Elena L Glassman, and Finale Doshi-Velez. 2021. Evaluating the interpretability of generative models by interactive reconstruction. In *Proceedings of the 2021 CHI Conference on Human Factors in Computing Systems*, pages 1–15.

Manuela Sanguinetti, Alessandro Mazzei, Viviana Patti, Scalerandi Marco, Dario Mana, and Rossana Simeoni. 2020. Annotating errors and emotions in human-chatbot interactions in italian. In *The 14th Linguistic Annotation Workshop*, pages 1–12. Association for Computational Linguistics.

Burr Settles. 2011. Closing the loop: Fast, interactive semi-supervised annotation with queries on features and instances. In *Proceedings of the 2011 Conference on Empirical Methods in Natural Language Processing*, pages 1467–1478.

Ben Shneiderman. 2020. Human-centered artificial intelligence: Reliable, safe & trustworthy. *International Journal of Human–Computer Interaction*, 36(6):495–504.

Patrice Simard, David Chickering, Aparna Lakshmiratan, Denis Charles, Léon Bottou, Carlos Garcia Jurado Suarez, David Grangier, Saleema Amershi, Johan Verwey, and Jina Suh. 2014. Ice: enabling non-experts to build models interactively for large-scale lopsided problems. *arXiv preprint arXiv:1409.4814*.

Alison Smith, Varun Kumar, Jordan Boyd-Graber, Kevin Seppi, and Leah Findlater. 2018. Closing the loop: User-centered design and evaluation of a human-in-the-loop topic modeling system. In *23rd International Conference on Intelligent User Interfaces*, pages 293–304.

Nisan Stiennon, Long Ouyang, Jeff Wu, Daniel M Ziegler, Ryan Lowe, Chelsea Voss, Alec Radford, Dario Amodei, and Paul Christiano. 2020. Learning to summarize from human feedback. *arXiv preprint arXiv:2009.01325*.

Gaurav Trivedi, Esmaeel R Dadashzadeh, Robert M Handzel, Wendy W Chapman, Shyam Visweswaran, and Harry Hochheiser. 2019. Interactive nlp in clinical care: identifying incidental findings in radiology reports. *Applied clinical informatics*, 10(04):655–669.

Imke Van Heerden and Anil Bas. 2021. Afriki: Machine-in-the-loop afrikaans poetry generation. *arXiv preprint arXiv:2103.16190*.

Eric Wallace, Pedro Rodriguez, Shi Feng, Ikuya Yamada, and Jordan Boyd-Graber. 2019. Trick me if you can: Human-in-the-loop generation of adversarial examples for question answering. *Transactions of the Association for Computational Linguistics*, 7:387–401.

Zijie J Wang, Dongjin Choi, Shenyu Xu, and Diyi Yang. 2021. Putting humans in the natural language processing loop: A survey. *arXiv preprint arXiv:2103.04044*.

Max Wiechmann, Seid Muhie Yimam, and Chris Biemann. 2021. Activeanno: General-purpose document-level annotation tool with active learning integration. In *Proceedings of the 2021 Conference of the North American Chapter of the Association for Computational Linguistics: Human Language Technologies: Demonstrations*, pages 99–105.

Xingjiao Wu, Luwei Xiao, Yixuan Sun, Junhang Zhang, Tianlong Ma, and Liang He. 2022. A survey of human-in-the-loop for machine learning. *Future Generation Computer Systems*.

Zexuan Zhong and Danqi Chen. 2020. A frustratingly easy approach for entity and relation extraction. *arXiv preprint arXiv:2010.12812*.

Author Index